The Frontier in Latin American History

Alistair Hennessy is professor of comparative American studies at the University of Warwick.

To Mellor

The Frontier in Latin American History

Alistair Hennessy

University of Warwick

HISTORIES OF THE AMERICAN FRONTIER
Ray Allen Billington, General Editor
Howard R. Lamar, Coeditor

UNIVERSITY OF NEW MEXICO PRESS
Albuquerque

First published 1978 by
Edward Arnold (Publishers) Ltd
25 Hill Street, London W1X 8LL

Published in the United States of America 1978
by the University of New Mexico Press
Albuquerque

Library of Congress Catalog Card Number 78-58816
International Standard Book Number 0-8263-0466-4
  (clothbound)

Library of Congress Catalog Card Number 78-58816
International Standard Book Number 0-8263-0467-2
  (paperbound)

Foreword

The appearance of this book signals a new direction in the Histories of the American Frontier Series. It also introduces a new publisher, a new coeditor, and an expanded publications program that promises to make the Series even more useful—and respected—than in the past.

The Histories of the American Frontier Series was first conceived in the mid 1950s. It was the brainchild of Ranald P. Hobbs, vice-president of the firm of Rinehart & Company, who believed that the story of American expansion had been sufficiently investigated in monographic studies to justify a multivolume synthesis summarizing modern scholarship and suggesting fields for future investigation. The Series, as originally planned, was to comprise eighteen volumes, each prepared by a specialist, tracing in chronological and regional sequence the advance of settlement across the continent from the arrival of the Spanish in the sixteenth century to the "closing" of the frontier early in the twentieth century. Distinguished authors were found for all the volumes, and writing began.

The first volume in the Series appeared in 1963—Rodman W. Paul's *Mining Frontiers of the Far West*. By this time Rinehart & Company had merged with two other concerns to form the publishing house of Holt, Rinehart and Winston, Inc. Under the auspices of this firm eight more volumes were published over the next seven years, all of them well received by scholars, teachers, and readers of western history who appreciated sound narratives, readably presented. Several have become standard works in their fields, and all are widely used both in and out of the classroom.

In 1973, economic considerations led Holt, Rinehart and Winston to reduce the number of its highly specialized academic publications. The Series was then transferred to the University of New Mexico Press, its present publisher. At the same time both the Press and the Series' editor felt that a coeditor should be named to ease the burdens of handling manuscripts, and to conceive fresh ideas for books that would reflect current trends in historical interpretation. Fortunately Howard R. Lamar, William Robertson Coe

Professor of American History at Yale University, was persuaded to accept this post. A highly respected scholar and teacher in the field of western history, he has proven a steady source of stimulating insights and challenging ideas.

Thus restructured, and with the enthusiastic cooperation of Hugh W. Treadwell, the able director of the University of New Mexico Press, the Histories of the American Frontier Series has launched an ambitious program of expansion. Reluctant authors whose books were planned for the original Series have been prodded into completing their volumes, with results that will soon become apparent. Even more important is a redefinition of the Series as an open-ended medium for the publication of seminal books exploring new approaches to frontier studies. These volumes are designed to supplement rather than to displace the original core volumes, and, we hope, to play an even larger role in defining and stimulating the study of frontiers in all their varied aspects.

With this as their goal the editors, with Hugh Treadwell's hearty approval, have explored a number of possible topics for future books, and have corresponded widely with prospective authors deemed worthy by their peers. As a result of this flurry of activity, volumes are either under way or being considered on the Mexican-American Borderlands, the Indian-White Frontier, the Pacific Basin Frontier, the Frontier Family, the Lumber Frontier, the Urban Frontier, and Women in the West. Other books are projected for the future, in the hope that the Series can remain useful in updating the traditional story of American expansion, and can lead scholars into significant new areas of investigation.

It is singularly fitting that this fresh departure should be inaugurated by Alistair Hennessy's superb book, for no work could better exemplify the revised purposes of the Series. With his doctoral degree from Oxford, extended service in the classroom as lecturer, reader, and professor at the Universities of Exeter and Warwick, and a distinguished list of publications in Spanish and Latin American history to his credit, Hennessy brings to his writing a background of experience and learning ideally suited to his task. He brings also proven mastery of a difficult subject; so familiar with the nuances of history is he that his challenging interpretations are completely persuasive.

But Professor Hennessy offers us more than sophisticated scholarship. As the founder of a comparative American history program at the University of Warwick, he reveals a grasp of historical patterns beyond the reach of the typical specialist. He draws his examples from one country after another, weighs them against theories developed in the United States by Frederick Jackson Turner and his successors, and presents them in sparkling prose (in what other historical study does one find such a delightful phrase as "heavy-uddered placidity"?). His perspective on the entire Latin American frontier gives us a needed perspective on our own, especially because he has focused on recognizable American frontier themes: the problem of territorial space and its conquest, and the kinds of heroes and myths that emerge from that conquest. The result is a book that not only teaches and entertains, but challenges. The conceptual web that Professor Hennessy weaves in his opening chapters advances mind-tingling theories on the nature of frontiers; the later chapters offer convincing proof of his theories.

As the original editor of the Histories of the American Frontier Series, and as one who shaped its initial structure, I am particularly proud to present a book of such distinction to inaugurate the new direction of the Series with a supportive publisher and a gifted coeditor. The appearance of this volume presages a future of achievement and service that will benefit not only frontier studies but our knowledge of the world's past in all its aspects.

Ray Allen Billington

The Huntington Library

Contents

Preface

My interest in the frontier in Latin America grew out of four main concerns. First, all those who teach Latin American history must have experienced the frustration of trying to organize a mass of intransigent material in coherent form. The contrast between the particular and the general which is a major theme of Latin American history can confuse teacher and taught alike. Is Latin America more than a metaphysical concept or a geographical expression? Can Latin American history be taught without obscuring the continent's diversity? Is there any purpose in considering it as a unity and, if so, what are the unifying factors? Are they mainly those resulting from colonial and neo-colonial domination? Or is it more realistic, and more manageable for the student, to study the history of separate countries, treating them as so many autonomous entities?

The problem is certainly not unique to Latin America: Europe also has deep divisions, wide linguistic variations and disparate cultural traditions. But European history revolves round certain well defined themes—the rise of nation-states and the relationship between them in the subsequent balance of power; the expansion of those states outside Europe and their rivalries; the origins of industrialization. The teaching of the history of Latin America may follow similar lines but it is not always easy to persuade students or the general reader that the intricacies of growth of its separate states merit the same sort of attention as a European power with considerable influence outside its own boundaries. Thus, in studying Latin American history the comparative approach to the twenty republics can have greater attractions. But it also has pitfalls, especially that of making too neat typologies, beloved of political scientists but distrusted by historians. I think a more fruitful approach could be to study the problem of territorial space and its conquest. This has been common to all Latin American countries, large and small, and it is something which they share with the United States and Canada. The history of the Americas has been one of European immigration, to an extent unparalleled elsewhere except in a few other areas of white settlement, such as Australia, New Zealand and southern Africa. In the case of Latin America the constant movement of peoples into unsettled regions provides a major continuity between the colonial and independence periods.

It could also be argued that success or failure to solve the problems of settlement lies at the root of many of the continent's difficulties and that an analysis of those successes or failures and of what is cause and what effect takes us to the heart of the Latin American predicament. If this diagnosis is accepted, then the study of frontiers of settlement in the North American sense can be a useful heuristic device for organizing and giving coherence to a mass of otherwise intractable material. It can be argued further that frontier studies must be an integral component of any general theory of dependency which seeks to explain the mechanisms of peripheral capitalism. I would certainly not want to argue that it is the only way but, as development-conscious governments become aware of the enormous potential of their unsettled regions, attention should be focused on that interplay between metropolis and frontier which is the heart of the Latin American historical experience.

The second concern arose out of my puzzlement that it is by no means normal for students of United States history in North America (or in Britain for that matter) to be taught Latin American history as well. Herbert Bolton's observation in 1932 has gone largely unheeded:

> There is a need of a broader treatment of American history, to supplement the purely nationalistic presentation to which we are accustomed. European history cannot be learned from books dealing alone with England, or France, or Germany, or Italy, or Russia, nor can American history be adequately presented if confined to Brazil, or Chile, or Mexico, or Canada, or the United States. In my own country the study of the thirteen English colonies and the United States in isolation has obscured many of the larger factors in their development, and helped to raise a nation of chauvinists.[1]

It may seem impertinent to labour this point for there are motes in the English eye. It was partly to offset the insularity of both traditional 'Americanists' and Latin Americanists that my own university inaugurated a degree in comparative American studies in 1974. This book is to some extent an outcome of planning that degree and of teaching a course on comparative frontiers within it, and it is directed as much at North Americanists as at Latin Americanists in the hope that the bait of the magic word, frontier, will lure them into the challenging fields of Latin American history and comparative study. Inevitably, an ambitious synthesis on a small scale, with little space to develop points or anticipate objections, invites the ire of specialists; but if it serves the purpose of enticing those who might otherwise have continued to paddle in shallow waters, I shall be well pleased.

Thirdly, I have long been interested in the relationship between myth and history in the modern period and in the social function of historians in different societies. The case of Frederick Jackson Turner and the extraordinary place he has occupied in American historiography illustrates more clearly than possibly that of any other historian in the last hundred years the interweaving of history and myth. It might be objected that Turner's name has been invoked too often for the good health of historical scholarship and that no useful purpose is to be served by dragging him into Latin America, which he himself was careful to avoid. It is not my intention to apply his thesis to that continent but rather to use it as a starting point for comparison, as comparisons need not necessarily be confined to similar situations but may be used to provoke discussion and open up new perspectives. These are the aims of this book.

'Frontiers' are not the same as *the* frontier. Some useful purpose might have been served by defining the term frontier more precisely but it is difficult to do so without hedging it with qualifications. Precise definitions can cramp and distort as well as pinpoint and illuminate. It may seem that my use of the word here is too elastic, that almost every thing in Latin American history has been subsumed under a capacious umbrella. But this arises from the peculiarities of the original settlement pattern which did not give Latin American frontiers that identifiable cutting edge distinguishing most frontiers in North America. The majority of Latin American nations today are still in the frontier stage of development but unlike the United States—this is a crucial difference—they are frontier societies lacking a frontier myth. This may be partly explained by the all pervasive influence of the past. The persistence of cultural traits on the frontiers of Latin America makes it difficult to talk in terms of the environment fashioning a 'new man'. If, as Richard Hofstadter argued, United States history is dominated by a sense of space rather than of time, then that of Latin America is dominated by a complex interweaving of both space and time. It is not easy to jettison cultural baggage in the Latin American environment. Monuments, whether pre-Columbian or colonial are ubiquitous and the greater degree of racial intermixing has bequeathed a complex pattern of varied cultural traditions and contrasting ways of looking at the past. There is over all—many ideologists of the Hispanidad and Luso-Tropical variety have exploited it—an Iberian *modo de ser*.

In the United States, the optimism born of revolutionary messianism bred a faith among people in their own institutions. But in Latin America the euphoria of independence from Spain took the form of embracing the ideas of Europeans (but non-Hispanic) and North Americans, imitating their political forms, copying their constitutions, adopting their dress, borrowing their money and following their writers. Slowly, however, a recognition of the irrelevance of most foreign ideas drove thinkers to realize that Iberian legacies could not be sloughed off so easily and that political, social and economic behaviour ought to be explained in terms of pervasive cultural influences—a sort of Iberian equivalent of the 'germ-theory'. A major problem confronting the comparative frontier historian is how to evaluate the significance of these cultural factors as against those of the environment.

The frontiersman of legend is the *reductio ad absurdum* of the individualist ethic and, when Turner refers to America as being another name for 'opportunity', he is saying something more profound than when he says it is the breeding ground of democracy. Democracy and opportunity are not synonymous as many nineteenth-century North Americans liked to believe. Opportunity on the frontier too often meant ignoring the claims of those who did not fit into his tidy evolutionary scheme. It is still an uphill struggle to escape from these assumptions. Frontiers have encouraged dichotomies; they are invitations to Manichaean schemes of thought. The historian's responsibility is to help us escape from these shackles. Comparison with very different frontier experiences in Latin America combined with new insights derived from ethnohistorians and anthropologists should make this task more rewarding.

The fourth concern developed from my own training in and teaching of European history where I often felt that current Cold War categories, emphasizing differences between East and West, have tended to obscure what for most of the modern period has been perhaps an even more fundamental split—that between north and south. Although the Reformation is probably the most studied part of the history curriculum in British schools, the presuppositions that lie behind the politics and behaviour of southern Catholic Europe can still elude those who, like myself, have been brought up on the assumptions of Protestantism and the Enlightenment. There is a growing interest among academics in the United States in corporatism (what one enthusiast has termed the 'third great "-ism"'), but I see this not as necessarily reflecting a swing to a new right but rather as a long overdue attempt to come to terms with the categories of Mediterranean and specifically Iberian thought, with its roots in Thomism and the behavioral patterns of peasant society.

The history of the Americas reflects this division between north and south; European experience is mirrored there and by studying the different responses of European migrants in a northern and southern environment we can perhaps learn something about ourselves as Europeans. As for the insular British, there is some virtue in breaking with the traditional twinning of English and American studies, which can too easily lead to a distorted approach to United States culture. By replacing the horizontal comparison with a vertical one between North and South America, there may be a better chance of getting students to realize that the United States is a foreign country and not just an eccentric version of the British experience.

There are clearly dangers in the comparative approach; one has only to think of an explanation which seeks to account for the discrepancy in economic performance between the United States and Latin America in terms of Weber's Protestant ethic hypothesis. But if the major division of the next decades is to be that between the northern and southern hemispheres, between those countries which are exhausting their natural resources and those which still have vast unrealized potential, the sooner we begin to broaden our vision and think comparatively the better. Latin Americans may not yet be living with a frontier myth; it is possible that soon North Americans will not be living with one either. Myths only flourish if they contain a germ of truth. In the era of the post-oil crisis and the growth of cartels among the primary producers of the Third World, the frontier has now closed in a far more meaningful way than that announced prematurely in the United States census of 1890. This is not said in any spirit of an *Untergang des Abendlandes* but as a challenge to face up to the underside of the myth and to examine what in the context of slavery has been referred to as the 'fungoid region of our past'. In doing this no one should neglect the historical experience of Latin America, and in studying that experience to open up new perspectives for looking at our own history.

I

The Turner Thesis and Latin America

In the United States, frontier is a trigger word invested with potent incantatory meanings. This potency derives from a cluster of images and from an amalgam of expectations and aspirations which are embedded so deep in the layers of the American consciousness that Americans seem ill at ease without new frontiers to conquer; their literary imagination is dominated by the restless search for new Wests, finally discovering in science fiction a 'new inexhaustible West among the stars'.[1] The frontier is associated with westward expansion and it has been suggested that the west, with the magnetic pull of the setting sun, has a cosmic significance for all cultures. But a belief in cosmic forces is not needed to appreciate that the imaginative appeal of the West is intimately linked with the idea of freedom from restraints, of limitless opportunities, of dimly perceived yearnings and of recapturing the innocence of arcadia lost in the unyielding march of industrialization. For European peasants burdened by feudal obligations the West was the lure of free land; for workers penned in by industrial cities it provided an illusion of the carefree life, perhaps echoing a recently lost rural past. In Latin America, by contrast, there is no West; there is no Frontier; there are only frontiers.

After Frederick Jackson Turner read his essay, 'The Significance of the Frontier in American History', in 1893, putting into shape a good deal of thought which had been floating around rather loosely, the word frontier became endowed with mythical significance, gathering to itself a range of attributes which expressed all that was admirable in the American national character; at the same time the concept enunciated by Turner became a yardstick by which United States history could be interpreted and against which the histories of less fortunate nations could be measured. The extraordinary influence exerted by Turner's thesis—his original paper has a claim to be the most important ever read to a historical gathering—may be explained partly by the fact that it is a nationalist manifesto, stressing as nationalism does, the unique features in a nation's past. It was both an assertion of the Mid-West against the domination of the eastern sea-board and a repudiation of the European criteria by which American history and institutions had previously been judged.

Turner's North American frontier lay at the 'hither edge of free land' and was a frontier of settlement. The American usage of the word has none of the restrictive connotations of European frontiers which were seen as 'fortified boundary lines running through dense populations', the outer limits of state sovereignty beyond which one cannot pass without the formalities of passport control. It implies rather an expansive domain, open-ended and constantly yielding new vistas. The word frontier in its European sense is not used to describe the boundaries between the United States and Canada or Mexico; the word border is used.

Turner argued that the frontier continually pushing into free land was the most important factor moulding the American character. The frontier experience was what distinguished American history from that of Europe. When faced with untamed nature, with forest, plain and mountain, the inherited skills and book learning of Europe had no relevance.

> American democracy is fundamentally the outcome of the experiences of the American people in dealing with the West. Western democracy through the whole of its earlier period tended to the production of a society of which the most distinctive fact was the freedom of the individual to rise under conditions of social mobility, and whose ambition was the liberty and well-being of the masses. This conception has vitalized all American democracy, and has brought it into sharp contrasts with the democracies of history, and with those modern efforts of Europe to create an artificial democratic order by legislation.[2]

Survival demanded fresh values; the cultural baggage of the Old World had to be discarded and new skills learned and applied. Under the influence of the frontier environment, characteristics were developed on which rested the greatness and uniqueness of the nation—individualism, a democratic spirit, hard work, inventiveness, optimism, a distrust of government intervention and a belief in self-help. A crucial aspect of Turner's thesis was the idea of 'perennial rebirth'. The frontier was a magic fountain of youth in which America continually bathed and was rejuvenated. The frontier also fulfilled a critical function by constantly renewing democracy as each wave of settlement touched a new frontier. It is a measure of Turner's influence that his misgivings about the prospects for the future of American democracy once this process of renewal had become impossible with the closing of the frontier were shared by many public figures and were invoked to justify governmental regulation of American life as a substitute for the frontier.

Many objections have been raised to Turner's propositions—that only a small proportion of Americans were subjected to frontier influence; that by concentrating on the frontier he deflected attention away from the problems of race and the city; that it reflected widespread nativist prejudices of the 1890s; that the frontier did not act as a 'safety valve' for industrial discontent and that this cannot explain the reasons for the absence of an American socialist movement; that his 'closed-space' assumptions were exaggerated; that his use of metaphor was misleading; that his definition of frontier was imprecise; that there are inherent contradictions in the evolutionary presuppositions of his thought; that he indulged in the 'rhetoric of exaggeration'; that the innovatory and unique features of frontier democracy were overemphasized and that his agrarian utopia had already been undermined by the land speculator and the railway promoter. There is also the criticism that the values taken to the frontier were more important than the frontier environment; that ideas and institutions had been carried to the frontier and that the East shaped the West, turning pioneer Wests into developed Easts; that there was an element of pre- and self-selection in those who became frontiersmen and thus the frontier confirmed pre-existing traits and did not create them.

But even after 'nearly every attempt to impose conceptual structure upon the lyricism of Turner and his followers had been abandoned',[3] Turner's views still confirm what observers had been remarking for the previous hundred years—that there was an organic connection between American democracy (which, in common with European observers, he distinguished sharply from democracy in Europe) and the American frontier. The problem lies in establishing exactly what this connection is. Subsequent scholarship has refined the concept and has rescued something from the wreckage of earlier demolition, even in the case of the once seemingly totally discredited safety-valve hypothesis. However, the concern here is not to discuss the validity of the arguments but to look at Turner's thesis as a problem in intellectual history as well as an analysis of the American past, and to suggest that his popularity is related to the fact that American historians have been compelled to answer ontological questions which, many will argue, is not the job of a historian at all. However, historians do not operate in a vacuum; their social function (which is implicit even in the case of the recluse devoting himself to 'pure scholarship') changes from age to age. Turner believed that the historian must provide answers to questions which should be and were being asked by his contemporaries.

His achievement was to give metaphorical formulation to the crisis of the 1890s, and the resonance which this sounded may be partially explained by the dual nature of its appeal—on one side, the optimistic evocation of past collective endeavour, on the other, the pessimistic anticipation of a period when the frontier would no longer be present to rejuvenate American democracy. Nor would the frontier be able to 'Americanize' the hordes of new immigrants from southern and eastern Europe whose lack of democratic traditions and religious obscurantism seemed to the Anglo-American Protestant establishment, at least, with its social darwinist assumptions, to pose a direct challenge to the American democratic ideal. The thesis found an echo in a public, both academic and at large, avid for an *American* interpretation and explanation of contemporary problems. It was, too, a consensus thesis in so far as it could supersede sectional interpretations of the ante- and post-bellum eras. The curious fact that Turner allowed subsequent reprintings of the original essay to remain unchanged and that he kept aloof from much of the later controversy around it raises interesting psychological questions; but it is more apposite here to notice the almost complete lack of interest outside academia, in his theory of sections on which he spent much of his later life, in spite of what might be considered its greater explanatory potential. The contrast between acceptance and indifference gives some insight into the different relationship between the historian and a public welcoming the answer it wants to hear, as well as into the relationship between myth and history. A non-metaphorical argument which stresses conflict and division is less palatable to the nationalist mood than one couched in metaphor and stressing communal effort.

In Latin America, by contrast, the complex interweaving of historical exegesis and public need is largely absent: high illiteracy rates, a limited readership and the existence of only a small professional historiat, often operating from an insecure institutional base, has reduced dialogue between the historian and a wider public to a minimum. New nations needed myths, and historians stepped in to provide them, in eulogies of liberators like Bolívar or San Martín or of the role of Indians in Mexican independence. It was still difficult to find themes which could command total assent and round which consensus historiography could coalesce. Even in the case of Cuba where the war of independence had created a highly developed sense of nationalism the figure of José Martí, the hero of that war, was to be used indiscriminately by everyone from dictator to revolutionary to justify his own legitimacy. Heroes were pre-empted by factions to serve particularist ends; interpretations were skewed to justify parties in power or those in exile and, although Latin America had no monopoly in such matters, party histories there had a polemical bite hard to equal elsewhere.

The questions asked of Latin American historians will be different in kind from those asked of United States historians (except possibly in the case of defeated Southerners or of depressed ethnic minorities). Explanations of

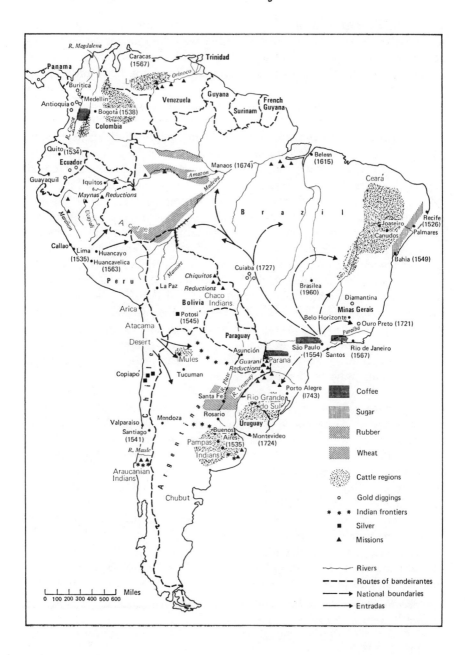

backwardness, underdevelopment, defeat and failure, rationalizations of feelings of inferiority or clarion calls to arms demand a different type of historiography from one concerned with accounting for material progress and democratic advance. History becomes, in Eric Williams's words, 'a manifesto for a subjugated people'. The history of independent Latin America has not been one of economic success or political stability. Whatever criticisms are levelled against the Turner thesis in the US, they have normally been made within the framework of capitalism, the basic postulates of which are not called into question. But Latin America's experience of capitalism has produced failures and dependence on outside powers, the more difficult to accept when compared with North American successes. Thus it is not surprising that Latin American historians have come to be critical of those processes which produced frontier expansion in the United States, nor will the word *frontera*, although it has connotations of an expanding area of settlement, deriving from medieval Spain, echo through the halls of the mind. Indeed, the multiplicity of political frontiers—*límites territoriales*—after the break up of the Spanish Empire, makes Latin America approximate more closely to Europe than to the United States.

A balance of power operates in Latin America which gives a European-style sensitivity to frontier disputes such as those between Argentina and Chile and between Peru and Ecuador, and hence any vision of unlimited territorial expansion is inevitably restrictive. Brazil, for example, cannot expand to the Pacific, only to the frontiers of her western neighbours, while conversely their expansion is blocked by Brazil. It is true that United States expansion was blocked by Mexico and Canada but this was overcome by superior power in the case of one and diplomacy in the case of the other, both underwritten by the expansionist ideology of Manifest Destiny. After 1850 all impediments, apart from natural obstacles and Indians, had been removed. Manifest Destiny not only legitimated the incorporation of Mexico's northern states and Oregon but finds an echo later in the 'spill over' frontier whereby the Canadian Prairie Provinces were seen as a legitimate sphere of activity for migrating farmers in the 1890s and northern Mexico for filibusters, cattle companies, miners and hoodlums. Although extreme expansionists argued for the incorporation of all Mexico and Canada, economic domination over both was to be achieved by indirect means, akin, in some ways, to Britain's 'informal empire'. From a Latin American perspective the expansionism implicit in the frontier concept did not stop with the closing of the frontier of settlement but was carried over into 'imperialist expansion' abroad. It would be surprising if the Turner thesis were not regarded from this perspective with a jaundiced eye, for its ideological implications have usually been insufficiently recognized by its North American defenders and detractors.[4]

In spite of this, Latin Americans have seen some relevance in Turner's views. One of the earliest to do so was the Peruvian, Victor Andrés Belaúnde. In 1923 he argued that the absence of a frontier in Turner's sense was one cause of the rigidity of the social system in Latin America, but he nevertheless recognized that the frontier idea could provide useful insights into Latin America's development.[5] He was not without subsequent influence and his nephew, Fernando Belaúnde Terry, was the first Peruvian president to incorporate the idea of an expanding frontier into the development programme of a political party—the Acción Popular.

It is in Brazil, however, that the frontier concept has had most resonance and relevance. Brazilian history has consisted of a number of sequential frontier pushes, corresponding to cyclical booms in different commodities. Thus brazil-wood was replaced by sugar which was replaced by gold which in its turn was replaced by coffee. Interspersed with these were other localized booms such as cotton, rubber or cacao. A pattern of exploiting a product in a near-monopoly situation until either it runs out, as gold did in the eighteenth century, or is undercut by rival producers, as in the case of sugar in the late seventeenth century and rubber in the early twentieth century, coupled with a shortage of labour, has contributed to the mobile migratory nature of Brazilian society—a trait shared with North Americans rather than with Spanish Americans. But a major difference between Brazil and the United States is the way in which frontiers have often been not consolidated but abandoned as migrants move on to the next boom product, thus creating the phenomenon of a 'hollow frontier'.

The epitome of mobility were the *bandeirantes*. Brazilian historians have regarded them as their frontiersmen par excellence, exploring the interior, discovering gold and staking out political claims for the Portuguese crown. Vianna Moog has pointed out, in a suggestive but pessimistic comparison between them and the North American pioneer, that they were essentially rootless plunderers not wanting to settle or put down roots; nevertheless their aggressive 'get up and go' mentality made them culture heroes for the inhabitants of São Paulo who like to model themselves on their forbears. Other historians have taken a less jaundiced view and stressed their essentially democratic qualities which, transmitted to their descendants, became an integral component of the Brazilian national character.

In the more densely settled northeast, Gilberto Freyre's *Masters and Slaves*, emphasizing the mixing of the early Portuguese settlers with the indigenous peoples and with African slaves, seemed a more appropriate text to explain historical influences. But common to both the *bandeirante* and Freyre school of historians is the emphasis on adaptation to environment through miscegenation—one primarily Indian and European, the other European and African. Freyre's influence has been greater because, by extolling the African heritage, he helped to overcome the stigma caused by a slave past. While Brazil's younger social historians criticise his argument for its overemphasis on continuities and the processes of accommodation and underemphasis on conflict, its importance as myth is comparable to the frontier of Turner's thesis. The Brazilian equivalent of the frontier myth is the myth of racial harmony, and this comes to provide both an explanation of the 'non-violent' nature of Brazilian history in contrast to that of Spanish America and a legitimation of present policies. Now, however, with the opening up of the Brazilian west, quite as violent as its North American counterpart, this myth is being replaced by a frontier myth with Manifest Destiny overtones. Whether frontier expansion is all that different under authoritarian military rule as opposed to democratic government will only be clear when more research has been done. On present evidence it appears to be perpetuating a two-class system rather than producing a viable rural middle class comparable with North America.

If the importance of the Turner thesis lies in its mythic force and its ability to provide a legitimating and fructifying nationalist ideology, then the absence of a Latin American frontier myth is easy to explain. Without democracy, there was no compulsion to elaborate a supportive ideology based on frontier experiences and their putative influence on national character and institutions. But the non-existence of a frontier myth is not necessarily proof that frontier communities in Latin America did not have democratic traits; at present we lack detailed studies which would enable us to offset the image of the frontier as dark and menacing, and the dichotomy between the 'barbarism' of the interior and the 'civilization' of the cities, forcibly expressed by the Argentinian, Domingo Sarmiento, in *Facundo* in 1845, is one that dies hard. The work of social anthropologists has shown that, even in the case of cattle societies, there are methods of control which are very far removed from the stereotype of unrestrained *caudillismo*. It is likely, in fact, that these other disciplines, with readily accessible evidence, will be able to throw more light on the influences of environment and on the mechanisms of social control than history can. One explanation for the neglect of frontier history has been paucity of material. Disorganized archives, incomplete runs of statistics and destroyed documents are obstacles which are not easily overcome. Walter Prescott Webb complained, in answer to criticism that he had only given the Anglo version of the Texas Rangers, that it was impossible to reconstruct the Mexican version through lack of archival material. Yet there is a sense in which archives are not discovered or organized until there is a compulsion to do so. Bolton's Borderlands school, for example, because of reliance on traditional archival research, did not uncover those sources which are needed to reconstruct the recent history of the forgotten minority of the Borderlands. The task of the first generation of Chicano historians, seeking answers to different questions from those posed by Bolton, is to ferret out these sources.

The problem of writing history from below is more complex in Latin America where we are dealing with a culture of *expresión oral* rather than the *letra impresa* of North America and Europe, with its insatiable market for memoirs and travellers' accounts of all and any aspects of North American frontier life.[6] The North American frontiersmen were voluble and often literate as tourists early attracted to the American West described them (readers will recall the English party encountered by Parkman on the Oregon Trail as early as 1846). But for descriptions of popular life in nineteenth-century Latin America, which the cultured elite there either anathematized, romanticized or ignored, we must still rely to a very great extent on foreign travellers.

Even if frontier societies had possessed democratic traits it is unlikely that these values would have flowed back and influenced thinking in the cities, given the state of communications, lack of information and absence of any agrarian myth comparable to Jeffersonianism, which predisposed many in the United States to conjure up a 'garden' image of the newly opening West. Without such influences the hierarchical, corporatist values of the colonial period remained unmodified or were covered over by a veneer of foreign importations such as liberalism or positivism. Peripheral areas were never strong enough to modify the centralizing, authoritarian tendencies of the Spanish state or to challenge these without breaking its unity; thus when Bolivia and Paraguay chose to become independent, the local elite established its own particular brand of authoritarian centralism. The centralizing tradition is still deeply rooted as may be seen in the artificiality of Latin American federal systems.

Stressing as he does the uniqueness of North American frontier experience and enunciating an exceptionalist interpretation of American history, Turner has often been accused of parochialism. However, he was aware of other frontiers and recognized, for example, that the Canadian experience had produced a different kind of society. He was also aware of the potentialities for research on frontiers in Latin America—although he did not follow this up, possibly because the absence of American-style democracy made comparison seem irrelevant. But frontiers do not necessarily produce democratic societies, as was shown even in the United States by the expansion of the slave plantation frontier in the Gulf Plains of the Deep South.

An exception to this lack of interest, however, was Herbert Bolton. His seminal article on 'The Mission as a Frontier Institution in the Spanish-American Colonies', published in 1917, seemed to presage a school of frontier historians of Latin America; but with few exceptions his graduate students concentrated their attention on the Spanish Borderlands and their influence was limited.[7] Nor did Bolton's address to the meeting in Toronto of the American Historical Association in 1932 on 'The Epic of Greater America' strike a responsive chord. A rather vapid liberal pan-Americanism was not the answer to questions most people were asking in the Depression years—except possibly for the State Department in formulating the Good Neighbour Policy of two years later. Bolton did not become another Turner, nor did he achieve his ambitions to 'Parkmanize' the Spanish contribution to American history. But had a school of frontier historians of Latin America developed they would have found a fertile field for their investigations.

Latin American frontiers show a greater diversity than those of North America. To mention only the most striking, there were mission frontiers in northern New Spain, Paraguay, on the Amazon and the Orinoco, silver mining frontiers in New Spain, Honduras, Upper Peru and Chile, gold frontiers in Colombia and Brazil, base metal frontiers throughout the

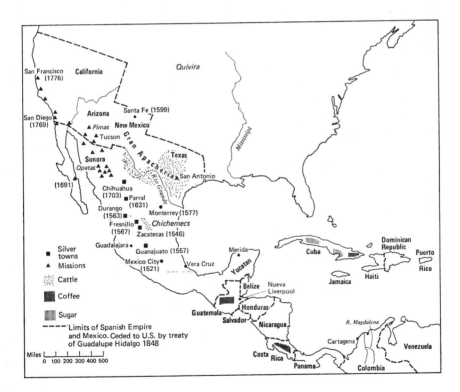

Andes, northern Mexico and Brazil, cattle frontiers in New Spain, Venezuela, the pampas, northeast, southern and now western Brazil, farmers'
and coffee frontiers, the Amazonian rubber frontier, the frontier of
religious sects and, on the periphery of settlement, Indian frontiers.

It would be wrong to think that each type of frontier produced similar
societies. In this respect Latin America reveals a yet wider range than the
United States. The difference between various precious metal frontiers and
the difference between various coffee frontiers, to take two examples, are
to be explained by contrasts in their respective labour systems. Thus the
silver mines of Mexico were largely dependent on free labour whereas
those in Upper Peru relied on the forced labour system of the *mita*. In the
case of gold, frontiers could range from the North American style
individual or family prospector in Colombia to the slave system of the
gold diggings of Minas Gerais in Brazil. Similar contrasts may be seen on
coffee frontiers. The expansion of coffee plantations in the Guatemalan
highlands relied on Indian peons, in Colombia the coffee frontier consisted
of family homesteads, in Oriente in Cuba *cafetales* were worked by slaves,
and in Brazil they were at first dependent on slaves and then, after
abolition, on cheap European immigrant labour, and in Venezuela on
casual labour. A major contrast, therefore, between North and Latin
American frontiers is that those in Latin America were differentiated by
availability of labour in varying forms whereas, in the United States,
opportunity provided the stimulus, attracting to the frontier labour which
was always available because of a constant flow of new immigrants
(although not too many to inhibit a high-wage economy or render
technological invention unnecessary) and the highly mobile nature of
North American society. What is significant and needs explanation is the
question why, in Latin America, scarcity of labour did not increase labour's
bargaining power but, on the contrary, led to its virtual enserfment.

What is a frontier? Even in the United States where it seems fairly
simple to identify it as the cutting edge between settled and unsettled
land, there was still vagueness and many ambiguities. When, for example,
does a frontier cease to be a frontier; at what stage does the metamor-
phosis occur? Turner himself seemed to use the concept in three different
senses—as a geographical region, as a process of adaptation and as a
condition, the existence at the edge of settlement of an unused area of
land. If one uses the definition of the United States Bureau of Statistics, that
a frontier exists when the density of population is less than two persons
per square mile, then much of Latin America has been and still is frontier
territory. Take out the metropolitan areas and we are left with perhaps
as much as two thirds of the continent which could be described as
frontier. As Isaac Bowman put it in the 1930s: 'One of the most extraordinary features of Spanish American life is the persistence of frontier

conditions through the centuries since the Conquest. It is still a continent of pioneer fringes.'[8]

The problem is complicated by the original settlement pattern. There are few examples of a 'cutting edge' frontier. Turner could write of the United States lying 'like a huge page in the history of society. Line by line as we read this continental page from west to east we find the record of social evolution.'[9] Even discounting the nineteenth-century evolutionary assumptions, there is still a sense in which frontier expansion was cumulative with settlements succeeding each other as the flow of immigrants created a self-generating momentum of expansion, inexorably pushing on and filling in. In contrast, the most striking feature of early Spanish American expansion was its centrifugal nature. The lure of El Dorado drew expeditions into the interior of the continent so that within fifty years Spaniards had penetrated into the most inaccessible regions—from Coronado's expedition of 1540 to Quivira, in what is now Kansas, in search of the Seven Cities of Cíbola, to the expeditions into wind-swept Patagonia in search of the 'City of the Caesars'. These 'cities', the product of febrile imaginations nourished on medieval fantasies, did not materialize except in the by-product of squalid isolated settlements which the disappointed searchers were compelled to establish; by 1600 the continent was dotted with over three hundred towns although some of these might consist of only fifty or a hundred families. By any definition these were frontier settlements but, instead of the frontier line creeping forward under irresistible pressures of immigration from Europe, expansion has consisted of a painfully slow 'filling-in' process between these original settlements. What R. M. Morse has written in respect of Brazil is equally applicable to Spanish America:

> The frontier is not a line or a limit or a process either unilateral or unilinear. We must, in fact, speak not of a frontier but of multiple complex frontier experiences, transactions and mutations. We can draw no fixed line between white man and Indian, civilization and primitivism, settled and unsettled areas, imperial outpost and autonomous community. Settlement occurred and still occurs in an archipelago pattern.[10]

An important factor both determined by and in itself determining this extended settlement pattern was the slow rate of immigration to Latin America. Some 243,000 may have emigrated to Spanish America in the first hundred years (with possibly one million African slaves legally imported and some half million smuggled in over the whole colonial period, together with some three and a half millions into Brazil). In the hundred years between 1820 and 1920 only seven millions voluntarily emigrated to Latin America in comparison with thirty-three and a half millions to the

United States. To these factors must be added geographical and climatic conditions: there was no Mississippi, Missouri, Ohio or St Lawrence to carry settlers into the heart of the continent; impenetrable jungle and Indians deterred settlement on the banks of the Orinoco and Amazon. Although the River Plate, as the name implies, was thought to lead to fabled silver mountains, early adventurers found their way barred by the arid wastes of the Chaco desert. Asunción, founded in 1535, stands as a symbol of the failure to reach their goal. The only rivers to have played a role comparable to those of North America were the São Francisco in northeast Brazil, which was the main entry into the cattle highlands of the interior and the gold diggings of Minas Gerais and, less important, the Magdalena in Colombia. Moreover, North America did not have the disadvantage of vast areas subject to incurable tropical diseases (although the Mississippi delta was sufficiently insalubrious to encourage migration to healthy Texas). But it would be unwise to overstress geographical obstacles except in the crucial question of relative transportation costs. These obstacles could deter, but could also provide a spur and a challenge. The Great Plains and the Rockies in the United States, and the Canadian Prairies with their hazardous climatic conditions were no barrier to the determined, nor did geographical perils hinder figures like Cabeza de Vaca, Coronado, Gonzalo Pizarro, Orellana and a host of others. What is important is not the environment but the motivation. The extraordinary feature of the Spanish and Portuguese experience was the early restlessness and rootlessness, a consequence of peninsular antecedents, of miscegenation and of pastoralism. This mobility is all the more striking because of its contrast with the telluric, earth-bound qualities of sedentary Indian communities and the near-mystical significance which the earth has for the Indian. If we are looking for a genuine rural culture in Latin America we must look, with only rare exceptions, to Indian communities.

Another contrast lies in the availability of 'free land'. Whereas free land was the magnet attracting pioneers into the North American wilderness, in Latin America most available land had been pre-empted by landowning patterns set in the sixteenth century. The *latifundio*, not the homestead, became the typical rural institution. Undercapitalized, worked with a primitive technology and by a virtually enserfed, debt-ridden peon labour force, the *latifundio*, although not necessarily inefficient by the standards of the colonial period, nevertheless set the pattern and saddled most Latin American countries in the nineteenth and twentieth century with an inefficient and retarded agriculture. Rural life offered few prospects for land-hungry European peasants yearning to become yeomen farmers.

Excessive concentration of land was a consequence not only of the colonial period but also of the redistribution of properties in the early years of independence. In many countries where there was no provision for the occupancy of lands until the late nineteenth century, those with political contacts were able to buy up huge expanses of public domain at minimal cost. Much of the early land policy of independent states was designed to attract European immigrants but the failure of most of these schemes underlined the need to discourage indigenous labour from taking to the frontier as a way of escaping from unprofitable share-cropping or onerous peonage. This was done by legislation making it difficult to obtain land legally.

Spanish emigrants in the sixteenth and seventeenth centuries went to the New World not to become farmers or to build a 'City on a Hill' but, in Bernal Díaz's much quoted, succinct phrase, 'to serve God and his Majesty, to give light to those in darkness and also to get rich'. Many settled in areas of sedentary agricultural Indians. They needed the Indians' labour at the same time as they strove for their souls and mated with their women. Thus in Spanish America we find a 'frontier of inclusion'. With the Church, Crown and settlers all having different interests in the Indian population, there could be no sharply defined racial frontier—a 'frontier of exclusion'—such as we find in the United States. Neither Indians (except as a 'consolidating agent') nor blacks have any place in Turner's adaptation thesis: the Mountain Men might acquire trapping techniques and women from the Indians but they were an exception. They were the 'users' rather than the 'subduers' of nature. It could be argued that the racial exclusivity of the North American frontier reveals as much about the 'national character' as the supposed virtues promulgated by the Turner thesis—democracy for us but not for them.

The Latin American frontier involved an adaptation to peoples as well as, and perhaps even more than, to environment. Hence the crucial importance of the distinction between 'frontiers of exclusion' and 'frontiers of inclusion'. In the former, a geographical frontier is also an ethnic, cultural and economic frontier with little impermeability between the two sides. In the latter, ethnic, cultural and economic facets of the indigenous society are absorbed within Westernizing society and find expression in a whole variety of eclectic cultural forms in dancing, music, plays and folk Catholicism, reaching the most sophisticated early expression in the historical work of Garcilaso de la Vega. From this vantage point, it is justifiable to subsume under the generic 'frontier' those cultural and ethnic frontiers which are to be most brutally exposed when the impact of expanding *haciendas* disrupts Indian communities.

In Spanish America and in Brazil miscegenation created a new human type, and it is on peripheral frontiers in Latin America that racial mixing most readily occurs in spite of many attempts, especially by the Church, to prohibit it. A form of 'racial apartheid'—to protect the Indians from exploitation by labour-hungry settlers—could be enforced where the policy of reductions was successful, as in the Jesuit missions in Paraguay or in their *aldeias* in Brazil; but where control was looser it went by default. Few white women faced the perils of exposure to Indian raids and the frontier missions sometimes closed a blind eye to soldiers and settlers taking Indian wives as this was one way of 'civilizing' them. There was also a centrifugal tendency, and particularly in northern Mexico, for rootless *mestizos* to drift to the frontier where work could be had as itinerant cattlemen and where the subtle gradations and distinctions of the *casta* society carried little weight. Similarly, in northeast Brazil (and indeed wherever there were unsettled hinterlands behind slave plantations) the cattle frontier of the *sertão* became a haven for runaway slaves and a racial melting pot of great complexity. These frontier regions tended to be highly volatile as was the case in the Orinoco valley during the Wars of Independence, in northern Mexico which became the cradle of revolution in 1910 and in northeast Brazil with its endemic banditry and religious messianic movements.

Although it would be misleading to suggest that miscegenation did not occur elsewhere, it is on the frontier that it found free expression. Under Darwinian and racialist influence, this intermixing was regarded by many Latin American thinkers as a major cause of backwardness in the nineteenth century and this reinforced the dichotomy between a 'barbarous' interior and a 'civilized' coast. Arguments for stimulating European immigration, especially from northern Europe, were based partly on the assumption that it would serve to offset congenital deficiencies of a mixed population; the inherent qualities of European immigrants would overcome the drawbacks of the Latin American social and physical environment. It was not until the new nationalist upsurge of the 1920s and 1930s that thinkers like the Mexican, José Vasconcelos, and the Brazilian, Gilberto Freyre, began to make a virtue out of racial necessity and to argue that 'miscegenation', far from being a drawback, was a positive gain in that a mixed population adapted more easily to an environment hostile to pure Europeans. Thus, in contrast to Turner's stress on environment, Latin American thinkers have stressed biological factors.

In the United States, the frontier environment, not a biological fusion of races or a declining Indian population, provided inspiration for a nationalist mythology at a time when the 'new' immigration from southern and eastern Europe seemed to pose a threat to traditional American values. For Turner as well as the agrarian populists, real wealth was created by honest farmers working close to the soil, not by financial speculators or the sweated labour of unassimilated immigrants in the ghettoes of eastern cities. There were echoes of Germanic nature—romanticism in this view that the frontier would be a bulwark against the insidious and incurable corruption of city life.

In Latin America an accelerating flow of immigrants after the 1880s, especially into Argentina, Brazil, Uruguay and Chile, posed similar problems of assimilation. The majority of these new migrants, and especially those from southern Europe, settled in cities as in the United States, thus sharpening the rural-urban split. The extent to which only foreigners could bring life to isolated frontier regions was one of the central issues in the debate over immigration. Cities were still, as in Sarmiento's day, symbols of civilization and modernity with their opera houses, bourses, railway termini and Parisian boulevards. But they were now regarded as breeding grounds of subversive doctrines—their immigrant populations the carriers of Spanish and Italian anarchism or German socialism with an implied threat to the dominant creole oligarchy. Throughout the Americas cities now seemed to threaten the purity of American ideals— individualist democracy in the United States, paternalist authoritarianism in Latin America.

In Turner's response to this threat the frontier was a great simplifier. Latin American responses were more complex; there was no frontier experience which could provide the basis for a nationalist myth. The frontier had either crushed those who had ventured to it, or in those cases where it had expanded successfully it had done so under the aegis of foreign capital—British managed railways pushing into the pampas and the Andes, nitrate and rubber companies with their financial headquarters in London. Frontiers expanded or contracted in response to external market demands almost to the exclusion of internal markets which were too restricted in size, purchasing power and industrial potential. This was not material from which nationalist myths could be spun. Such prosperity and progress as there was in Latin America seemed to come as much from foreign technical expertise and capital as from native efforts.

Most Latin American thinkers were still mesmerized by Europe. In 1900, for example, the Uruguayan José Enrique Rodó published *Ariel* with its juxtaposition of Latin America as Ariel representing the ethereal spirituality of European culture and Caliban representing the materialism of the United States. In Rodó's view, Latin America was the true heir to the European cultural tradition. The popularity and influence of this book, at first sight difficult for the foreigner to fathom, was due to its being a compensating ideology of sublimation on the part of a small nation in the face of the overwhelming material power of the United States whose financial and political influence had been increasing in Latin America in the 1890s. The attractions of Rodó's book were obvious to an elite fearful of the levelling influence of North American democracy, at the same time it glossed over the more unattractive materialist aspects of European influence in South America represented by money-grubbing immigrants, avid to make their fortune and then return to the Old World. It also contributed to the myth of incorruptibility of youth (Rodó was known as the '*maestro de la juventud*') and the idea—to be influential in later student movements—that salvation would come from the younger generation imbued with the teachings of classical European culture. Whereas in the United States the frontier was the great rejuvenator, constantly revivifying democratic idealism, in Latin America rejuvenation would come from an intellectual and spiritual elite. In this process there was no role for the common man, for the Indian, mestizo or mulatto.

This was to change in the Latin America of the 1920s in the aftermath of widespread disillusion with Europe caused by the First World War. Under the influence of the Mexican Revolution's revindication of the Indian, *indigenismo* became a vogue among writers, especially in the Andean countries with their large Indian populations. It had its counterpart of Afro-Brazilianism and Afro-Cubanism in the two countries with large African minorities while in the writings of Vasconcelos and Freyre miscegenation acquired intellectual respectability. In so far as the interior had been tamed it was argued that it had been largely due to mixed races. Forbidding environments had been settled by those who accepted, learnt from and mixed with the indigenous inhabitants.

The history of frontier expansion in the Americas is the history of the expansion of European capitalism into non-European areas. European expansion involved the interlocking of the economies of peripheral frontier regions with those of European metropolises, gradually creating a unified worldwide trading system. Walter Prescott Webb put this most succinctly in *The Great Frontier* when he argued that modern western European civilization was a direct consequence of the opening up of world frontiers.[11] Webb referred to the four hundred year-old boom that resulted from 'windfalls' of vast natural resources discovered in the unsettled parts of the world, the Americas, Australasia, South Africa. In Webb's nomenclature, Europe is the metropolis dominating the exploitation of these frontiers in its own interest. Because of these windfalls, Europe was able to afford the luxuries of democracy, individualism and 'high culture'. Marxists and neo-Marxists have elaborated similar approaches but many historians do not take very kindly to macro-explanations of this sort. Nevertheless, Webb's thesis serves a useful purpose in drawing attention to the transitory nature of European dominance and may perhaps be viewed a little more sympathetically for its insight in these days of the post-oil crisis era.

Frontier expansion introduced European property concepts and the idea of profit and monetary exchange into societies where previously these had been unknown. Once a region had been touched by frontier expansion, there could be no turning back. For the indigenous peoples the choice was limited: they might reject modernity by withdrawing into mountain or jungle but this could spell extinction. The irony of the phrase 'free land' is that land was only free if the pre-emptive claims of indigenous peoples were ignored. What might appear to be empty lands could well be buffalo hunting grounds; Indians were marginal to the frontier—useful initially to the fur trader or as auxiliaries in colonial wars but ultimately expendable and troubling few consciences if they became extinct. Yet as the history of submerged minority groups comes to be written we are becoming aware that there is an underside to the democratic myth. Freedom not only meant freedom from European class systems, it also meant freedom to break those unable to compete. The frontier symbolized not only democracy but the rage for property, dressed in the postulates of Lockean individualism; physiocratic notions of agriculture as the source of wealth, together with nineteenth century evolutionary views, meant that hunters were relegated to the status of non-people. From this perspective, the land speculator and not the rugged pioneer appears the more significant frontier figure.

At this point it is worth suggesting that the distance between North American and Latin American frontier experience as far as land policy was concerned was not as wide as might at first appear. In the United States land was less equitably distributed than the Homestead Act of 1862 might lead one to expect because of loopholes in the legislation (land companies in Argentina were not unique in nullifying the intent of homestead laws), while in Latin America some of the long accepted truisms about the inefficiency of haciendas and the uneven distribution of land are now being questioned. The model of the northern Mexican hacienda during the colonial period is not a reliable one even for the rest of Mexico let alone South America, where recent research is emphasizing wide regional variations in landholding patterns caused by both environmental and demographic factors.

Farming in the United States eventually became hyperefficient, after the wasteful methods of the mid-nineteenth century but, when it did so, the bonanza farms and the political attitudes of their owners bore little relation to the Jeffersonian agrarianism and Jacksonian democracy on which Turner, with his eyes fixed mainly on the old Northwest, was nurtured. Nomenclature, too, obscured the fact that poorer rural dwellers in the United States could just as well have been described as 'peasants' as 'poor farmers'. Debt peonage based on the crop-lien system was not unknown in the Deep South during the twentieth century[12] and the availability of a huge migrant agricultural proletariat, which helped to ensure the profitability of Californian agri-business, would have been the envy of any sugar corporation in pre-revolutionary Cuba. Finally, in the case of Indian lands, the opening of reservations to white settlement was the equivalent in the United States of the encroachment of Latin American haciendas on Indian communal lands. In the former it was caused by a superfluity of land-hungry migrants and in the latter by a paucity of labour often resulting from the failure to attract European immigrants.

If historians focus attention on the dominance of foreign capital in the expansion of the cattle frontier in Argentina or the base metal frontiers of the Andes, it is as well to recall the very large investment of foreign capital on both the cattle and mining frontiers in North America. What needs to be explained are the mechanisms by which one perpetuated economic dependence but the other stimulated autonomous economic growth.

One of the most controversial aspects of the frontier thesis has been the extent to which the frontier served as a safety-valve for urban discontent. It has been argued that the obverse was true and that the cities became an outlet for agrarian discontent, especially in the depression years of the later 1880s and 1890s. Migrants to cities do not have the same capital requirements as migrants to rural areas. Thus the experiences of the United States and Latin America are not as diametrically opposed as they would be if the Turner hypothesis retained its validity—although it is true that the 'psychological safety-valve' of the 'open West' was denied to most Latin Americans.

Turner virtually ignores the role of capital but it was of crucial importance in mining and farm technology, a field where contrast between the United States and Latin America could not have been wider. North Americans had scarcely any skills when the mining frontier opened with the Californian gold rush (except those acquired in the lead mines of Galena or the copper mines of Michigan). Techniques were copied from Mexican miners but the slowness of their methods stimulated new technologies requiring heavy Eastern and foreign investment. With the challenge of hard rock and quartz mining, North American mining technology shot ahead and was pre-eminent in the world by 1900. Inventiveness is not a prerogative of frontier societies but the list of inventions stimulated by the challenge of the opening of the Great Plains is impressive, ranging from the six-shooter to portable windmills, barbed wire (with its consequent stimulus to selective breeding and the destruction of the Spanish inherited open-range) as well as an enormous variety of mechanical appliances from improved ploughs to harvest combines.

T. Lynn Smith has argued that advanced plough culture, using an improved plough was 'probably the factor which did most to generate the immense differences between the levels of living in northern Europe and southern Europe and between those in the United States and Canada and those in Latin America'.[13] Whereas the unimproved wooden rooting plough was the mainstay of Mediterranean and Latin American agriculture, the North American colonies were the recipients of advanced plough culture based on the moldboard plough, cutting and turning at the same time. Wherever European immigrants introduced a similar system as in Chile, Argentina and southern Brazil they made significant contributions to efficient agriculture and a pattern similar, in some respects, to North American experience emerges. Elsewhere, methods proved resistant to change because of peasant conservatism, geographical intractability and lack of capital and farming expertise.

Part of this resistance to innovation may be explained by the processes of acculturation to a new environment whereby Spanish culture had to be simplified in America because of the need to transmit its rudiments to the native population. George Foster cites the case of the adoption of a single plough type instead of the wide regional diversity found in Spain at the time of the Conquest.[14] Cultural patterns crystallized very early and, mainly because the immigrants were comparatively homogeneous (in spite of regional variations which, on occasions, were divisive), there was not the same compulsion as in the Thirteen Colonies to accommodate widely differing cultural and religious traditions and so create the need for compromise and debate. The extended nature of Latin American settlement with settlers exposed to marauding tribes or outnumbered by sedentary Indians among whom they lived were additional factors in discouraging divisive innovation. There was a correspondingly strong compulsion towards making later arrivals conform to an established conservative culture, particularly in face of an expanding and potentially rebellious mestizo population. Thus were perpetuated the hierarchical, corporatist and patrimonial assumptions of late medievalism, together with the cultural norms of Mediterranean peasant society and the religious beliefs of the Spanish Catholic Church.

Perhaps the most striking fact about the economic development of Latin America in contrast with North America is the perpetuation of many archaic economic and social forms on the frontier.[15] Part of the explanation for this process, which reaches into the nineteenth and, in some cases, the twentieth century, is the very unfavourable man-to-land ratio prevailing in large parts of Latin America. Inflexible attitudes were bred by a super-fluity of land in a situation of labour scarcity. Big estate owners made land artificially scarce by restricting access to it and so forcing labour to work for them. Labour scarcity stemming from the demographic catastrophe of the sixteenth century coupled with the slow rate of immigration from Europe and the difficulties of attracting capital to frontiers made many of these regions deserts of exile and despair, where rural bosses exercised domination virtually independent of the control of the central government; this was the case in Mexican California, whose isolation made it a lotus eater's paradise. When capital did move to frontier regions it was usually foreign capital impelled by the demand for raw materials from the industrializing powers in the latter half of the nineteenth century—copper and nitrates in Chile, copper and zinc in Mexico, tin in Bolivia, oil in Venezuela. The mines and oil fields were enclave economies, connected directly with ports, skewing transport systems and in general producing few multiplier effects on the economy. Expansion and export sectors failed to transform an economic life which consisted of export cycles and localized booms. Exports were mostly controlled by foreign merchants, financed by foreign banks and left little room for local initiative in foreign policy making. Domestic manufacturers were sacrificed to agricultural export interests. Intellectuals were often seduced by the siren song of laissez-faire which was widely regarded as the key to prosperity because of British success, but which, in practice, crippled artisan industry, disrupted regional economies and linked coastal metropolises to foreign metropolitan centres rather than to their own hinterlands. It is scarcely surprising that this socioeconomic environment did not engender political liberty, social mobility or the other reputed effects of the North American frontier.

It is tempting to reverse Turner's hypothesis by asserting that, far from stimulating democratic values and creating a democratic myth, the frontier in Latin America has bred a spirit of lawless anarchy and perpetuated outworn forms of social and economic organization whose typical political expression is pastoral despotism. It could be argued that it is these frontier regions which have bred *caudillismo* or strong man rule; that power and prestige derive from ownership of land and domination over a serf-like rural following; that in the struggle between the 'barbarism' of the interior and the 'civilization' of the city, it is the former which has triumphed; that, instead of an expanding frontier, Latin America has produced a contracting frontier in which cities are being engulfed by a rising tide of peasant migrants escaping from the misery of poverty in the countryside and are importing into the cities the residual legacies of rural boss-rule; and that the prevalence of dictatorial government is directly related to the failure of frontiers to produce viable rural communities.

This is to put the case in extreme form and such generalizations are too simplistic; nevertheless the relationship between developed metropolises and underdeveloped frontiers requires elucidation. Looked at in historical perspective, the failure to generate dynamic frontier expansion, for whatever reasons, has bequeathed a legacy of structural imbalances and lopsided growth which some writers have explained in terms of 'internal colonialism'.[16] The capital cities are seen as the legatees of colonial power; their relationship to the rural interior is similar to that between industrialized and non-industrialized countries in that the gap between the two under the impact of modernization is widening rather than narrowing. Once there is an initial imbalance between the metropolis and the periphery—or the frontier—it proves extremely difficult to restore any balance. Capital flows to where profits are guaranteed, foreign investment is attracted to where there is already an infrastructure of roads, railways, skills, credit institutions. The city acts as a magnet for the able-bodied; push factors of poor educational facilities, bad housing, inadequate medical care, inequitable tenancies and generally restricted opportunities combine with pull factors of greater opportunities and excitement in the city, educational possibilities and the dream of social advancement. A reversal of the capital and population flows of the magnitude experienced by every country in Latin America would require a massive commitment of resources as well as acceptance of revolutionary change which the beneficiaries of the present system are unlikely to accept without a struggle.

Although frontier settlement has become a prime concern for Latin American governments, there is no frontier myth to stir massive migration to the countryside and this is unlikely to occur without an avalanche of potential farmers from outside. At present in Latin America, socially and politically conscious historians seem more concerned, as in the United States, with urban problems. Faced with spiralling urban growth and with the spectre of urban terrorism in one case, and with prohibitive costs and urban decay in the other, an understanding of the dynamics of urban growth in historical perspective has assumed a new urgency. Latin America's salvation might seem to require a rural myth: there might well be a role for a Latin American Turner but he would be hard put to fashion a progressive myth out of past agrarian history. Perhaps the discovery of new mineral resources, as, for example, in the Venezuelan Oriente, will be the magnet to reverse the flow to the cities; this, after all, would be in a well-worn tradition for mines were a motor of frontier expansion throughout the colonial period.

2
Conquistadores, Crown and Church

The Spanish background

In the same year that the peninsular frontier closed with the conquest of the last Moorish stronghold of Granada in 1492, a new frontier of limitless possibilities opened with Columbus's discovery of America. Within fifty years an area between thirty and forty times that of the Iberian kingdoms had been claimed by a few thousand adventurers. In medieval Europe, the seven hundred years' Reconquest had been a rare example of an expanding frontier in which the Moors were pressed back and lands were opened up for settlement and colonization. In this medieval enterprise two contrasting concepts of the frontier intermingled —a politico-military boundary between two hostile powers and an expanding frontier of settlement.

The triumph of the Reconquest sanctified the virtues which had made success possible. The perpetuation of the values of a military and clerical aristocracy was considered integral to the future triumph of Spanish arms in Italy and against the Ottoman Empire. The response to these challenges might have been different had Spain not become the heir to an overseas empire. Without its supply of American silver, the Crown could have been forced by the nascent bourgeoisie to make a political bargain. As it was, the bonanza of New World wealth breathed fresh life into the values of the successful Reconquest.

Military success legitimized the levying of tribute on the defeated and the enslavement of captives taken in war. The private nature of the early expeditions of the *conquistadores*, with their personal followings, gave the Conquest a medieval military character in which gifts of *encomiendas* and *repartimientos* were regarded as rewards for services. Mentalities were conditioned by the warfare of an expanding frontier, and to many conquistadores the conquest of America was simply an extension of the Reconquest in the peninsula. The crusading spirit was transferred to the New World. Victory against the Moors bred the conviction of righteousness and confirmed the Spaniards' view of themselves as God's chosen people with the right to reap an economic reward for doing his work.

Settlement patterns in America echoed two distinctive features of peninsular experience—the process of colonization by towns rather than by unprotected rural settlements, and by extension of a cattle and pastoral economy into the newly liberated areas. Chronic instability and the threat of attack from raiding parties were responsible for the peninsular pattern of municipal settlement which resulted in a society markedly different from the villages and manorial economy of northern Europe. In Spain we can talk of an 'urban frontier' with such towns as Plasencia and Cáceres providing the market centres for a pastoral economy. Scarcity of labour, the hazardous nature of crop farming as well as climatic and geographic conditions favoured pastoralism, either of sheep or cattle. A growing demand for the wool of Spanish merino sheep in northern Europe finally gave the victory to sheep farmers, consolidating the powerful Mesta sheep guild. The passage of herds from summer pastures in Asturias southward to winter pastures in Andalusia was such a fiscal boon to the Crown that agricultural interests were sacrificed to those of the Mesta. West-central Spain, especially Extremadura, suffered from the depredations of trans-humant sheep to such an extent that it became the region from which a high proportion of early settlers in the New World was drawn, carrying with them over the ocean some of the instability and restlessness of a mobile herding economy. Further south in Andalusia, which also provided a large number of early settlers, cattle predominated.

Andalusian cattle-ranching was unique in medieval Europe, apart from the Hungarian Plain. Elsewhere cattle tended to be subordinated to a manorial crop agriculture. The heavy-uddered placidity of the milch cow in a mixed farming economy contrasted with the feral bulls and lean, tough-hided cattle of Andalusia and the Algarve of southern Portugal. The exigencies of long-distance grazing on open ranges led to a unique cattle culture with round-ups, branding and the bull-fight which was perpetuated from the sixteenth century onwards as an urban court spectacle and surrogate for a frontier that had closed. Thus stock-raising was more important than tillage and agriculture languished in Spain. So also in America, Indian agriculture declined and armies of ravening pigs, goats and cattle, which had been introduced into the New World by the Spaniards, rampaged over unfenced fields.

Two other factors conditioned the nature of Spanish emigration. Firstly, many of the conquistadores were *hidalgos*—the lesser aristocracy whose exaggerated social pretensions precluded them from making a living from commerce. Out of the 168 in Pizarro's original expedition to Peru, some twenty-five per cent could be described as such.[1] Owing to the Crown's policy of selling titles for ready cash, competition for office in Spain itself became acute, and many a young person opted to try his fortune in the New World rather than enter the army or the Church or live off his wits in the fashion depicted in the picaresque novel. Secondly, few women emigrated (although not as few as was previously thought). Penurious *hidalgos* married late and, with dowry payments forcing many fathers to put their daughters into convents, few were available to risk the perils of an Atlantic crossing or unknown diseases. Thus, in contrast to the largely family emigration to North America, Spanish emigration consisted of lusty bachelors who imparted a further element of instability and restlessness to the early years of settlement. Once *encomiendas* had been granted to the conquistadores, the viceroys encouraged women to come out and marry the *encomenderos* as a way of quelling their restlessness. This brought over many unscrupulous fortune hunters and led in some cases to friction when it was discovered they might have to share a household with an Indian ex-mistress and even, perhaps, to accept the legitimation of bastard mestizo children.

The Caribbean frontier

The Caribbean phase of the Conquest lasted from 1492 when Columbus first landed to 1519 when Cortés mounted his expedition to Mexico. It shows the motivations and aspirations of those involved in the early probes and, as it was here that most of the conquistadores of later mainland expeditions were to serve their apprenticeship, illustrates in microcosm some of the processes of the Conquest. Once this initial phase was over the Caribbean relapsed into somnolence, its gold exhausted, its indigenous peoples decimated and drained of Spanish settlers, attracted away by the richer pickings on the mainland. For the rest of the sixteenth century the calm was intermittently disturbed by the plundering raids of British, Dutch and French pirates, foreshadowing the feverish activity of the seventeenth century when sugar became firmly established as the staple export crop. After that, it knew no peace. It became the cockpit of European rivalries, a trash-can for footloose adventurers and a paradise lost.

Antecedents for the early expedition to the Indies may be found in those which had been mounted a few years earlier against the Canary Islands and the Barbary coast of North Africa. The small scale of the operations in the Indies did not require substantial modification of these precedents. Privileges were embodied in *capitulaciones*, granting to Columbus, for example, a percentage of the royal profits gained by commerce, as well as jurisdictional and administrative privileges. The initial purpose of the expeditions was not to settle but to probe for sources of immediately realizable commercial profit and to establish monopoly trading posts as in Portugal's trading empire. However, Columbus's early reports, couched in traditional metaphors of the Earthly Paradise, offered visions of endless delights and give an indication of why this policy changed. Rather than establishing Portuguese-style entrepots, with the Crown enjoying the monopoly of barter trade in gold, the emphasis became one of settlement by Spaniards enjoying the services of Indian labour, with the Crown drawing a fifth of the precious metals mined. The abundant labour of a meek population together with readily available placer gold deposits provided the basis of the *encomienda* system (see below p. 39). Hispaniola enjoyed a brief moment of golden glory from 1505 to 1510 with Santo Domingo as the first administrative centre and the springboard from which those unlucky enough not to have obtained *encomiendas* set out for other islands.

Bernal Díaz, alive to popular motivation, tells us that *encomiendas* were the prize and stimulus to the migratory movements from island to island. In 1499 Hojeda discovered the pearl coast of Venezuela. In 1509 Jamaica was explored but offered little realizable wealth. From 1511 Diego Velásquez occupied Cuba over a period of three years, founding Santiago. Puerto Rico was occupied by Ponce de León who was sidetracked by attempts to settle Florida in 1514. In 1513, Núñez de Balboa led an expedition to Tierra Firma which crossed the Isthmus of Panama and discovered the Pacific. Finally, in 1519, Cortés, set out from Cuba to begin the conquest of Mexico, and this was to put an end to these early intra-Caribbean migrations. New vistas of wealth stimulated an exodus of two streams, one to Mexico and the other to Panama and eventually on to Peru.

Santo Domingo remained the most important city in the Caribbean until the navigational advantages of the Florida channel led to the rise of Havana. Hispaniola then became a depopulated backwater, its indigenous population exterminated, having dropped from a possible eight millions in 1492 to 1,000 in 1524, and its Spanish settlers moving on to the mainland.[2] Those who stayed raised cattle to supply ships for the transatlantic crossing or, alternatively, experimented with the new crop of sugar introduced from the Canary Islands in an attempt to find a staple on which to base an agricultural economy once gold had been exhausted. As neither the island's natives nor those brought in by slaving expeditions from other islands could meet sugar's labour demands, African slaves began to be imported. Although the Dominican sugar industry did not flourish and could not compete with that of Brazil, this early development was later to determine the future of the whole Caribbean area.

Alternative policies were proposed but overruled. In 1517 Hieronymite friars, again citing a Portuguese model, this time in Madeira and the Azores, recommended unlimited immigration and family farms as a solution to the settlers' restlessness and the exploitation of Indian labour. Bartolomé de las Casas, realizing the devastating effects of forced work on Indians, recommended the introduction of slaves: 'If necessary white and black slaves can be brought from Castile to keep herds and build sugar mills, wash gold, and engage in other things which they understand or at which they can be occupied.' But he scarcely knew what the effect the 'lesser evil' would produce.[3]

Thus even before the Conquest of the mainland, precedents had already been established—private expeditions, financed by Italian or Spanish merchants, reward of booty with the Crown drawing off its share; the grant of jurisdictional and administrative privilege; settlement based on planned towns with elected *cabildos*, supported by the *encomienda* of Indian labour; a devastating population decline caused by disease, over-work and culture shock; resort to African slave labour as a solution to heavy manual work; concern of churchmen about the Indian population, ruin of a flourishing and highly productive native agriculture by wild cattle and hogs introduced by the Spaniards, and a restlessness which was not to be assuaged until a source of wealth was found, be it Indian labour, gold, or both.

The sustaining myths of expansion

El Dorado

The discovery of a new world gave an enormous stimulus to the imagination, but in order to encompass the idea of a huge *terra incognita* people had recourse to traditional imagery. The New World became the repository of the myths and legends of medievalism. One of the most striking features of the new discoveries was not so much that they liberated men's minds as that they confined them within the straitjacket of medieval conceptions which embellished and nourished a starved imagination.

The Spaniards' sense of mystery and fantasy was fed by rumours spread by returning sailors: Seville abounded in tales of gorgons, Amazons and mermaids and of the fauna and flora of the unknown continent. These rumours were matched in the popular novels of the day—the chivalric literature of the mystical exaltation of adventure and romance. When Bernal Díaz first saw Tenochitlán, the greatest praise he could bestow on its wonders was to say that it even surpassed those of Amadis de Gaul. The first version of Amadis de Gaul, with its vista of exotic lands and strange peoples, an epic of honour and faithfulness in love, appeared in 1508 and was followed by many sequels which soon degenerated to the travesties that became the butt of Cervantes's satire.

Religious ideas also shaped men's reactions; Columbus believed that the mouth of the Orinoco was one of the four rivers of Eden and that the gold district of Veragua in Panama was the region from which David and Solomon quarried precious stones. The way in which a crude desire for gold could be mystically spiritualized is further shown by Columbus's view that gold could be hallowed by rebuilding Jerusalem and Zion.

The mirage of geographical legend constantly enticed men into wild and uninhabited regions and made them capable of superhuman feats of endurance. The New World became the locus of geographical myths— the Fountain of Youth, the four rivers of Eden, the seven cities of Cíbola, the City of the Caesars and the Enchanted City of Patagonia, the island of the Amazons and the Land of Cinnamon. The most persistent of these myths was that of the Amazons and some contractual agreements for expeditions even included a clause concerning them. The Greeks had reported their existence; they are mentioned by Marco Polo and Mandeville. Amazons find their way into romances and are located in the 'island' of California where Queen Calafia's various weapons were 'all of gold as well as the trappings of the wild beasts which they ride after taming, for there is no other metal in the whole island'. In the accounts of the Amazons, sexual fantasy is inextricably linked with fantasies of unlimited wealth. When expeditions to Lower California failed to locate either Amazons or gold, the search shifted to South America and here Orellana, the first European to traverse the length of the Amazon, named that river after a supposed conflict with them.

Most seductive of all, however, was the legend of El Dorado himself, the leader of a native tribe who lived in the area round Lake Guatativa some fifty miles north east of Bogotá. Every year, at the climax of a religious ceremony the chief was coated with gold and dived into the lake in an act of ritual purification. Indian accounts of this rite reached the Spaniards, and substance was given to the rumours by the existence of the superb gold artifacts of the Chibchas. The El Dorado myth helped to perpetuate the idea of the inexhaustible riches of Spanish America. This was to exercise a compulsive fascination over generations of Europeans like Sir Walter Raleigh, whose imaginations fed greedily on the putative riches of the Orinoco and on the easy booty to be gained on the Spanish Main; it found practical expression in the great South American boom in England in the 1820s when Spanish American trade opened up vistas of limitless wealth.

The myth of El Dorado and the idea of quick windfalls exercised a potent fascination on those who valued making a sudden fortune more than political or religious liberty and hence it played some part in later centuries in determining which emigrants chose to go to South rather than North America. Many who chose South America did so not to settle but in order to *hacer América,* and having made a fortune to return to their native region as *americanos* or *indianos,* buying up land and with it social prestige.

Gold was power and was coveted by all the Atlantic states but the *auri sacra fames* seems to have been peculiarly Spanish—that disease of the heart to which Cortés referred, 'which can only be cured by gold'. The search for the source of the Nigerian gold which came to Europe via the Saharan caravans had prompted the Portuguese voyages down the African coast, but its discovery by the Spaniards fulfilled a Spanish dream, firing the imagination and steeling the will of the conquistadores. Spaniards were not necessarily more acquisitive than other European peoples, but the ferocity of their drive seems to require some explanation. Spain was less fertile and at a disadvantage in the commercial revolution of the early sixteenth century; war had absorbed its energies and starved the development of manufactures and agriculture; it had, therefore, few goods to export and was hampered in the trade for eastern luxuries. Europe, on the other hand, was short of silver and gold which in mercantilist thinking constituted real wealth until challenged by the eighteenth-century physiocratic view that agriculture was the basis of a country's wealth and power. Gold and silver therefore were needed for foreign exchange. Hence the excitement when the first consignment of gold from Hispaniola was succeeded by Aztec loot and tales of the untold riches of Peru. The discovery of silver in Zacatecas in northern New Spain in 1546 and at Potosí in 1545 seemed to be final confirmation of the El Dorado myth. The Spanish Empire was now saddled with a silver economy. By the beginning of the seventeenth century, bullion comprised 80 per cent of exports and in some years, 1595 for example, it rose to 95 per cent. By contrast, the value of hides, cochineal, indigo, and other tropical products was miniscule.

Will to empire
The New World presented a challenge for which there was no precedent in Spanish or European history, either in terms of the geographical immensity of the new conquests or of how to control enormous subject populations. The actual conquest of sedentary Indians posed few problems for the Spanish Crown. In Mexico, for instance technological superiority in firearms, the horse, the conquistadores' self-sufficiency, the leadership of Cortés, alliances with Indians who were discontented with their Aztec overlords and diseases against which Indians had no resistance, combined with the doom-laden cosmology of the Aztecs, facilitated the collapse of an otherwise highly developed militarized society. The Crown's involvement came only in the immediate succeeding period of consolidating Spanish rule.

The New World not only seemed to bring the medieval yearning for universal empire within the bounds of possibility but also offered the opportunity to establish in a new environment a state unfettered by the cramping restrictions of customary law and representative institutions. The Spanish Crown entered the sixteenth century with a polity peculiarly unsuited to the needs of an expanding national state with a wide range of foreign commitments. The crushing of the Comunero and Germanía revolts in 1519–21 confirmed the Crown's hegemony but the bonanza of New World wealth made it even easier to bypass the Cortes and escape from attempts to make grants of money dependent on redress of grievance, although Charles V was still to have trouble with the intractable Cortes of Aragón.

Sovereignty, as viewed in Roman law and the principles of Renaissance statecraft, was harnessed to force the undirected spontaneity of the early conquest into the framework of the patrimonial bureaucratic state. In the conflict of the Crown with the conquistadores bent on carving out feudal-style domains, the main instrument of royal power was the imperial bureaucracy. This was formed from the new caste of *letrados*, scions of a professional middle class, without titles and antagonistic to privilege, the products of the ebullient Spanish universities. Under Isabella, the *letrados* had been organized into a powerful, independent juridical and administrative class. In the spirit of the New Monarchy in contemporary Europe, they consisted of men bound to the Crown through personal, non-hereditary office rather than through feudal obligations. With these bureaucrats, the Crown was enabled to establish a sophisticated system of government throughout its new dominions and to assert its will in every sphere of activity by controlling trade, by administering justice, by distributing land, by protecting the indigenous peoples and by ensuring uniformity of belief.

The royal fifth, the tax levied on all silver entering the monopoly port of Seville, gave the Crown an independent source of income. Precedents could be discarded and a planned polity came within the bounds of possibility. The limitations of the *fueros*, traded in return for the support of towns and social groups in the struggle against the Moors, could be ignored. Statutory law could create a new society administered by an uncorrupt centrally appointed bureaucracy whose loyalties would be to the home government and not to the colonists. The will to empire was especially evident in the claims asserted by the Crown over its new Indian subjects, and in its attempts to control the relationship between them and Spanish settlers. All lands were the property of the king as monarch and not of private persons, and all land titles, Indian and European, were granted as royal concessions, at first through the viceroys and later through the town councils.

An important aspect of Spanish imperial policy was the Crown's use of the clergy, especially the missionary orders, as instruments of further expansion. The *Patronato Real* gave the Crown unlimited authority in ecclesiastical patronage to an extent unrivalled in Europe and this was a major source of royal power. The Crown nominated to benefices, controlled all movements of clerics to the Indies and channelled appeals to Rome through the Council of the Indies. The *Patronato* came to be regarded as a royal prerogative rather than as a revocable papal grant. With this control, the Crown had an invaluable source of political patronage and it was never necessary for it to resort to the Inquisition as an instrument of state policy on the scale that it did in Spain. The monastic inquisition operated between 1522 and 1532 and was succeeded by the episcopal inquisition (1535–71) and finally, by the Holy Office of the Inquisition in 1571, aimed to tighten up on subversive literature.

In trying to explain the Spanish Crown's will to empire in the sixteenth century, it is difficult to disentangle the secular, Machiavellian raison d'êtat from other worldly concerns. It has been argued that the Crown never allowed religious considerations to interfere with the achievement of secular goals. The gradual abandonment in the latter half of the sixteenth century of the earlier collusion between the missionary orders and the Crown, as financial considerations came to dominate Spanish policy, is often cited as evidence of this. Nevertheless, both Charles V and Philip II did regard themselves as the instruments of God's purpose—to such an extent that, on occasion, defiance of the papacy could be justified. Both believed in Spain's providential mission, and secular activity was justified by reference to this mission. The discovery of a new and unknown humanity and its incorporation into the Spanish Empire increased the receptivity of sixteenth-century Spaniards to the eschatalogical currents which enjoyed a vogue among theologians at the end of the medieval period. These stemmed from the Old Testament Book of Daniel which prophesied that four kingdoms would be destroyed but that the fifth would survive and would dominate the world. It was widely agreed that the four mortal kingdoms were the Assyrian, the Persian, the empire of Alexander the Great and the Roman Empire. The fifth was in dispute. Some theologians envisaged the age of Anti-Christ; others that Christ would return and that in preparation the task of conquering the world would be entrusted to men. What more natural than that the Spanish Crown should see itself in this role?

Religious messianism

The desire for gold and imperial ambition by themselves are insufficient to explain the dynamism of the Spanish Conquest; this derives in large measure from the apocalyptic messianism of the missionary orders on whom ultimately much of the onus for further frontier expansion would devolve. The late fifteenth and early sixteenth century in Europe was a period of religious ferment and apocalyptic expectation. To many it must have seemed as if Europe would survive the onslaughts of Islam only to be torn apart by internecine religious strife. Under Ferdinand and Isabella, Spain was comparatively immune from religious dissension. The Church was able to capitalize on the struggle against the Moors at the same time as Archbishop Cisneros, Isabella's confessor and a Spiritual Franciscan, reduced the need for more radical reform. When reform currents did infiltrate Spain in the early years of Charles V, they were to be those of Erasmus's Philosophy of Christ, not of Lutheran or Calvinist extremism. Furthermore, the conquest of Granada, combined with the discovery of the New World, opened up new fields of missionary endeavour which channelled the surplus energies of the Church.

The orders, and especially the Franciscans, responded to the evangelical challenge. The first Franciscan missionaries to the Indies, the Apostolic Twelve, arrived in 1524, to be followed two years later by the Dominicans and in 1533 by the Augustinians. But it was the Franciscans who set the pace. The Twelve represented Cisnerian Spain while Juan de Zumárraga, the first bishop of Mexico and also a Franciscan, represented the mild Erasmian current and not the Dominican Inquisitors.

The missionaries, schooled in the apostolic tradition of Joachim of Flora, saw in the innocence and openness of the Indians an opportunity to create a terrestrial paradise, the religious counterpart of the secular Renaissance recreation of the classical golden age, an escape from the incurable corruption of Europe and a revival of the primitive simplicity of the early Church. The mendicant orders, wedded to the apostolic cult of poverty, expected to achieve immediate success among an Indian population which appeared untainted by the acquisitive spirit and unaware of European concepts of private property.

There is an obverse side to this messianic urge. The yearning for a land without evil was not confined to Europeans. The religious history of Indian tribes is full of messianic turbulence, caused by the impact of foreign occupation and the threat to native traditions, customs and religious beliefs. Some of the best examples of these, handed down by oral tradition, are to be found in Brazil. The case of the Tupinambas is both the earliest and the most striking as it resulted in a massive and extraordinary migration. In 1539 they abandoned their coastal settlements in eastern Brazil where the Portuguese were beginning to settle, to seek the Land of Immortality and Perpetual Rest far to the west. Nine years later they arrived on the borders of Peru where the imagination of Spaniards was stimulated by the rumours of fabulous cities and enormous riches to the east.

The significance of these Indian messianic tendencies is illustrated by the case of the high point of Jesuit achievement. In their missions in Paraguay part of the Jesuits' success with the Guaraní Indians can be explained by the highly charged emotional atmosphere within which conversion took place; here, Jesuit messianic notions of a return to the conditions of the primitive church merged with the Guaranís' urge to achieve a haven of peace in which responsibility for decision would be removed from them.

The proselitizing aims of the orders were all too successful but not in the way envisaged by the first missionaries: the earthly paradise proved illusory. The problems of genuine conversion were far more intractable than was originally thought. As the process of consolidating Spanish power moved into a new phase, the orders lost many of their privileges. The emphasis of Crown policy changed as Spanish commitments in Europe increased and the need to ensure a constant flow of bullion became imperative. For this a servile labour force was needed, and the alliance between Church and Crown in the face of settler power was replaced by a new understanding between settlers, the secular clergy and the episcopate who had always looked askance at the orders' privileges and their freedom of action. In 1583 the seculars were given preferential treatment in nomination to benefices. The orders were subordinated to the authority of bishops—a consequence of the Tridentine Decrees—and bishops were permitted to collect tithes from Indians. The loss of their privileged position and the cooling of the Crown's evangelizing ardour forced the orders to make the choice of either retiring to their monasteries and cultivating their estates or of switching their energies and enthusiasm to remote frontiers and proselitizing among nomads. In the case of the Jesuits the choice was not mutually exclusive for their haciendas, perhaps the best managed of all colonial estates, provided the finance for their frontier missions. On the frontier, at least, friars might be free from episcopal control and for strategic reasons also might receive Crown support. After the *Ordenanzas* of 1573 which forbade armed *entradas*, the responsibility for pacifying the frontier was in fact placed on the orders. The Church in the heartland now comprised an integral part of the colonial establishment, whereas the exposed frontiers of northern New Spain, Paraguay, the Amazon and the Orinoco became the new fields of missionary endeavour. Here the milliennial dreams of the early missionaries could be realized but this time largely under the inspiration and control of the Jesuits, who first arrived in Brazil in 1549 and in Spanish America in 1568 and who, in Counter-Reformation spirit, were prepared to reconcile religious messianism with a realistic geopolitical role.

Colonization and early settlement

Encomienda, hacienda and plantation

The conquistadores expected remuneration for their hardship and sacrifice. During the early years of the Conquest land by itself had little value. After the exhaustion of the early windfalls and before the discovery of silver mines in the 1540s, wealth and power lay in access to Indian labour. Without an adequate labour supply the new settlements would collapse. Hence the crucial importance of the *encomienda*, the institution used by the Crown to regulate and control the labour supply. Unlike its peninsular precedent, the *encomienda* was not a land grant but entitled the *encomendero* to the tribute and labour of Indians.

In return for the Indians' labour, *encomenderos* were expected to instruct them in Christianity and generally to be de facto administrators, responsible for their welfare and control, using the *caciques*, the Indian chiefs, as go-betweens. The *encomendero* was a feudal figure only in so far as he owed military service to the Crown; in the Mixton War of 1540–41, for instance, the first serious Indian rising was put down by the *encomenderos'* levies. The *encomienda* system was shortlived: its importance declined as the fall in population reduced the availability of Indian labour, and the Crown, fearing the growth of a new feudalism, began to gather the reins of power and control into its own hands. As early as the 1530s, the Crown had started to whittle down the *encomenderos'* power. The New Laws of 1542 marked the climax of this policy when the *encomienda* was limited to payment of tribute, the hereditary aspect was curtailed and labour services were forbidden. In any case the *encomienda* was geared to the survival of traditional Indian society and, being ill-adapted to the needs of a growing capitalist economy, was largely inoperative in mining areas. It was mainly in the peripheral frontier regions such as Paraguay or Yucatán with a fairly high population density and minimal external market demands that the *encomienda* continued to fulfil its original function.

The relationship between the *encomienda* and frontier expansion is seen most clearly in Peru where the flood of Spaniards, attracted by the lure of Peruvian gold, outran the availability of *encomiendas*. The civil wars which raged in the 1540s were fundamentally conflicts between the first conquistadores who had received *encomiendas* and latecomers who had not. As the Indian population continued to decline and the prospects of becoming an *encomendero* diminished, the latecomers were compelled to seek openings elsewhere. Armed expeditions, *entradas*, often deliberately encouraged by viceroys as a means of draining off potential troublemakers, provided the origins of many scattered settlements in Upper Peru, Chile and Argentina. In northern Mexico in contrast, it was not frustrated *encomienda* seekers who were drawn to the frontier (Peru siphoned off most of these) but rather Indians wishing to escape the burdens of *encomienda* service who could obtain employment in the mines.

The decline of the *encomienda* led the Crown to replace it with the *repartimiento*. This put the allocation of labour firmly in the hands of the Crown's officials, the *corregidores*, who were responsible for administering the compulsory recruitment of labour, now in increasingly short supply. With population decline and the diminishing importance of the *encomienda*, land became the visible means to wealth and position and the hacienda, or landed estate, developed on the ruins of the *encomienda* system. As Indian agriculture was largely geared to supplying Indian needs, the hacienda originally developed in response to the food needs of the Spanish community or of the mining communities; in addition to foodstuffs, they provided wood, leather, salt, tallow and draft animals. The hacienda emerged in a situation of capital and labour scarcity but abundant land.

In order to attract and keep its labour the hacienda had to rely on a series of economic and social devices such as the monopolization of land to prevent labourers from finding alternative employment, and debt-peonage which prohibited the peon from moving away so long as he was in debt to his employer. Whereas the *encomienda* depended on the continuance of traditional society, the hacienda flourished on the break up of Indian communities. During the colonial period the Crown guaranteed the Indian's communal holdings and there was some equilibrium between hacienda and community; but this was upset after independence when communal land holding was regarded by the liberals as an obstacle to economic progress. During the nineteenth century, therefore, there was growing conflict between haciendas anxious to pre-empt vacant lands and ensure a labour supply, and Indian communities whose lands might abut on to or were enclosed within hacienda territory. The insatiable expansionism of haciendas also brought them into conflict with *rancheros*, small farmers living in the shadow of their more powerful neighbours.

The historical controversy now raging round the exact role played by the hacienda in Latin American economic history is evidence of its importance as well of its Janus-like quality. This is well summarized by Eric Wolf:[4]

> Organized for commercial ends, the hacienda proved strangely hybrid in its characteristics. It combined in practice features which seem oddly contradictory in theory. Geared to sell products in a market, it yet aimed at having little to sell. Voracious for land, it deliberately made inefficient use of it. Operating with large numbers of workers, it nevertheless personalized the relation between worker and owner. Created to produce a profit, it consumed a large part of its substance

in conspicuous and unproductive displays of wealth. Some writers have called the institution 'feudal' because it involved the rule of a dominant landowner over his dependent labourers. But it lacked the legal guarantees of security which compensated the feudal serf for his lack of liberty and self-determination. Others have called it 'capitalist', and so it was, but strangely different from the commercial establishments in agriculture with which we are familiar in the modern commercial and industrial world. Half 'feudal', half 'capitalist', caught between past and future, it exhibited characteristics of both ways of life, as well as their inherent contradiction.

The hacienda had a sociopsychological significance transcending its economic importance. The *hacendado* and his peons existed in a symbiotic relationship, with the peons drawing psychic satisfaction from identifying with the *hacendados*' prestige. Hacienda society was deliberately modelled on the patriarchal family with peons often linked to their patron by ties or *compradrazgo* (god-parenthood). Obligations were mutual and in return for security the patron expected absolute obedience from his peons.

The hacienda, with its emphasis on conspicuous consumption, appears irrational by the standard of maximizing profit, but nevertheless made economic sense in the period of recession in which it emerged. On exposed frontiers its compact, interdependent society and fortress-like adobe walls provided protection against marauders while its self-sufficient economy was a protective shield in times of depression. In boom years, lands held in reserve (and these unused lands were the major cause of agrarian discontent among the landless, particularly as population rose during the nineteenth century) could be brought into cultivation. But there were limits to its productivity: hampered by low-level technology and lack of capital, the hacienda was ill-equipped to meet the demands placed on it by rising population, and it must bear some of the blame for the retarded state of much Latin American agriculture today.

It is important to emphasize that there was considerable regional variation in landholding patterns. In Mexico the haciendas of the 'Great Men of the North' were probably an exception. In the valley of Oaxaca, by contrast, Indian caciques and *pueblos* retained a considerable amount of land. Even at the end of the colonial period Spaniards held under fifty per cent of the land. In the valley of Mexico the decline in Indian population meant that Indian agriculture was unable to meet the demand for European grains so Spaniards had to develop their own estates, as happened in the case of the wheat farmers of the Puebla region.

In contrast to the hacienda which was geared to producing a variety of crops for subsistence and the local or regional market and only became involved in specialization after market opportunities opened up with transport improvement (for instance, *pulque* in late nineteenth-century Mexico), plantations were specialized from their inception and were geared to producing tropical products for an external market. Attempts to turn easy-going haciendas into efficient plantations invariably caused severe tensions as patterns of work-discipline were changed and relationships with the surrounding small producers were strained—the classic example of this being Morelos in the years leading up to the Mexican Revolution.

In the present state of research it is unwise to generalize about the hacienda; both its dominance of the colonial rural economy and the ubiquity of debt-peonage are being called into question as research reveals the wide variety of labour arrangements used on them. Haciendas certainly had their rationale in an age of limited demand and slow population growth, but in comparison with them the plantation was a model of economic rationality. Geared to producing tropical products for an international market and worked in most cases by slave African labour, it was highly capitalized and, lacking the haciendas elasticity, was sensitive to fluctuations in the international economy. Often under absentee ownership, the personal liens of the hacienda were replaced by impersonal sanctions; the work discipline was that of the factory. There was a specialized division of labour and necessities such as dried beef for the slaves often had to be imported. But even in the case of plantations, generalizations are unwise. Some plantations produced for an internal market and, in the case of central American cacao plantations, for an Indian market at that. These plantations on the Pacific coast relied on the fact that highland Indians needed to work on them in order to pay taxes to the colonial authorities. Some had their origins in pre-Columbian days and some were even under Indian ownership during the colonial period.

It was not until the fad for chocolate developed in Europe in the eighteenth century that African slave-worked cacao plantations, often financed by peninsular merchants as was the Caracas company formed in 1728, produced for an external market.

But even the voracious sugar plantation was not wedded to slave labour. Soil exhaustion and declining yields demanded a more economical form of labour which was met by contracting East Indians to work in Trinidad and Guyana, or Chinese to work in Cuba. Whereas haciendas had their origin in supplying the demands of the local market and so had a functional relationship with the surrounding region, the plantation was essentially an enclave economy increasingly dependent from the seventeenth century on foreign capital and unrelated to its locality. These tended to be in low-lying tropical regions, close to ports and so it is difficult to talk of plantations as frontier institutions, except in specific cases such as Cuba where the sugar plantations began to expand into virgin land or the coffee plantations of Brazil.[5] Although the Jesuit reductions in Paraguay shared some of the plantations' characteristics they were sufficiently distinctive to be considered as a case apart.

Confrontation with the Amerindian

Frontier expansion involves physical displacement and cultural deprivation for the indigenous inhabitants. Even where physical uprooting of native communities does not occur, changes in the ecological balance between man and nature can have devastating results on the way of life of nomads; the Great Plains Indians, for instance, were deprived of buffalos and the Indians of the Central Valley in Mexico had their crops ruined by the Spaniards' herds.

Settlers feel little sympathy for those they displace. The advance of 'civilization' is equated with their own well-being and those beyond the frontier are relegated to the status of non-people or, in the Spanish phrase, *gente sin razón*. Indians were regarded as a commodity, an exploitable labour force. Native customs and practices such as human sacrifice, cannibalism, polygamy, aberrant sexual habits, drugs or ritual drinking heightened the sense of moral superiority of colonists, underpinned the imperialism of righteousness and justified enslavement. Spanish laws prohibiting enslavement of Indians excluded maneaters from their protection; thus it was to the advantage of adventurers to attribute cannibalism to any tribe which could be subdued. Crude culture-bound arguments rationalized a situation where labour was scarce for colonists who had left Spain to escape from the restraints of manual work and had gone to America to enjoy the fruits of the cheap labour of others. The indolence of natives, so frequently observed by foreigners and justifying forced labour in the eyes of settlers, was due, however, not so much to innate characteristics as to loss of purpose, to psychological unemployment under the traumatic impact of conquest when a series of unpredictable burdens replaced the predictable burdens of their own culture.

Settler attitudes were not shared by the early missionaries who attempted to protect Indians from avaricious and acquisitive settlers. The missionary orders were the voice of conscience in the Conquest and under their prodding, especially Las Casas in Spain and Father Vieira in Portugal, the two Crowns legislated on Indian matters. A unique feature of the Spanish Empire was official concern over the new humanity, exemplified in the debate over the rationality of Indians and hence the legitimacy or otherwise of enslavement, even though in practice much of the subsequent protective legislation was ignored.

Over the question of evangelization the friars were deeply divided. Their fascination with Indian customs entitles them to be called the first modern anthropologists. Toribio de Motolinía, Diego de Landa and

Bernardino de Sahagún produced detailed studies of Indian mores which are still important sources for ethnologists. The purpose of these studies was, of course, to comprehend the Indian mind and society as a prelude to proselitization but it represents a unique approach to a conquered people. The destruction of temples, statues and codices was the first horror-struck reaction of a militant church to paganism and human sacrifice but it was followed by an evangelical approach which preached a gentle Christianity; yet throughout the history of relations between the Church and Indians those who submitted were admired for their meekness and humility and those who resisted were condemned as savages.

The main division among the friars was between those who believed that there must be a total break with the former culture, for whom conversion involved total renewal and the end of native traditions, and those who recognized elements of worth in pagan culture and sought to incorporate them into the Christian plan. The Franciscans, interested in ethnological and linguistic studies, were concerned to train a native clergy, the Dominicans were less sanguine about the Indians' religious capacities, while the Augustinians were interested in giving converts more advanced spiritual training.

These attitudes stemmed from differing assessments of the Indian mentality, beliefs, capabilities and potential. In contrast to the secular clergy, the orders tended to think that the virtues of the Indians could best be preserved by reducing contacts with Spaniards. Hence they tried to interpose themselves between Indian communities and settlers and, by learning Indian languages and not teaching Spanish, they hoped to reduce contacts to a minimum. The Franciscans went furthest by trying to educate the sons of great Indian families in the College of Tlatelolco in order to provide a native clergy; but the enterprise was doomed in the face of great hostility and not a single native priest graduated. This failure to develop a native priesthood resulted in effect in two religions—the official Church which, as the Counter-Reformation gathered momentum, exerted its power and influence through the secular clergy, and a syncretic folk catholicism in which idols still lurked behind altars.

The logical consequence of trying to seal off Indians was the establishment of self-sufficient communities. The most famous was founded by Bishop Vasco de Quiroga at Santa Fe near Lake Patzcuaro in New Spain and modelled on Sir Thomas More's *Utopia*. But the colonists' demands for labour and for the products of Indian agriculture made it difficult to repeat that type of experiment except on those frontiers where few settlers ventured—in Paraguay, the Amazon and the far north of New Spain and California. The most that could be achieved was to establish Indian pueblos, the *República de Indios*, protected in theory by legal safeguards and administered by special officials, the *corregidores de indios*. But the poor salaries of the latter and links with merchants tended to turn them into exploiters of the Indians they were supposed to protect.

The policy of congregation—the concentration of Indians in urban settlements—was initiated by the Crown in the latter half of the sixteenth century. Although this facilitated social control and the collection of taxes as well as proselitization, it was also designed to protect Indians from unbridled exploitation both at the hands of *encomenderos* and from the bands of wandering mestizos who were a scourge of Mexico at that time. One of the side effects of this policy was the centrifugal dispersal to the fringes of colonial society of Indians who refused to be congregated, and some of the villages in isolated mountainous regions of Mexico today owe their origins to this dispersal. Some Indians, though, seem to have welcomed a policy which gave them legal protection and guaranteed their communal land—the *ejido*—and excluded mestizos, blacks and mulattos who were the main losers. But there was a dark side to urbanization. The herding together of Indians helped the spread of diseases against which they had no resistance. In effect, it was only in the missions and especially those of the Jesuit reductions in Paraguay that the segregation policy became a reality.

A unique feature of the Spanish Conquest, as well as the Portuguese settlement of Brazil, distinguishing them from all other European colonizing ventures, was that they were sexual conquests. The absence of white women, the submissiveness of native women and the lack of an inhibiting Puritan ethic encouraged a sexual bonanza. Miscegenation early resulted in a mestizo population. As few such unions were legalized they bequeathed a legacy of family instability and homelessness and also imposed a pattern of sexual attitudes which has only been slightly modified to this day. Mestizos became marginal men in a highly stratified society, many of them vagabonds, wandering through the land, squatting in and sponging on Indian villages.

Colonial authorities in both Spanish America and Brazil were obsessed with the vagrancy problem and were constantly inveighing against vagabonds who seemed to constitute a perennial threat to social stability. The predatory nature of life in the New World derived from the rapid expansion of a rootless population of mixed blood. It has been estimated that a sixth of the population of New Spain in the sixteenth century had no fixed abode, and that between twenty-five and fifty per cent of the Spanish population of Peru were unemployed in the middle of the sixteenth century. These vagabonds provided the recruits for the civil wars of the 1540s and for the bands that roamed the country, preying on Indian and Spaniard alike. These were also the men who comprised the *entradas*, like that of Rojas which roamed over northern Argentina for five years in the 1560s. In Brazil the floating population comprised poor whites like the *degredados,* convicts sent as punishment to Brazil, escaped slaves, free blacks and semi-civilized Indians; one observer wrote:

> The servants [who came from Portugal] deem it a better fortune to be vagrants or to die of hunger, to end up as soldiers or even as thieves, than to serve an honest master who would pay them well, feed and care for them, and all this not to do what negroes do in other houses.[6]

During the colonial period legal prohibitions not only discriminated against mestizos in the creole-dominated caste society but also forbade them from entering Indian villages. This had a centrifugal effect in impelling them towards turbulent frontiers where the writ of government scarcely ran, where they could become Indian fighters or adventurers in mining camps and where ruthlessness might bring them some social advancement which eluded them in settled society. The vagrants who remained in the cities helped to swell the unstable marginal population living off their wits, very much in the style of the *pícaro* of Spanish fiction.

Demographically the mestizos flourished as, unlike Indians, they were immune from European diseases. Disease was the great conqueror— European-born diseases such as measles, influenza, smallpox, typhus, the mysterious *matlazahuatl,* probably a kind of typhoid, and malaria and yellow fever from the African slaves, all carried off Indians in their millions particularly in the two great epidemics of 1545–6 and 1576–7. 'They died like fish in a bucket', commented one chronicler, and a missionary wrote, 'The Indians die so easily that the bare look and smell of a Spaniard causes them to give up the ghost.' The most striking aftermath of conquest was the decline in the sedentary Indian population in one of the greatest demographic catastrophes of modern times. From approximately 25 millions in 1519, the population of central Mexico shrank to a little over a million by 1600. Records are not so complete for the Andean region but the pattern was similar, and the population may have declined from possibly six millions to one and a half millions in the course of the thirty-five years after 1575; additional factors earlier were the murderous civil wars between Pizarrists and Almagrists and the depletion of llama herds.[7]

Population decline was the most damning evidence for the dislocation of Indian society caused by conquest. The equilibrium of resources and population was drastically changed. The introduction of the Spanish plough meant lower productivity than that of labour-intensive hoe-culture and it also broke up the soil and exposed it to erosion; in the case of Mexico, this was exacerbated by the deforestation of the Central Valley for building purposes. Livestock roamed over Indian reserve lands used for crop rotation. Land was converted from the Indians' staple of corn to wheat in order to feed the Spanish population. Water resources were diverted for the benefit of Spanish estates, and the highly efficient *chinampas* which could feed the city of Tenochitlán were allowed to decay. Indians used the land intensively, the Spanish extensively: 'sheep ate men', in the graphic phrase of the time.

The urban fixation

Spanish colonial society was essentially urban-oriented, a fact symbolized by the huge metropolitan centres of Mexico City and Lima and the three hundred or more towns founded before 1600. Although the Crown tried to encourage settlers to become farmers, few did so. A land-hungry peasantry anxious to acquire lands to farm with their own labour belongs to a later century of immigrants, many of them non-Iberians or Atlantic islanders. The ideal of most settlers was to live in urban ease from the products of windfalls, the profits of mines and the labour and tribute of Indians.

The Spanish American city was more than a pragmatic solution to the problem of how to prevent excessive rural dispersal in a virtually limitless geographical wilderness. It was also the visible sign of *imperium*, reflecting the ambitious pretensions of the Spanish New Monarchy and obeying the prescriptions of Renaissance town-planners. Civilization was conceived in essentially urban terms. America provided an escape from inhibiting medieval constraints and cities were unencumbered by encircling walls, except for those on the coast which were exposed to piratical attack. Spanish American towns were formalized abstractions, constructed on the grid-iron pattern, the rational geometry of empire, which was a revival of Graeco-Roman practice and owing something perhaps to Aztec example but little to immediate European precedents, apart from the armed camp of Santa Fe built during the siege of Granada. Towns had to be built according to the strict specifications laid down in the Royal Ordinances for the Laying Out of Towns of 1573, which codified practices applied since the 1520s.

The Spaniards were heirs to the Romans in identifying municipal office with nobility. The municipal council, the *cabildo*, was to be the one institutional focus for representing the views of creole landowners. It was also the institution which controlled the distribution of land, subject to confirmation by *audiencia* or viceroy. Municipal government took on new life in America at the moment when it was beginning to decline at home, although the vitality of New World municipalities was to fall sharply as fiscal needs led to the sale of office and the consequent growth of self-perpetuating urban oligarchies.

However cramped and inconvenient, medieval cities were organic growths, their expansion obeying the imperatives of commercial and manufacturing needs. In contrast, Spanish American towns were mechanistic creations, bureaucratic centres established for strategic or administrative purposes. They might rise symbolically on the ruins of pre-Spanish cities as in the case of Mexico City, or be deliberate new creations like Lima. A feature of early Spanish American urban history is the number of false starts in town-building, begun on arbitrarily chosen sites and then moved for commercial, strategic or administrative convenience to a more favoured site. Mining camps and staging posts on the *caminos reales* also provided the nuclei of new settlements but these were isolated from each other, separated by journeys of weeks or even months over forbidding terrain. Population was too thin and the complementarity of economic exchange too tenuous to encourage the development of articulated regional economies. The 'filling-in' process which might have occurred as a result of settlement by homesteaders did not occur because of the pre-emption of land by big landowners who, through their domination of town councils, controlled the distribution of land. Thus, there are many regions of Latin América where to this day the settlement pattern has changed little over the past three hundred years, and it now tends to be the cities and not the countryside which are absorbing the increase in population.

The geometrical monotony of Spanish American town plans contrasts markedly with the haphazard nature of Brazilian towns. They were often sited on hills in imitation of Lisbon and Oporto, whereas the Spaniards tended to choose level sites. This contrast reflects the looser nature of Brazilian urban settlement and the way in which towns developed in response to commercial needs rather than to the dictates of imperial necessity. In Brazil, the big house of the plantation was the major nucleus of settlement until the mining frontier shifted the centre of economic gravity inland; the architecture of these houses epitomizes a society which was more patriarchal and less dependent on the colonial government for administration and political direction.

Brazil

The pattern of Brazilian settlement and colonization was completely different from that of Spanish America. The main thrust of Portuguese expansion was to the Far East. Domination of the spice trade was the aim of Portuguese policy and for this a series of trading and military posts was established, ringing the Indian Ocean and the Persian Gulf and stretching away to Macao in China, with footholds on the African coasts serving as stages for the long sea journey. Portugal itself was too small to undertake the responsibilities of formal territorial empire and, without the political and dynastic commitments of the Spaniards, the Portuguese Crown lacked the same will to empire.

Portuguese expansion also lacked the self-justificatory sanctions of crusading zeal, except in Morocco which was the major field of Portuguese crusading activity until the disaster of Alcácer Kebir in 1578. But there was nothing comparable to the Habsburg's arrogation of the role of defender of the West against Ottoman expansion. The Portuguese aristocracy was not noted for its clerico-military fanaticism: the conquistador mentality was alien to it and the *fidalgo* did not share the hidalgo's contempt of commerce. Nor did the Portuguese have the proselitizing zeal of the Spanish Church. A minor role was played by religion in the early days of Brazilian settlement where there was no huge captive population awaiting salvation. Erasmus's Philosophy of Christ, which inspired the religious zeal of the Spanish missionary, did not fire the Portuguese. Not until the towering figure of Father Vieira in the 1650s do we find an apocalyptic messianism comparable to that of Spanish American experience. In the economic sphere too there was a difference in that the Church in Brazil never played a comparable role to the Church in Spanish America as its power was not rooted in extensive landholdings.

Nor did the myth of El Dorado exercise a hypnotic spell as it did for the Spaniards, confronted with the visible golden wealth of Aztecs, Chibcha and Incas. It is true there were similar Indian legends such as the fabled Sabarabussu, a Potosí of the imagination, but Crown support for the search for this hidden wealth was intermittent and half-hearted. Once it was clear that there were to be no sudden windfalls of gold or silver, Brazil occupied a peripheral position in the Portuguese Empire until the efforts of the *bandeirantes* were finally rewarded by the gold strikes of the 1690s in Minas Gerais and the Crown at last became aware of the enormous potential wealth of the country.

Attempts by the French to oust the Portuguese and capture control of the brazil-wood trade, which the Portuguese Crown claimed as a monopoly, roused it to send an official expedition in 1530 in the first attempt at settlement. The system established then was aimed at diverting initiative and responsibility away from the Crown to private entrepreneurs, using a model which had already proved successful in Madeira. Huge grants of land, *sesmarias*, were made to *donatorios* who were each responsible for one of twelve captaincies; in practice these were separate colonies with no overland communication with each other and they thus inaugurated the regionalism which was to become such a feature of subsequent Brazilian history.

During the early years of the captaincies the donatory was empowered to divide the lands of his *senhoria* among applicants of any social status. The grant was made in perpetuity on payment of a tithe to the Crown until 1695 when the last *donatorio* holders paid a quit-rent. The holder was obliged to cultivate the land, the title being confirmed on inspection after three years.

Sesmarias were granted for participation in conquest and defence, and as a reward for developing land, but religious orders and clerics were ineligible and this meant that the Church did not become the all-powerful landowner it was to be in Spanish America. Although in principle it would have been possible for a smallholding class to develop, in practice the high cost of slaves meant that only the richer landowners could work lands adequately to get their titles confirmed. These landowners were also able to use their influence in the *câmaras*, the local municipal governments, to squeeze out the smaller agriculturist. The choice open to a smallholder was either to become dependent on the *senhor de engenho*, receiving land in return for producing cane or grain for the plantation, or to try his fortune in the backlands.

The absence of tribute-paying precedents among the native population as well as their elusiveness precluded a labour system comparable to the *encomienda*. The replacement of the early barter system by attempts to enslave Indians had resulted in a confrontation between them and settlers which caused exports of brazil-wood to decline. This, with continued French interest, prompted the Crown to establish royal control in 1549 and to revoke and whittle down the donatories' rights. Bahia was established as the capital of the colony and seat of a governor-general, the Crown's powers of Church patronage (exercised through the *padroado*, the Portuguese equivalent of the *patronato*) were used to compel the Church to play a more active role in the colonization process, and authority was given to commence trading in black slaves with Portugal's West African trading posts; this inaugurated Portugal's South Atlantic Empire based on a triangular trade and parallelled that of the North Atlantic in the eighteenth century. Imports of African slaves, coupled with Portuguese sexual preferences and shortages of white women, resulted in early growth of a racially mixed society.

In the absence of minerals, land became the prized possession once a labour supply had been assured. Although *donatorio* grants had been partly feudal in character, they presupposed a high degree of capitalist enterprise. The course of Brazil's economy and the pattern of settlement were conditioned by the economic view prevailing at the time of the country's discovery. The Portuguese thought in terms of accumulating wealth by trading in scarce products. The smallness of their ships encouraged a concept of profit in terms of the scarcity of supply, in contrast with wealth created by increasing productivity. Thus Brazilian economic history has consisted of a series of cyclical export booms—brazil-wood, sugar, gold and diamonds, cotton, cacao, coffee and rubber—based on an extreme sensitivity to market demands in Europe and later in North America.

The first of these booms, that of brazil-wood, soon broke as stands near the coast became exhausted and Indian determination not to be enslaved made it dangerous to seek new stands inland. Favourable soil conditions and Europe's rising wealth encouraged settlers to introduce sugar from Madeira, thus starting the sugar cycle, but sugar required heavy capital investment for equipment and African slave labour. As much of Portugal's financial resources were tied up in the eastern trade, foreign capital and expertise became necessary to the expansion of their economy at an early stage in its history, thus locking it into the newly emerging international trading system. In this respect Brazilian experience differed markedly from that of Spanish America.

Sugar production was linked to a comparatively narrow coastal strip but the demands of the plantations for meat and draught animals led to the growth of a cattle industry in which cowboys and ranchers ranged inland in search of new pastures. The *sertão*, the arid hinterland, became an area of scattered settlements, based on ranches and supporting a population of mixed bloods. Throughout Brazilian history the *sertão* has been an exporter of migrants, providing manpower for the rubber boom of the 1870s and 1880s, for the Bahian cacao boom of the 1890s, and a source of cheap labour for the industrialized heartland bounded by Rio de Janeiro Belo Horizonte and São Paulo. Most recently, it has provided migrants for the colonization of the Brazilian highlands which are being opened up by the new transcontinental highways.

During the first fifty years Brazil offered nothing comparable to the extended settlement pattern of Spanish America, and the majority of urban settlements were confined to the coast. An exception was São Paulo, founded as a Jesuit mission in 1554 and later the springboard for exploration of the interior. The early *paulistas* were poor immigrants who had failed to make a living on the coast, and mixed bloods. From the earliest days *paulistas* were noted for their restlessness, roaming over hundreds of square miles in search of slaves and precious metals. Organized in bands (*bandeiras*) the *bandeirantes* were the Brazilian pathfinders, the frontiersmen who were a striking example of adaption to the New World environment, identifying with the interior and rejecting the effete ways of coastal society (see below, p. 120). When *paulistas* discovered gold in Minas Gerais they sparked off a mass migration from the coast to the new mining camps. This migratory movement inland during the first half of the eighteenth century is comparable to the crossing of the Appalachians. The São Francisco river valley is the nearest Latin America has to offer to a Cumberland Gap. As a result of this migration the centre of economic gravity gradually moved inland and away from the sugar plantations of the coast, already severely threatened by the challenge from Caribbean sugar. When the mining boom burst at the end of the eighteenth century, Minas Gerais itself became an exporter of migrants with groups moving southeast to develop cotton, south and north to start cattle ranching and southwest to grow coffee. The mining boom deflected *paulista* energies away from developing their own region, whose future prosperity became associated with the cultivation of coffee only after the 1830s.

The general pattern of land exploitation was of a latifundiary nature but the important exception was the Crown's policy in the eighteenth century of encouraging small peasant proprietorship in the far south where empty lands needed population in order to prevent the Spaniards moving in. In Santa Catarina and Rio Grande do Sul, state-supported migrants, mostly from Madeira and the Azores, were settled on family farms, thus creating a distinctive pattern in which slavery played a less dominant role than in other regions. Frontier settlement in the south was prompted by similar strategic considerations to those in the far north of Mexico threatened by British, French and Russian encroachments. Unlike the Spanish Crown in Paraguay where the Jesuit reductions were the spearhead of empire, the Portuguese Jesuits were reluctant to play that role on the Portuguese side of the border, thus avoiding what could have been an embarrassing confrontation between members of the same order.

One question not easily answered, posed by the extended and scattered nature of Brazilian settlement, is the role it played in preventing Brazil from breaking apart at independence. *Prima facie* it would seem that the isolation of regions and the virtual autonomy of country estates together with the looser, less rigid bureaucratic structure of the Brazilian state would have made Brazil more prone to fragmentation than Spanish America, but although regional feelings put down strong roots they never led to secession. Why was this? The stock answer tends to emphasize the peaceful transfer of power under the umbrella of British diplomacy and the consequent dynastic continuity which provided a focus for loyalty and so avoided a legitimacy vacuum, which in Spanish America had been filled by rival warring *caudillos*. Furthermore, it is suggested that national feeling was stimulated by the occupation of the northeast and French threats in the early eighteenth century—a stimulus absent in the case of Spanish America (with the exceptions of the British occupation of Havana in 1762 and of Buenos Aires in 1806). The Dutch were expelled from Brazil by Brazilian not Portuguese efforts, by a rallying of inland frontier regions and by cooperation between the three races of American, African and European extraction.

Whatever importance is given to these factors, they are insufficient explanation in themselves. Nations are created and held together by mutual complementarity between their separate parts. The explanation must be sought in the growing interdependence of widely separated regions. Rio Grande do Sul, with a distinctive settlement pattern and a strong regional feeling, did not break away because its economy had become linked to that of the developing centre and because strategic importance gave it a bargaining counter with the national government. Paradoxically, the loss of the Banda Oriental after the creation of Uruguay in 1828 may well have ensured Rio Grande do Sul's continued loyalty: with the port of Montevideo to export its cattle products, Rio Grande do Sul would have had less need of markets to the north. As it was, it continued to be dependent on the expanding economy of São Paulo especially in the demand for mules which, until the coming of railways in the 1870s, were the mainstay of the inland transportation system. None of Rio Grande do Sul's southern or western neighbours were interested in cattle products which duplicated their own. In the northeast the hinterland had been linked to the coast by a satellite cattle economy. The opening up of Minas Gerais had also linked the mines via the São Francisco with the coast and, although the development of Rio de Janeiro as capital of the colony from 1763 led to a comparative decline, this route retained importance, especially when the inter-provincial slave trade developed in the middle decades of the nineteenth century. Isolated Maranhão, which experienced cotton booms both during the Napoleonic Wars and American Civil War, was deterred from seceding by the thinness of settlement and by growing overland trade with the northeast.

The vast river and jungle area of Amazonia has been an exception to settlement patterns in the rest of the country. River and jungle were a barrier to settlement but not to exploration. After the capture from the French of San Luis at the mouth of the Amazon and the foundation of Belém in 1616, the Portuguese set out to exclude Spain from consolidating its power in the Amazon basin. Slave expeditions and missionary activity were the typical forms of penetration, giving the Portuguese pre-emptive rights, but it was not until the rubber boom of the 1870s onwards that there was any large-scale migration into the region. Those immigrants who did not die finished up either in small riverine settlements or in Manaus, the great Amazon emporium and a monument to a boom which was extraordinary even by Brazilian standards.

3
Types of Frontier

The mission frontier

The mission was the Spanish American frontier institution par excellence. Gold and silver may have provided the initial impetus, drawing conquistadores and settlers into the far interior, but the work of consolidation, pacification and trail-blazing was taken up by the missionaries. Until the end of the sixteenth century Franciscans played the major role, but increasingly the Jesuits came to regard missionary work on the frontier as their preserve. After the Jesuits were expelled in 1767 the Franciscans once again took the initiative. Even today it is often the missions, now swollen by a confusing array of Protestant sects, who are the only white people in isolated regions.

The era of proselitization among sedentary Indians was comparatively shortlived. By the middle of the sixteenth century the core areas of Aztec and Inca domination had been brought under the spiritual control of the Church, symbolized by a spate of church building in which the practical and aesthetic skills of Indians were harnessed to help create an elaborate architecture of spiritual domination. From this period the orders gained valuable experience for their later activities.

A new challenge to missionary endeavour soon came from the Chichimec attacks on travellers on the Zacatecas silver road. The discovery of silver mines at Zacatecas in 1546 pushed the frontier beyond the limits of settlement into the hunting lands of the Chichimecs. As this area came within the Franciscan sphere of influence they began to move into the turbulent northern deserts. By 1600, they had a strong foothold in the province of Zacatecas with some twenty-five houses. Nine Franciscans accompanied Juan de Oñate's expedition into what is now New Mexico and pressed the Crown to accept responsibility for protecting the converted Indians from the attacks of the unconverted. As a result Santa Fe was founded in 1609, isolated some 400 miles from the nearest Spanish settlement to which it was linked by an annual caravan. Until the opening of the Santa Fe trail in the 1820s, Santa Fe was the terminal point of the great *camino real* stretching to Vera Cruz.

The early successes of the friars in their work of pacification so convinced the Crown of their worth as colonizers that they became prime agents of frontier expansion in northern Mexico. The mission was recognized as a distinctive frontier institution in the New Laws of 1543 when missions were given ten years to proselitize before moving ahead to begin a new cycle. The original mission would then be taken over by civil authority and the secular clergy.

The Franciscan missions were supported by the Crown in various ways. The annual stipends of missionaries were paid by the government; by the 1750s, 123 friars were on the payroll in the northern provinces. Soldiers were allocated to mission stations from the *presidios* and new missions received capital grants for bells and other equipment. A Crown subsidy was a pump-primer: missions were expected to become self-supporting except where there might be a clear strategic reason for bolstering them, in Texas, for example, as a barrier against French expansion or in California against Russian incursions. The expenses of both *presidios* and missions were debited to the War Fund account. The defensive purpose of many of these missions is shown by their fortress-like architecture.

Conflict between friars and uncivilized Indians and between the latter and pacified Indians was endemic even after the process of hispanicization and christianization was far advanced. Revolts were often led by *hechiceros*, the witch doctors whose power had been whittled away by missionary activity. Discontent was particularly virulent among tribes such as the Tarahumaras in northwestern Mexico to whom congregation in pueblos had proved irksome and who longed for the freedom of the deep canyons. The *hechiceros* were able to use the ravages of disease and physical disturbances such as bad weather and earthquakes to stir up discontent, as in the great Tepehuana and Tarahumara revolts of 1697 which destroyed the Jesuit missions in that area.

Jesuit activity had been concentrated between the Pacific coast and the western Sierra Madre, and in Sinaloa, Sonora, California and Arizona. In 1596 the Tepehuana mission had been founded from Sinaloa and by mid-seventeenth century some estimates put the number of converts as high as 400,000. Cattlemen and miners followed in the wake of the missionaries and it was often their attitude and behaviour towards Indians, pacified or not, which undermined the friars' achievements.

The most famous of the Jesuits, Father Kino, gave a fresh impetus to missionary activity with the drive into Arizona. In the early years of the eighteenth century Jesuits had also started the thankless task of evangelizing the arid Baja California peninsula.

These northern missions played an important role on the strategic frontier when the Spanish Empire seemed to be threatened by French, English and Russian expansion. In Texas, French threats stimulated the establishment of *presidios* and the foundations of missions whose Indian converts could act as auxiliaries in case of conflict. It was not until Spain acquired New Orleans at the end of the Seven Years' War that the threat to Texas was removed, only to be revived again when New Orleans reverted to French rule in 1800.

The last expansionist surge in the north came after the report of José de Gálvez alerted Spanish authorities to the threat from English and Russian penetration of Upper California. In 1769 Junipero Serra founded the Franciscan mission at San Diego and in 1776 at San Francisco. When the Spanish Empire collapsed some twenty-one missions and four *presidios* had been established.

Opinions are divided about the success of the Franciscan missions. On the eve of secularization in 1834 they comprised 30,000 converted Indians, tending 400,000 cattle and 300,000 sheep and pigs; but California still remained a largely subsistence economy and Russian and English accounts refer to the miserable aspect of Indian converts.

How would the new Mexican state tackle the problem of the northern provinces after independence? Distance, thinness of population and political instability meant that the writ of government scarcely ran in the border regions. This did not imply that the frontier became a cradle of democracy on independence. Governors behaved like *caudillos* and other military commanders like lesser *caudillos*. In 1824 a Colonization Law was passed to encourage settlement and in 1834 the missions were secularized in accordance with liberal laissez-faire views and under pressure from colonists enviously coveting mission lands and the labour of mission Indians. Secularization threw these lands open to occupation and broke up Indian society, much as it had done when the Jesuits had been expelled in 1767. In both cases the secular latifundia increased in size; another consequence was a massive slaughter of cattle by the newly liberated Indians, many of whom reverted to their former nomadic way of life in the hills. Those who remained were impressed as cheap labour by the four thousand ranchers who had established ranches under the Colonization Act. For the next few years Mexican California was an indolent, illiterate, hospitable and pleasure-loving society, in no way equipped to deal with the challenge from North American infiltration.

There was even less to show of the mission frontier in Arizona: the withdrawal of troops during the independence wars exposed the few scattered settlements to Yuma and Apache attacks until finally only the *presidios* at Tubac and Tucson were left holding out.

By the 1830s New Mexico had a human population of 44,000 outnumbered by four million sheep scattered on ranches between El Paso and Taos, together with a few small gold and copper mines; but it remained as isolated at the end of the *camino real* as on the day when Santa Fe had been founded in 1609. Santa Fe's future lay in trade with the frontier posts of the Missouri, only 700 miles away, and in 1822 the Mexican government, breaking with Spanish practice and bowing to realities, opened up New Mexico, so inaugurating the twenty-year era of the famous Santa Fe trail.

In Texas the problem was again one of underpopulation with only 4,000 settlers strung out along the frontier, tending herds of longhorn cattle. Further north in the United States the westward movement had been temporarily blocked by the barrier of the Great Plains and the Indian reservations beyond Missouri and Arkansas, and this turned the attention of settlers to Texas where rumours of the success of early settlements started a migratory movement southwards. Although new settlers had to acknowledge the authority of the Mexican government it was a Trojan horse situation. Whereas the old missions and *presidios* had provided some sort of barrier against Indian incursions, nothing could resist the flow of settlers coming from the north, and the Mexican state was too enfeebled to prevent the breakaway of Texas in 1835 and its incorporation into the United States after the war of 1846–80.

With the late arrival of the Jesuits in Spanish America much of the initiative for frontier expansion passed to them. Part of the Jesuits' success lay in their ability to acquire funds which made their missions self-supporting. Initially, the Crown subsidized their efforts but in the financial depression of the seventeenth century they were expected to become self-sufficient. By educating the sons of the creole elite they amassed resources which, together with bequests, enabled them to buy haciendas; soon the Jesuits had established a reputation as efficient estate managers. For example, within a decade of arriving in Zacatecas in 1574, they had become the largest ecclesiastical landowner in the region and in 1616 founded a college there.

In Ecuador, income from the Jesuits' extensive haciendas herding sheep for the *obrajes* (sweatshops) in the Sierra was used to finance their Amazonian missions; these received no support from the Crown in spite of their strategic value in pushing Spanish claims in unclaimed jungle territory. The first half of the seventeenth century saw attempts by Spaniards to explore and settle the upper Amazon, nearly a century after the initial expeditions by Gonzalo Pizarro and Orellana in 1541. Here, as in Paraguay, the limits of Spanish power were marked by Jesuit missions, fanning out from the Presidency of Quito.

To the east of Quito, Spanish settlement was very thin. A few dozen *encomenderos* farmed cotton with Indian labour but any prosperity was swept away in 1579 when Indians rose against the *encomenderos'* attempts to increase burdens on them. Quijos cotton had been exported as fine cloth to Peru but the thinness of the Indian population prevented any substantial expansion of this trade. To the south in Maynas a punitive expedition to avenge Indian raids on isolated settlements was the prelude to deeper penetration. This resulted in the foundation of San Francisco de Borja, some 900 miles east of Quito but it suffered a similar fate to Quijos in 1635 when, only fourteen years after its foundation, an Indian rising wiped out all but twelve of its families.

Failure, however, was a challenge and not a deterrent to the Jesuits whose discipline, dedication and centralized control provided the drive which the Franciscans often lacked. From 1638 onwards twenty-one Jesuit missionaries pushed down the Marañon and into the Amazon, setting up riverside missions, claiming thirty years later to have baptized 100,000. The conception with its geopolitical overtones was grandiose. By the Treaty of Tordesillas the Amazon basin belonged de jure to the Crown of Castile but de facto occupation, albeit thin, had been undertaken by some Portuguese. When two Spanish Franciscans arrived in Belém after travelling down the Amazon from Quito, the governor despatched a huge expedition of some 2,000 men under Pedro Texeira to establish Portuguese claims to Amazonia. Two years later he returned to Belém after setting up a settlement at Franciscana to mark the westward limits of these claims. Texeira's actual appearance in Quito in 1639 alerted the Spanish authorities to the Portuguese threat and this became more acute the next year when Portugal revolted against the union with the Spanish Crown and began the Portuguese War of Independence.

The Spanish mission experience in Amazonia afforded an opportunity to create a perfect society without the presence of settlers with their labour demands or the corrupting influence of soldiers. But the success of missionary endeavours depended on more complex factors than this and in particular on the nature of the culture of the Indians under mission influence. The unit of Amazonian Indian society was a very small one, based on kinship relations between half a dozen or a dozen families. Thus the policy of congregating Indians into settlements of four to five thousand lacked any sociological justification, particularly in view of the enormous linguistic and cultural diversity among different groups. Nor was a system of agriculture based on the shifting cultivation of manioc and maize conducive to permanent settlement. The success of the Jesuits' congregation policy affecting 100,000 Indians in thirty-two pueblos was impressive but shortlived. Smallpox epidemics and other European diseases carried off nearly half the mission population in the 1660s. Frequent revolts against attempts to abolish head hunting and polygamy climaxed in the great rising on the Ucayali river in 1742 when 40,000

Indians broke away in a messianic revolt under an Indian from Cuzco, Juan Santos Atahualpa, a Jesuit neophyte who had been educated in Spain. The Jesuits had no means to suppress the revolt. They could call on no soldiers and lacked the sanctions of a forced labour system. The missions were also a prey to Portuguese attack

The other major area of Jesuit activity was in Paraguay and what is now the Bolivian Oriente. In 1610 the Jesuits established missions there and on the banks of the Paranapanema and Guaira. The subdued and congregated Indians were now tempting prey for the slave-raiding *bandeirantes* of São Paulo. In 1629 an expedition of 3,000 *paulistas* with their *mamelucos* and Indian auxiliaries raided the reductions and threw the Jesuits out of Guaira thus ensuring that this region would eventually revert to Portuguese control, although it remained uninhabited until *paulistas* began to move into it in the 1760s. Pressure from the *bandeirantes* constantly pushed the Jesuits and their wards further south. They founded fifteen more reductions in Rio Grande do Sul, planning to expand eventually to the Atlantic coast, but this again was blocked by the *paulistas*. In 1641 after receiving permission from the Crown to arm their neophytes, the Jesuits made a stand at the battle of Mbororé when the defeat of the *paulistas* finally ended their harassment. In the 1680s the Jesuits founded a further seven missions in Rio Grande do Sul where they remained unmolested until the Treaty of Madrid in 1750 which exchanged the missions for the smuggling port of Colonia.

Whereas Spanish Jesuits were active on the political frontiers of South America, Jesuits in Brazil were active inland, especially in Maranhão at the mouth of the Amazon where they were locked in a threefold struggle with settlers and the Crown. The settlers in Maranhão who lived mostly from cotton cultivation were too poor to afford highly priced African slaves and so depended on Indians brought in by *resgates* or slaving parties. But with the arrival of Father Vieira in Belém in 1653 the Brazilian Indians found their Las Casas.

When the Crown implicitly permitted slavery Father Vieira went to Portugal to dispute the decision and as a result succeeded in getting a *Junta dos Missões* established, by which the settlers had to submit to Jesuit oversight of their labour demands. By the end of 1654 the Jesuits had set up 54 *aldeias* under such tight control that in 1662 angry colonists rose and expelled them. New legislation the next year permitted the Jesuits to return with curtailed powers. When the Jesuits were again expelled in 1684, the Crown was forced to draw up new regulations for the conduct of missions. These regulations of 1686 were a compromise. Settlers were permitted to undertake peaceful expeditions, organized by Jesuits, in order to attract natives to the *aldeias*, the mission villages near Portuguese settlements, where they would be available as labour at the same time as they remained under Jesuit supervision. Only in the case of Indians who persisted in 'unnatural practices' or who resisted efforts to convert them was violence justified.

The success of the Jesuits brought hostility from the other orders, the secular clergy and the hierarchy who resented their freedom from episcopal control, from landowners who were jealous of their high profits and competition for available labour and from the government which in the tradition of the enlightenment saw them as a barrier to rational progress. In Portugal, where the blow fell first, Pombal was more receptive to the complaints of the colonists than João V had been and was prepared to sacrifice them in the interests of winning their cooperation in his scheme to overhaul the Portuguese Empire. When the expulsion did come in 1767 it was unpopular with ordinary people. In Mexico, for example, it was greeted with riots among mine workers in Guanajuato and San Luis Potosí, by risings of Indians as well by numerous popular demonstrations.

The secularization of the Jesuit missions threw their land on to the market, released Indians for labour and left a vacuum in the missionary field which the Franciscans (who alone of the big orders had not amassed landed property) were now to enter. The purpose of the Franciscans was not to take over the Jesuit missions but to undertake further expansion of the frontier into Alta California.

In the area of Jesuit reductions in Paraguay the frontier contracted after their expulsion as they no longer pushed further afield in the search for new supplies of yerba maté which was their major crop. Their eleven missions with 11,000 Indians in Entre Rios and Misiones were divided on their expulsion among French Dominicans and Mercedarians but continuity was destroyed and the discouraged Indians fled to the jungle and even to Spanish communities. These jungle locations became an Indian stronghold and unsafe for European colonists for a hundred years or more. But European colonists were eventually tempted into the region to take up where the Jesuits with their remarkable agricultural skills had left off and most of the techniques, such as a method of speeding up the germination of yerba maté plants, were adopted by these later colonists. Indirectly, therefore, flourishing agricultural communities today are a legacy of the Jesuits' pioneering achievement while the sad ruins of their great churches are the visible reminder of one of the most remarkable episodes in Latin American frontier history.

The Indian frontier

The easy conquest of the Aztec and Inca empires gives a misleading picture of the powers of resistance of Amerindians to Spanish rule. Miscegenation encouraged the view that there was no Indian problem which hispanicization and christianization would not cure, but many sedentary Indians were reluctant to be assimilated, even in Mexico where the races had commingled since the sixteenth century. However, the problem of the 'Indian frontier' discussed here is not that of the cultural line dividing the European and Amerindian but those of warlike, nomadic hunting and gathering tribes on the periphery of settlement who not only blocked the way to further expansion but whose incursions into settled areas compelled the authorities to divert men and money to provide defences against them. It is often forgotten how long some of these Indians resisted. The Araucanians in southern Chile and the pampas Indians in Argentina were not finally subdued until the 1880s, and in northern Mexico the Apaches continued their raiding until the end of the nineteenth century. In the sixteenth century Araucanian resistance had so roused the admiration of the Spaniards that Ercilla made them the subject of *La Araucana*, one of the few epic poems to have been written in Latin America.

In New Spain it took the Spaniards a mere five years to establish their power in the Aztec-dominated central valley but over fifty years to subdue the Chichimecs. The expansion of the frontier into the northern deserts with the discovery of silver at Zacatecas created a situation for which the Spaniards were ill-prepared. They were legatees of a problem which the sedentary tribes before them had never managed to solve. The Spaniards adopted the Aztec word Chichimec meaning 'dirty uncivilized dog', a generic term referring to the 'four nations' of the Paines, Gaumaca, Zacatecas and Guachachile tribes who had obduratedly remained outside Aztec influence. The 'hard frontier' between nomadic hunter-gatherers to the north and the sedentary agriculturists to the south lay on the 20–21st parallel with no intervening buffer zone. To the north of this line was

> a place of misery, pain, suffering, fatigue, poverty, torment. It is a place of dry rocks, of failure, a place of lamentations: a place of death from thirst, a place of starvation: it is a place of much hunger, of much death. It is to the north.[1]

Without the enduring hostility of sedentary Indians towards the nomads it is doubtful if the Spaniards by themselves could have mastered the turbulent northern frontier.

The Mixton War of 1541 had strained the resources of the Spaniards to the limit but at least a military solution had been possible against the sedentary Cazcab Indians. The elusive nomadic Chichimecs were a different proposition. The first serious attack on travellers on the Zacatecas road which opened the Chichimec War occurred in 1550 and immediately underlined the difficult problem of highway defence caused by shortage of men. Military service was uninviting when there were possibilities of striking silver in the mining regions. Small forts were built which became the nuclei for towns, and heavy armoured waggons provided some protection for convoys of travellers, but the major problem was how to conduct offensive warfare.

The Chichimecs were fine, ruthless warriors, fighting to defend their gathering grounds 'as if they were Moors of Granada'. 'Long-haired, with dyed bodies, graceful, robust and beardless', they lived in caves and rude huts, eating a form of bread made from *mesquite* shrub and drinking the juice of the *agave*. The introduction of cattle into the Zacatecas region provided an added incentive for raids on settlements once a taste had been acquired for beef as a relief from desert rat. The Chichimecs' practice of ritual cannibalism, scalping and indiscriminate torture struck terror into the settlers and the only inducement to serve in campaigns against them was the prospect of capturing prisoners who could be used as slaves. However, pacified Indians provided the bulk of the Spanish forces as fighters, porters, interpreters and scouts, and their role was crucial to border defence throughout the colonial period, providing in many cases a 'soft frontier' between Spanish settlements and hostile nomads.

One of the most distinctive features of the northward advance was the colonization of conquered lands by Indians. Once nomads had been pacified they were absorbed into settlements of northward moving Tarascans, Otomís and Colultecans. The Otomí chief Don Diego de Tapia assumed the title of Captain General of the Chichimec Warfare and was one of the discoverers of the San Luis Potosí mines. As the price for cooperation he was relieved of tribute payment and personal service. The most important native group were the Tlaxcalans who had been specially favoured by the Spaniards since assisting them in the assault of Tenochitlán in 1521. In 1590, four hundred families moved north to establish eight settlements, demanding hidalgo status in perpetuity and freedom from tribute and personal service.

This colonization marked a shift away from the policy of *guerra a fuego sangre* or war of extermination to one of conciliation. Until 1590 hardliners had pushed for a policy of extermination but as military success seemed impossible to achieve the viceroy tried killing by kindness. 'Peace by purchase' involved a vast aid programme by which the Chichimecs were provided with maize and beef, textiles and clothing. At the same time a congregation policy was aimed at bringing nomads into settlements and teaching them to become agriculturists. The new approach represented a victory for the missionaries and their policy of using sedentary Indians to set an example for the Chichimecs to follow. After nearly fifty years of conflict the frontier was pacified and future expansion up to and beyond the Rio Grande was comparatively free from hostile attack. Whether in the long term the assimilation policy was successful or not is harder to determine. Indians from outside, and expanding haciendas took over the best land and pushed the Chichimecs out to the fringes. Many refused to be assimilated or to become pensioners of the state; others became absorbed into the peon workforce on the haciendas or drifted to the mining towns. In general they lost their sense of identity.

The experience of the Chichimec Wars provided the pattern for later missionary expansion. Pacified Indians were used to colonize new frontiers in Jalisco and Sonora. Opatas from south Sonora were sent into Arizona to teach agriculture to the Pimas and then the Pimas were used by the Jesuit, Father Kino, in the 1690s to defend his missions from Apache attack. Thus, in the expansion northwards into Arizona, California, New Mexico and Texas, we can talk of a moving Indian frontier which finds in the mission and the Indian pueblo its main institutional expression.

The factor which turned nomadic Indians into the most formidable obstacle to Spanish expansion was the 'horse revolution'. The Spaniards had tried to prohibit the sale of horses to Indians but nothing could stop them obtaining *mesteños*, wild mustangs. After the great revolt of Pueblo Indians in the 1680s, horses became readily available, transforming the economy and culture of the Plains Indians. The Apaches and Comanches in particular took advantage of their new mobility to raid deep into settled territory. The eighteenth century was the great age of the Plains Indians but in the nineteenth century the pressures of the expanding North American frontier and the destruction of the buffalo herds forced them to prey on Mexican border communities who tended to receive less protection from the central government than their more fortunate opposite numbers over the border.

The Apaches were probably the most intractable of all the tribes with which the Spaniards had to deal. Whereas the neighbouring Navahos were becoming shepherds and weavers, the Apaches, converted into fierce merciless raiders by the horse, became the scourge of the borderlands until the 1880s. The *gran apachería* over which they ranged was some 750 miles in length and some 550 miles deep and stretched from Texas to Arizona. Although linguistically a nation, the Apaches had no political unity and this complicated dealings with them. A truce with one group did not bind other groups. The Spanish response was to build *presidios* and to seek alliances with the Comanches with whom the Apaches were in competition for buffalos. By the end of the eighteenth century it looked as if the reservation system, in which Tlaxcalan Indians played some part as intermediaries, was at last bringing the relentless Apache War to an end. The Apaches now held the Spaniards in virtual tributary vassalage, extracting from settlers and subject Indians a never ending supply, but the system collapsed after the outbreak of the Mexican War of Independence against Spain in 1810 when garrisons were withdrawn to meet the rebel threat in central Mexico, thus leaving the frontier open once again to Apache incursions.

In Chile, as in northern Mexico, the Spaniards were heirs to a pre-Columbian Indian frontier. The Incas had not succeeded in conquering the tribes of southern Chile and their empire never extended beyond the River Maule which they reached seventy-five years before the arrival of the Spaniards. The stability of Spanish society in the fertile central valley contrasted with their precarious foothold in the south. Throughout the sixteenth century this southern frontier was an armed camp with local settlers having to serve in a militia because of the inability of the colonial authorities to supply regular troops. But after the great rising of 1598 when all Spanish settlements south of the River Bío-Bío were devastated, the Spanish authorites instituted a frontier force. Unfortunately, it guaranteed that conflict would continue as its members supplemented their meagre pay by raiding forays, *malocas*, in order to obtain slaves to sell to labour-starved estates. With the introduction of German colonists from the 1840s onwards, the farmers' frontier began to expand into the Indian territory in the southern rain forests. Unlike the pampas Indians, the Mapuches, as the descendants of the Araucanians are called, were not exterminated, and many Chileans who did not realize they had an Indian problem were rudely disabused when the Allende government supported the revindication of Indian rights.

In spite of some successes achieved by the frontier missions established by the Jesuit, Luis de Valdivia, in the early seventeenth century, the friars failed to soften the harsh impact of irreconcilable conflict on either the Chilean or the Argentinian Indian frontier.

In Argentina the lack of economic incentive, the prohibition of direct trade with Spain until the decree of 1778 and limited settlement had frozen the frontier along a line which was virtually the same in 1790 as it had been in 1590. Once the horse had crossed the Andes at the end of the seventeenth century the pampas Indians, superb horsemen, armed with the eighteen-foot lance and the *bolas*, were formidable opponents re-quiring, in one estimate, an army of 12,000 men to subdue them.

A precarious equilibrium between settler and Indian was achieved with the construction of a line of forts and ditches garrisoned by *blandegues*, in a type of military colony some of which provided the nuclei for later towns; but in practice the *gauchos*, mestizo cowboys who rivalled the Indians in their horsemanship, kept the Indians at bay, providing a 'soft frontier' or buffer between the areas of expanding settlement in the cattle *estancias* and the free range pampas. However, there was increasing competition for declining herds as the cattle economy began to accelerate in response to an almost unlimited European demand for hides; this upset the balance and sharpened conflict and the government began to conduct offensive campaigns to drive the Indians back. Rosas, the landowning *caudillo* who dominated Argentina from 1829 to 1852, made his reputation in command of the Indian campaign of 1833 when as many as 10,000 Indians may have been killed, and when the frontier was pushed back and salt pans for the needs of the *saladeros* were secured. Although the Indians were relentlessly pursued throughout the course of the century, it was only with the appearance of the repeating rifle that it became possible to mount a successful campaign of extermination in the War of the Desert in 1879–80—even more effective than the Indian wars of the mid-west.

There was another Indian frontier in northern Argentina where fierce Chaco Indians preyed on outlying settlements and pack trains. Owing to restricted economic activity in that region, it did not cause governmental concern, until in the late nineteenth century the cattle trade from the Chaco to supply the mines and nitrate fields of northern Chile attracted the attention of Indian raiders.

Discussion so far has centred on the conflict which occurred when an expanding frontier of settlement threatened the traditional hunting grounds of nomadic Indians. There are two other types of confrontation to be considered: one, where Indian communal landholdings which had been protected during the colonial period were threatened by liberal land legislation, thus enabling haciendas to expand at their expense: the other, where a frontier expanded into an area of hitherto free jungle villages.

The most striking case of the former occurred in the Mexican state of Morelos in the 1890s and 1900s. Sugar haciendas, established in the sixteenth century but geared to local markets, began to expand in response to a growing external demand caused by the decline of sugar production in Cuba during the Cuban War of Independence (1895–8). The need for additional land and labour could only be satisfied by encroaching on neighbouring village lands, by depriving previously free villages of their livelihood and so forcing them to become a captive labour force. Although the land legislation of Mexican Liberals had accelerated this process throughout Mexico, it was only in Morelos that resistance to it took an effective form, in the *zapatista* movement.

In the Andes too, Indians experienced dispossession as a result of hacienda expansion. In Bolivia, the process accelerated under the dictator Melgarejo's distribution of the lands of 70,000 highland Indians among eight hundred or so of his own supporters in the late 1860s and early 1870s. In Peru, where coastal cotton and sugar plantations were able to expand with migrant labour from the Sierra, the problem was less acute than in the Sierra itself. Here demand for alpaca and llama wool during the First World War, combined with the shortened sea route to Europe after the opening of the Panama Canal in 1914, stimulated the growth of highland haciendas at the expense of Indian communities and the enserfment of their members. The submerged history of countless risings in isolated valleys is only now being unearthed by historians, although echoes of this process are caught by such writers as Ciro Alegría in his novel *Broad and Alien is the World.*

The clearest case in Spanish America of the impact of frontier expansion on jungle Indians is provided by Yucatán: Yucatán had remained a backwater since the original Spanish conquest in the sixteenth century. Cut off from the rest of Mexico by thick jungle, it had developed at a slower pace, preserving both the language and cultural forms of the indigenous Mayan Indians. *Encomienda* interests there were very strong: ninety per cent of the towns were held in *encomienda* in comparison with only fifty-five per cent in the rest of Mexico, and the institution lasted until 1785, longer than anywhere else in the country. Little was produced for export: poor rainfall excluded European grains, but a few cattle were exported to Cuba. Social control was largely in the hands of Mayan caciques. The town of Valladolid marked the frontier between the tightly controlled villages of the north and the free Mayan villages of the south. These villages were a refuge for those escaping from Spanish, and later, Mexican rule, and a breeding ground for revolts which increased as demographic pressures as well as harsher labour exploitation pushed the frontier southwards towards Belize.

Free land and low taxes on sugar attracted white settlers who were less rigid in their social attitudes than the strait-laced creole elite of towns like Valladolid and Mérida. But the threat to the religion of the Huits, the backwoods Mayans, and the fear of enslavement were causes of the Caste War which convulsed Yucatán in the late 1840s and 1850s. To some extent frontier expansion was slowed down by the development of the *henequen* plantations in the barren northwest of the peninsular, where Indians had accepted *ladino* ways and did not identify with the aspirations of the jungle Mayas. The end of the nineteenth century were Yucatán's boom years as a result of demand for sisal to make the twine for the mechanical binders on the American prairies. The boom drew off Indians from the frontier region and also from far off Sonora where land grabbers, avid for the lands of Yaqui Indians, had conducted punitive expeditions. Thousands of Yaquis captured in these expeditions were transported to work as virtual slave labour on the *henequen* plantations.

When the frontier began to expand again in southeast Yucatán in the late 1890s, with the development of cotton, banana, sugar plantations and *chicle* gathering, it met with fierce resistance. Road and railway building accompanied a military expedition in 1900, and two years later the newly subdued area became the federal territory of Quintana Roo.

Brazil's Indian frontier has also been essentially a jungle frontier. There was no contrast between sedentary Indians, with a highly developed urban civilization, and nomads. Brazilian Indians have been nomadic hunters and gatherers, living for the most part in jungle clearings. Attempts by early settlers to enslave them for work on the coastal plantations drove them further inland but, in spite of their elusiveness, the Portuguese were determined to make them participate in colonizing vast open spaces, especially in those areas disputed by Spain. In 1751, for example, Pombal issued a decree encouraging Portuguese settlers in regions adjacent to Spanish territory to marry Indian women as a way of creating a stable mixed population. But most settlers, especially those unable to afford highly-priced African slaves, were more interested in enslaving the Indians or in using them as auxiliaries in conflicts against other powers; this was the case in the alliance between the Portuguese and the Tupiniquim against the French and the Tupinamba in the 1550s and foreshadows similar alliances during the Franco-English conflict in North America in the eighteenth century. Finally, the Jesuits, the order which consistently guarded Indian interests, had their own aims, the creation of a state within a state which ran counter to the aims of both settlers and the Crown. Apart from Amazonia, and even there they had to be satisfied with an uneasy compromise, Jesuit influence was unable to prevent the *resgates* or slaving expeditions which were both a cause and a consequence of the open warfare typical of settler-Indian relationships.

One of the most disturbed regions was Piauí, the hinterland of the coast between the Amazon delta and the northeastern hump. Here and in Maranhão to the north, colonists could not compete with the sugar plantations for African slaves and so were compelled to enslave jungle Indians. This provoked the great revolt of the Tapuayas of the north in 1712–13 when a quarter of the four hundred ranches there were destroyed and which was only finally suppressed through the loyalty of mission Indians. The Jesuits had no doubts that the rising had been largely caused by the depredations of *vaqueiros* who rode down Indians 'as in a bull-fight'. In contrast to the nomadic Indians of Northern Mexico or the pampas, very few Brazilian Indians took to the horse, a notable exception being the Guiacurus, the nomadic horsemen of the borderlands of the River Paraguay who had harassed border settlements since the 1620s. Indians were primarily jungle dwellers and, unless forced into the open, could not be defeated or enslaved. This was one reason why early settlers burned off jungle cover, so making the *sertão* the arid wasteland it is today.[2]

In numerous instances, fear of jungle Indians was a major deterrent to expansion as, for example, in northern Goias where attacks by the Arroas and Xicriabás on the west bank of the Tocantins led to the abandonment of many estates. As late as 1808 the Aimorés Indians launched a series of attacks in Espíritu Santo which compelled the government to declare official war against them, thus permitting prisoners to be used as slaves by their captors.

The reduction of missionary protection after the expulsion of the Jesuits in 1767 combined with a pastoral frontier pushing into their hunting grounds, as well as the rising price of African slaves caused by the British blockade, seems to have resulted in a sharp rise in the incidence of Indian slavery in the early days of independence. In Pará, especially, always plagued by labour shortages, conditions became so bad that in the middle 1830s, the state was convulsed by a series of guerrilla wars or *cabanagems*.

The maroon frontier

The Indian frontier was not the only frontier of resistance in the Americas. Wherever there were slave plantations—in the Carolinas, Florida, Central America, in the Caribbean or South America, there were also runaways who fled into uninhabited hinterlands to establish hideouts. These maroon communities, *palenques* in Spanish America, and *quilombos* or *mocambos* in Brazil were by definition frontier societies, sited in inaccessible un-settled and inhospitable regions.

Many were ephemeral, consisting of a handful of fugitives who were soon recaptured, but others were numbered in hundreds or thousands and proved impossible to destroy. Deprived of the simplest tools which other settlers could take for granted, maroons had to improvise, drawing on the limited modernizing experiences of plantation life, on memories of their African past or on borrowings from neighbouring Indians if these happened to be friendly. Those communities which managed to survive were remarkable examples of adaptation to forbidding environments, of cultural resilience and linguistic innovation.

In Brazil ten major *quilombos* are known to have existed but only three of these survived longer than two years. The most famous was Palmares in the northeast which lasted from about 1605 until its destruction in 1692. Two Dutch expeditions failed to recapture those slaves who escaped during the dislocation caused by the Dutch occupation and when Portuguese rule was re-established in 1654 the various hideouts had coalesced into a kingdom under a leader, Ganga Zumba, with a social organization based on African traditions.

This constituted such a threat that six further expeditions were sent against it in the 1680s. However, it was not until the government finally contracted *paulistas*, the most ruthless and renowned slave catchers, that Palmares was finally destroyed, even then only after two years' struggle and a final twenty days' siege. The head of Zambi, the war chief, was publicly displayed to destroy the legend of his immortality, as was that of the bandit Lampião in the 1930s.

Palmares was the largest but not the last *quilombo*. The gold rush into Minas Gerais in the early 1700s made it increasingly difficult to keep slaves under close control and a number of *quilombos* were established in the gold region, the total population of which numbered thousands. In no case in Brazil, though, unlike elsewhere, was the colonial government prepared to treat with maroons. The precedent was too dangerous for a society totally dependent on slave labour and where whites were in a minority. Had Palmares not been destroyed it might have provided an inspiration and model for other African states in the hinterland, confining the Portuguese to their original coastal possessions.

In Haiti, a large maroon community survived for some seventy years at Le Maniel, in the frontier area between French and Spanish Hispaniola, and was never subdued by the colonial authorities. In Jamaica maroons fought so successfully in the Maroon War which reached a climax in the 1730s after many decades of running skirmishes, that the British were compelled to acknowledge their rights by treaty. The Guyanas were the classic site for maroon communities and, although most of those in British and French Guyana were destroyed in the course of the eighteenth century, those in Dutch Guyana, now Surinam, survived, were recognized by treaty and exist today in six tribal entities, numbering some 40,000. In Colombia, one community was recognized but was absorbed in the early twentieth century as its members went off to work in sugar and banana plantations or on the Panama Canal. In Mexico, where black slaves had been imported in large numbers at the end of the sixteenth century to offset the drastic decline of the Indian population, the threat of slave revolts was a constant preoccupation of viceroys but only one community ever seems to have been recognized by treaty. In Cuba many hamlets and small towns in mountainous and heavily wooded Oriente owe their origin to *palenques*.

Many maroons, protected by geographical inaccessibility, tried to create self-sufficient communities; others were dependent for supply on the very plantations from which they had escaped; others entered into trading relationships with nearby settlers, offering to refrain from raiding in return for goods. Yet others cooperated with pirates, with Sir Francis Drake, for instance, in Panama, where thick jungles were a favourite hideout for slaves in the sixteenth century. Maroons benefited from inter-colonial rivalry: in Jamaica they helped the English in their struggle against the Spaniards in 1655 and Spanish frontiersmen supported the maroons of Le Maniel in French Hispaniola. Some were friendly with local Indian tribes but we know little about these Indian-black relations (the best known example is that of the Seminole Indians in Florida who mixed with fugitive blacks and whose descendants are a distinctive group today). Shortage of black women generally led to attempts to capture Indian women and this probably was the major obstacle to peaceful cooperation, making it easy for colonial authorities to use Indians to hunt down maroons. With the reluctance of European troops to adopt counter-guerrilla tactics,[3] Indian militias were the most favoured and successful slave-catchers; in Jamaica where there were no Indians, they were imported from the Mosquito coast of Central America, although there and elsewhere free blacks and even slaves were also used.

Cases can also be cited of Indian maroon settlements; in Yucatán where the jungle afforded shelter from the plantations of Campeche, in Peru where whole Indian villages might escape to the wilderness outside Spanish influence, as in the case of the Morocochas Indians who live today near Ayacucho and are a rare example of a surviving Amerindian horse culture, and in Cuba where there were many Indian maroon hamlets in the sixteenth century before the Indian population was wiped out.

Although colonial governments feared slave hideouts as springboards for offensive attacks, maroon communities were essentially defensive in conception and outlook, wishing to be left alone. Neither the maroons of Le Maniel in Haiti nor those in Cuba played an active part in their country's independence movements. Indeed they sometimes became slave owners themselves or agreed to become slave catchers as part of the bargain by which the colonial government recognized their autonomy, and they would not welcome more fugitives than their community could support.

Maroon communities could survive only so long as the interior remained unsettled. In the nineteenth century, as the frontier of settlement expanded, rebellion on the plantation became a more frequent form of protest in both Brazil and Cuba while *marronage* took the form of individual rather than mass flight. Runaway slaves in Cuba, whether blacks like Esteban Montejo,[4] imported Yucatecan Indians or indentured Chinese, could be left to be recaptured by groups of *rancheadores*, white peasants (*guajiro*) made landless by the expansion of the large sugar plantations, using fierce mastiffs to sniff out their prey. Another form of escape was to the cities which provided a refuge for the creole slaves who knew Spanish or Portuguese and whose skills might enable them to pass as freedmen. The city gave anonymity or, as in the case of São Paulo in the 1870s, the protection of middle-class abolitionists.

Although in retrospect the maroon problem may seem unimportant it was not so at the time. No colonial society felt safe as long as there was a potential focus for resistance and opposition. It was not so much that maroons preyed on communication routes and settler communities for in fact they often lived in a mutual relationship with them, but rather that their hideouts acted as a magnet for other slaves on the plantations.[5] While hideouts were known to exist there was always an alternative way of life and the risk to achieve it was worth taking.

The savagery of the slaveholding system was displayed at its most brutal in the punishments meted out to captured runaways—branding, public castration, dismemberment, roasting over slow fires, all the civilizing devices of frightened societies which sensed on what slender bases their legitimacy rested. The institutionalized terror of fugitive slave regulations decreed by colonial governors and their literal application was the response of colonists on the ground to the slave codes passed in the metropolis and designed in theory to afford the slaves some measure of protection.

Many maroons tended to be recent arrivals from Africa who could not or would not adapt to slave conditions. This was one reason why so many *quilombos* and *palenques* show a multiplicity of African influences but the influences of plantation cultures should not be ignored or over-simplified; the variety of cultural forms in maroon communities parallels the variety shown on the plantations. If any distinction is to be made between Afro-American plantation influence and that of Africa it is that the latter provided a rich storehouse of organizational forms which was lacking on the plantation except at a low level.

Maroon communities are significant in that they provide some of the longest and most persistent examples of resistance to colonial rule. But only recently has their historical experience been incorporated into the ideologies of nationalist movements. Their positive achievements help to offset the 'Sambo' image of the slave as contented, or the view that Africans showed a natural predisposition towards slavery. Conditions forced maroons to become masters of guerrilla warfare and in this respect they provide an ancestry to the rural guerrillas of the 1960s. Most maroon leaders were anonymous and so are not found in the pantheon of nationalist heroes. But the maroon experience and the adaptation of black frontiersmen to forbidding environments constitutes a myth which can have the function of liberating the historiography of newly independent black countries—such as the Guyanas—from independence on an interpretation of the past where blacks are always seen as the passive recipients of superior white values—a black equivalent of the Turner thesis.

Mining frontiers

The lure of silver and gold was the strongest pull drawing settlers into the desolate interior and extending the frontier of settlement. After the exhaustion of the gold beds of Hispaniola and Cuba, Spaniards began to search on the mainland in Central America where, for something like a century, we can talk of a patchy moving mining frontier, sustained either by *cuadrillas* of Indian slaves or by *güirises*, marginal prospectors working on their own or in small groups. Some of these were poor Indians or mestizos scavenging through abandoned mines and, as many did not register, were seen as a threat by established miners. *Entradas* into Nicaragua resulted in some gold panning in rivers between 1519 and 1542 but Central American mining was always bedevilled by labour shortages; the Indians declined through disease or overwork, had been sent as slaves to Peru or were drawn off to work on the cacao plantations of the Pacific coast. Although some Africans were imported, they were expensive for miners who could not compete with the higher prices offered in Mexico or Peru. Honduran mining, writes one historian, was an 'economy of fraud and evasion', common enough in regions of primitive placer mining everywhere but doubly necessary in Honduras where profit margins were minimal.[6] Nevertheless, the poverty-stricken mines round Tegucigalpa provided some nucleus for the settlement of central Honduras which might otherwise have remained a haunt of wild cattle.

Neither gold nor silver was to provide the basis for a stable society in Central America whose economy was conditioned by the search for a key crop such as cacao, sarsparilla or indigo. There were no 'silver cities' nor was mining much of a stimulus for other economic activities. It was but a part of a distinctive cyclical economic process, a microcosm of Brazilian experience but without the latter's limitless potential. Examples may be found elsewhere in Latin America of small mining camps—in Panama, at Buritaca in Colombia and in eastern Ecuador, and often in between larger mining regions; but the mining economy on which the wealth and importance of colonial Spanish America, and Brazil in the eighteenth century, rested did not depend on these small scale operations so much as on the big strikes which were also a major factor in promoting settlement. The first of these was sparked off by the discovery of the great silver mountain of Potosí in 1545, 15,000 feet on the Andean *altiplano* in what is now Bolivia. The second was the discovery of silver bearing lodes at Zacatecas, some 350 miles northwest of Mexico City and the third was the discovery of gold in the 1690s in the area now known as Minas Gerais in Brazil some 200 miles north of Rio de Janeiro.

The main distinction between gold and silver mining lay in the technology required. Gold, unlike the Rand in South Africa but in common with California and the Yukon, was alluvial, found in mountain streams and obtained by panning. Silver, embedded in rock required deep shafts and tunnelling and a complex refining process to separate silver from the ore. As the silver content declined, the importance of mercury increased since it was required in the amalgamation process, first used in Spanish America in the 1550s, enabling lower grade ores to be mined.

Hence the crucial importance to the mining economy of the mercury mines of Almaden in southern Spain and Huancavelica in Peru.

Silver in New Spain and Upper Peru

The mirage of the golden cities of Cíbola might draw adventurers into the desolate wilderness but only an actual strike of precious metal would lead to permanent settlement; even then news of another strike elsewhere often led to an exodus of labour and capital, as happened at Zacatecas on the discovery of silver at Parral in 1631. The original strike of silver at Zacatecas was sufficiently big to tempt settlers across the shifting pre-Spanish frontier between sedentary Indians and nomads to the north and into a forbidding waterless region. Zacatecas was a totally new phenomenon in the Americas. Within two years of its foundation it had five churches, fifty refineries and was attracting hordes of adventurers. As the shortest route from Mexico City lay through Chichimec country, it was necessary to found garrison towns to protect the silver route, and a string of new settlements owed their origins to frontier defence—San Miguel (1555), San Felipe (1562), Celaya (1571), León (1576). These towns also came to serve as centres of an agricultural and pastoral economy providing food and cattle products for the mining areas. Defence, supply and labour were the major problems for the mining towns, and of these the last was the most pressing. In central Mexico where mining communities had been established among sedentary Indians, as at Taxco, Pachuca or Sultepec, mine-owners recruited their labour by means of the *repartimiento*; but in the sparsely populated northern regions where there were no sedentary Indians to provide *encomienda* grants, they had either to use slaves or to attract free labour. Spanish law permitted the enslavement of Indians charged with armed resistance and rebellion, and one factor prolonging the Chichimec war was the possibility which its continuance gave to enslaving prisoners taken in the course of it. Negro slaves were also imported but they were expensive as well as being a source of disaffection. From an early date, therefore, free labour was employed in the mines of northern Mexico. At the end of the sixteenth century, for example at Zacatecas, free Indians constituted nearly two thirds of the total mining force of seven and a half thousand. Tarascans, Otomís and Aztecs from central Mexico were drawn to the mining settlements, many in order to escape the increasing burdens involved in church building and public works projects. They might live either in an *hacienda de minas*, receiving free supplies of meat and corn, or in one of the Indian *barrios* on the outskirts of mining towns. These *barrios* were distinctive, with each one comprising a separate Indian group. There was always as well a floating population, largely of mestizos, ready to move on at the news of a rich strike elsewhere. Hence the importance, as a means of keeping labour, of the *pepena*, a productivity bonus by which a miner might keep a proportion of his haul.

The food needs of the mining towns, although limited, were not met by small farmers. Few fortune hunters were interested in anything but discovering their own lodes. Agriculture was developed by the larger miners. The northern Mexican frontier is, therefore, in its beginning a 'big man's frontier'. Food production, at first a necessity, soon became a profitable investment under the stimulus of high prices. There was also the provision of materials needed in the mines—wood for charcoal used in smelting, for pit-props and machinery, mules needed for the ore-crushers, cattle to provide meat, tallow for candles to light the galleries (seventy tons a year were used in Zacatecas alone), hides for thonging, harnesses and buckets, fodder for draught animals. Wealthy miners founded haciendas to provide both agricultural and pastoral products. When mining production began to fall off in the middle of the seventeenth century the miners were able to fall back on their mixed haciendas for subsistence. From being a nascent bourgeoisie, miners could become founders of landed dynasties with estates protected for posterity by entail in the *mayorazgo*, although few in fact did so as land often proved to be a poor investment.

Zacatecas dominated Mexican mining until the 1630s. It was the 'mother of the north' and 'gateway to all the kingdoms of the north', the second city of New Spain. Mining profits subsidized the exploration and settlement of the northern provinces. The miner, Francisco de Ibarra, financed the conquest of Nueva Vizcaya and the foundation of Durango, and expeditions based on Zacatecas founded Fresnillo, San Martín, Sombrerete and Santa Barbara still further north. The strike at Parral in 1631 combined with a shortage of mercury needed to work the lower-grade ores marked the end of Zacatecas's domination, for miners were now drawn to regions with ores of higher quality and were less dependent on mercury supplies. Although a Colonization Law of 1573 promised the award of titles, the right to grant *encomiendas*, to make land grants and found *mayorazgos* as a reward for bearing the major costs of exploration and conquest, it was often the haphazard discovery of new lodes which proved the most effective magnet drawing people into inhospitable areas.

The rise and fall of the populations of the mining towns is indicative of the restlessness of many mining communities. The Mexican mining frontier encouraged extensive rather than intensive settlement. Towns were often oases in the northern scrub deserts, separated from each other by vast distances. In the eighteenth century the pattern changes as the silver boom then was centred on the densely populated Bajío rather than on Zacatecas, Parral or the northern mines; nevertheless, José de la Borda, with new techniques learned in his successful exploitation of the Taxco silver mines, brought a revival to Zacatecas in an attempt to revive his waning fortunes by a combination of fiscal exemptions, subsidized mercury, low labour costs and technical skill.

The initiative for further expansion northwards now came from missionaries and cattlemen rather than from prospectors and the motives were those of missionary zeal and strategic necessity rather than greed.

Imperial Potosí, 'the opulent pious and licentious city' with a population of 120,000 in its heyday in the seventeenth century was not only the largest city of the Americas but was also the motor of the Spanish economy between the first strike in 1545 and the 1660s—a lodestone attracting Spaniards, Portuguese and foreigners alike from all over the continent and beyond the seas. As befits a city which made and unmade European monarchs, its panegyrists vie with others in their fulsome descriptions—'the famous, always supreme, richest and inexhaustible Mountain of Potosí'; 'a rare creation of the power of God, a miracle of nature, a perfect and permanent marvel of the world'; 'an honour and glory of America'; 'I am rich Potosí, the treasure of the world, the king of the mountains, and the envy of kings'.[7]

Unlike mining towns in New Spain, Potosí was not part of a loosely knit network of isolated mining communities. These came only with the growth of mining settlement in the latter half of the nineteenth century when silver had given way to base metals and in particular to tin. Potosí was the greatest mining city of the Spanish Empire and the richest market of the Americas, an emporium knitting together commerce from Buenos Aires to Lima. It was a magnet attracting those unable to obtain *encomiendas*—adventurers and *pícaros* who hoped to live off their wits.

Potosí had no raison d'être apart from silver and, with the failure to revive the mines after the Nordenflicht mission of 1788 and after the destruction during the wars of independence, its fate was sealed. Its decline of population, falling since the peak in the mid-seventeenth century, was hastened by the epidemic of 1719 which carried off 20,000 and by the beginning of the nineteenth century it had barely 15,000. Today it is a museum town set in a forbidding treeless landscape. The great hill honeycombed with galleries still has a symbolic value as on the day when Bolívar climbed to its summit in 1825 after the Spaniards had been driven out and recalled how twenty years earlier on the Monte Sacro in Rome he had vowed to free America from the Spanish yoke.

Unlike the settlements of New Spain beyond the pale of the old Aztec Empire, the site of Potosí was within the orbit of the Inca Empire, lying near the old Inca road to La Plata (Sucre). In spite of the feeling of permanence conveyed by the solid and ornate Andean baroque architecture, it is doubtful if many Spaniards envisaged spending their lives there. Their ambition was rather to make a quick fortune and then retire to Spain or to invest their profits in a lowland hacienda in the temperate climate of the Cochabamba valley. There were few white women in the population because of the difficulty of bearing children at such an altitude; no Spanish child was born there in the first fifty years and Spanish mothers used to go to the lowland valleys to have their children. Part of the city's turbulence may perhaps be explained by the lack of balance between the sexes. Mestizos were also a cause of instability, provoking riots in 1586 and clamouring for legal recognition to avoid being recruited by the *mita*. The climax to endless feuding was reached in the Guerra de los Vascongadas between 1623 and 1626: Basques fought with Vicuñas, as those Spaniards were called who banded together to resist Basque domination of mining and politics, much as *paulistas* were to fight with foreigners in the Guerra dos Emboabas of 1708 in the gold mines of Brazil, although in this case the cause was bitter resentment by the *paulistas* at seeing their discovery being exploited by hordes of newcomers.

Many Spaniards who arrived in Peru too late to receive encomiendas drifted to Potosí where not being an *encomendero* was no handicap. In the early years much of the mining was done by *yanaconas*, Indians who were personal servants outside the framework of the clan and *encomienda* and relatively skilled in comparison with *mita* Indians. There may have been as many as 7,000 *yanaconas* in Potosí in the 1550s, each attached to a Spanish master operating on his behalf, extracting and smelting ore and delivering silver to his master each week. But, unlike northern Mexico, the majority of the labour force was made up of *mitayos*, Indians selected by caciques from each Indian community according to a scale laid down by royal officials, to work in the mines. These *mitayos* were drawn from all over the *altiplano*.

The provisioning of such a rapidly growing city in a barren landscape posed many problems. The *mitayos* used to bring their own food with them in the form of huge llama herds as well as *coca* to make working in the mines bearable. Wheat was imported from Chile, the granary of the Peruvian viceroyalty; wheat, fruit, cotton and cloth came from Tucumán and Salta, pork from Tarija, corn and fruit from the Cochabamba valleys and from the distant Mojos and Beni where estates were worked by enslaved Chiriguana Indians of the Chaco captured in fierce raiding forays. Fish, packed in ice, was brought from Lake Titicaca, grapes and brandy from Arequipa; food was also sent up from the Jesuit missions in Paraguay until their expulsion. Mules on which the whole Andean transportation system depended were bred in Salta and driven in their tens of thousands over the mountain passes. The key supplies of mercury, needed for the *patio* amalgamation process after its introduction in 1573, came from Huancavelica in Lower Peru. From there it was taken to the coast and shipped to Arica where llama and mule trains conveyed it in a month's journey to Potosí. Silver in bars was carried out by mules on a four-month journey to Lima for shipment to Spain in payment either of the royal fifth or for imported European goods. Alternatively silver might be transported illegally on a two-month journey to the smuggling centre of Colonia do Sacramento, opposite Buenos Aires—a process organized by Brazilian merchants known as *peruleiros*.

Merchants were clearly attracted by the prospect of a possible thousand per cent trading profit and the high prices tended to create dearth elsewhere. Goods from all over the world were sold in the Potosí fair—English cottons, Italian brocades, Venetian glass, eastern stones, spices and perfume, Ottoman carpets and Chinese silks.

The whole of this elaborate commercial network began to break up as mining declined in the eighteenth century and was finally shattered by the loss of Lima's monopoly, the opening up of Buenos Aires and the wars of independence. The subsequent shift in the axis of trade meant that northern Argentina, once a satellite to the Andean economy, went into decline and did not recover until Bolivian mining revived at the end of the nineteenth century and Chilean mines created a demand for cattle and agricultural goods.

Silver enjoyed a brief revival in Bolivia in the 1870s and 1880s but was then replaced by tin; yet the pattern of settlement remained largely unaltered and the economic centre of gravity remained located in the *altiplano*.

Gold frontiers

In spite of the wealth of gold found by the conquistadores in both Mexico and Peru, gold accounted for only some ten to fifteen per cent of the precious metals exported from Latin America over three centuries, and between 1503 and 1660 some 300 tons of gold were exported in comparison with some 25,000 tons of silver. Apart from the Brazilian gold boom of the eighteenth century, the bulk of this gold was exported during two gold cycles—between 1510 and 1530 and in the 1550s. Aztec loot and panned gold from Santo Domingo and Veragua comprised the first cycle; that of Buritaca in Colombia the second cycle. There were other fitful gold rushes such as one at Carabaya near Cuzco and one east of Quito in the 1540s but they did not prove fruitful.

In Colombia the Chibcha Indians had a highly developed culture and although they left few architectural remains they achieved an extraordinarily high expertise in working gold. The quest for gold was stimulated by the El Dorado myth and the fabled wealth of Zenu was the immediate cause of the sixteenth-century settlement of Colombia. Cartagena, one of the great Caribbean ports, owed its initial prosperity to the finds of gold at Buritaca in the Cauca valley. The 1550s were the great years of Buritaca gold but production was soon crippled by epidemics which carried off most of the labour force, first in 1588 and then again in 1626. The discovery of emeralds at Muzo stimulated one area of settlement but other gold strikes occurred in the Antioquia highlands and were to prove more significant in stimulating settlement. Antioquia became the main area of interior settlement and a disputed frontier area between gold-seekers coming up from Cartagena and others coming from Peru. Placer mining predominated; methods were primitive, based on the simple sieve, and labour was scarce. Until the development of steam navigation on the River Magdalena in the early nineteenth century, communication with the coast was difficult; it was cheaper, for example, for coastal towns to import wheat from abroad than from the interior.

The factor conditioning the nature of Antioqueño colonization was the shortage of labour: there were few sedentary Indians and miners could not afford to buy slaves in the Cartagena market in competition with the wealthier coastal plantations. Spaniards and mestizos, therefore, had to do much of the manual labour themselves. As a result, there emerged what has been described as a 'sort of Latin American puritanism' and a frugal and hardworking population; from this were drawn the entrepreneurs and pioneers who pushed the coffee frontier south and west and in the twentieth century helped to make Antioquia (with Medellín its capital) a flourishing industrial centre. By contrast, in the Chocó a different gold frontier developed where prospectors enslaved both blacks and Indians. This was predatory mining at its worst as evidenced by the region's backwardness today.

In Brazil the consequences of the discovery of gold in what is now Minas Gerais were very different. News of the discovery in the coast sparked off the first mass gold rush of modern history. Within a decade the economy and the attitude of the Portuguese Crown towards its previously neglected colony had been totally transformed.

The sugar plantation economy had been slow to recover from the effects of the Dutch War between 1634 and 1654. The expansion of Caribbean sugar in the late seventeenth century, especially after 1654 when the Dutch took with them their marketing and technical skills and the Jews their financial expertise, made competition difficult. Thus the news of a gold strike came as a welcome relief, drawing to the interior planters and their slaves, merchants and vagrants and causing a stampede from Portugal which assumed such serious proportions that the Crown was compelled to place a limit on emigration in 1720 in order to prevent depopulation. One estimate puts the number of people who emigrated to Brazil in the course of the eighteenth century at 300,000 possibly more than the total for Spanish America throughout the whole colonial period. The gold rush led to a price revolution as labour became scarce in the coastal regions. This became so serious that the Crown also attempted to prohibit the exploitation of the Jacobins and Rio das Coutas mining districts in the hinterland of Bahia for fear of depriving tobacco and sugar plantations of labour, as even annual imports of slaves into Bahia alone of 10–12,000 slaves were insufficient for both plantations and mines.

In the gold fields the miners had at first neglected to plant manioc or maize and famine was a real threat, but rocketing prices of food and other essentials in a virtually uninhabited and uncultivated region turned some prospectors aside from the hypothetical gains of mining to the more tangible profits of food production. As in New Spain, fortunes were consolidated by diversifying into farming, cattle-raising, slave-trading and commerce.

The early years in Minas Gerais were racked by conflict. There was no common enemy like the Chichimecs to make the prospectors close ranks. Feuding broke out in the Guerra dos Emboabas (called *emboabas* because of the leggings they wore) between foreigners and *paulistas* over the latters' complaint that outsiders were swamping the diggings and jumping *paulista* claims. As the *paulistas* had made the original discovery their resentment was understandable. Stability was not helped by the youthfulness of many of the recent arrivals nor by the shortage of women. Negresses were in great demand not only for sexual gratification but also because of their supposed gift for divining gold. One early consequence of the gold rush was the growth of a mulatto population.

With their fierce individualism, no *paulistas* could take kindly to increased government control, and their restless energies were soon directed elsewhere after the failure of their petition to Lisbon that land grants should be limited to *paulistas*. This restlessness was rewarded with the discovery of gold in Cuiabá in 1718 and 1725 and in Mato Grosso in 1734. These frontier areas of the eighteenth century are part of today's Brazilian 'West'. To reach it then took a seven-month canoe journey of immense hardship and danger from piranhas, malaria, mosquitoes and Indian attack. The fierce Piaigua Indians decimated convoys—*monçãos*—one, four-hundred strong, was massacred to a man. Safety lay in numbers and, in 1726, three hundred and five canoes set out from São Paulo with three thousand aboard. In 1727 Bom Jesus de Cuiabá was founded, 1,600 miles from São Paulo by river, a meagre collection of mud huts with a population of some 7,000 of whom 2,000 were negro slaves. Again the hated *emboabas*, many penniless with their slaves on credit, threatened to engulf the *paulistas*. Riots ensued as at Goias in 1736, but it may have been the threat of Indian hostility which prevented the deeper divisions of Minas Gerais. The Cuiabá diggings were in any case shallower than those of Minas and were quickly exhausted. Cuiabá virtually emptied as prospectors moved on to new sites, leaving behind the fruit of their illicit unions with coloured women.

The mining frontier now contracted, and Goais and Mato Grosso were depopulated. An eye witness in the 1820s refers to the mining camps as heaps of ruins and the capital city Vila Boa as a collection of tumbledown shacks. In the latter half of the eighteenth century the mining boom in Minas Gerais also slowed down and its population began to scatter centrifugally, some pushing south, others south eastwards, meeting a migratory movement up from Rio (which as the port for the mining region had begun to outstrip Bahia). To the southwest *mineiros* moved into areas traditionally within the influence of São Paulo.

The mines in Minas Gerais were mostly placer mines and, although they were worked by slave labour, few miners owned more than a dozen slaves. In 1752 the larger miners secured a privileged position when the Crown granted their petition to enjoy a similar immunity from restraint for debt as that enjoyed by coastal tobacco and sugar planters. The Crown anxiously watched the progress of the mining settlements, seeking to assert its authority and to ensure regular payment of the royal fifth, much to the disgust of the *paulistas* who 'desired to be free from justice'. But in spite of its vigilance the Crown never put an end to the smuggling activity of the *faiscador* and *garimpeiro*, two distinctive types of the Brazilian gold fields, and to prospectors working on their own account.

The situation was different in the diamond district further to the north in the barren and forbidding Serro do Frio where royal control was ruthlessly enforced. The unofficial importation of Brazilian diamonds into Lisbon in 1730 forced the Crown to intervene in order to prevent prices falling, and in 1734 a decree forbidding the mining of diamonds resulted in a severe economic depression in the diamond camps. When the price began to rise again the Crown permitted mining to restart on a limited scale only and on a Crown monopoly basis. The first contract, for a four-year term, ran from 1740 and limited the work force to 600 slaves instead of the previous 8–9,000. Many miners, now ruined, took to smuggling if they could escape the watchful eye of the specially recruited dragoons of Minas Gerais. In 1753 the Serro de Frio became a closed territory when the Crown converted all diamond mining into a royal monopoly; this was not abolished until 1882. When diamonds were discovered elsewhere these areas were also sealed off.

As the population began to drift away from Ouro Preto and the other gold centres, they left behind them sleepy country towns with superb baroque churches as monuments to the gold boom. The Brazilian gold rush was unique in its creation of a baroque civilization and in producing an artist of the calibre of Aleijadinho, the handless mulatto sculptor whose soapstone carvings and church decorations are one of the wonders of Latin American art. There could be no greater contrast than that between the baroque splendour and solidity of Ouro Preto and the tumbledown sleaziness of mining towns of the United States and the Canadian West.

Base metal frontiers

Gradually, base metal began to replace precious metals in importance as the needs of industrializing countries for raw materials increased from the middle of the nineteenth century. In Chile, for example, the silver strikes of the 1830s were soon eclipsed by the development of copper mining and nitrates, and in Bolivia the revival of silver mining in the late 1860s was shortlived after an enterprising mestizo clerk called Simon Patiño realized that the spoils from the silver mines, rich in tin ore, would become more valuable than the silver itself.

In Chile the discovery of the 'silver hill' of Chanarcillo sparked off a silver rush which became the basis of the wealth and growth of Copiapó. Other strikes followed and Copiapó, which had been an outpost of the Inca Empire and had never quite lost its frontier character, became a centre first for silver and then for copper. These new developments also revived its traditional function as a commercial centre for the trans-Andine mule trains which were now stimulated in response to the demands for / transport in the nitrate and copper workings. Meat on the hoof was also imported from Argentina and the new mining frontiers of northern Chile were knitted together, reviving, to some extent, the unity of the Andean colonial economy. The desert frontier between Peru, Bolivia and Chile, rich in nitrate, was disputed between the three powers in the War of the Pacific (1879–83).

For some years Copiapó was the world's richest copper town and outpost of European civilization, boasting the first opera house in Chile as well as the terminus of Chile's first railway and the country's first gas works. It also remained something of a frontier settlement, situated between the fertile central valley and the waterless Atacama desert to the north. The early exploitation of copper in Chile was technologically undemanding but, with the exhaustion of the oxide ores and their replacement by low-grade porphyry deposits, more sophisticated technology was required. There is, therefore, a marked change from small and medium mining to *gran minería* in the early years of the twentieth century. Both technical expertise and large capital investment had to be attracted from abroad, given the low level of Chilean technical education and the reluctance of Chilean capitalists to invest their money in enterprises involving long term risks. As in the Chilean case, so elsewhere, the new mining frontiers were dependent on foreign expertise, capital and markets.

The most important by-product of these new frontiers was the building of railways. Although ore was transported from Bolivia to Buenos Aires on the backs of mules as late as the 1870s, this method of transportation clearly had its limitations. In the Bolivian case the new tin mines were linked by railways to the Pacific ports—in Chilean hands after Bolivia's defeat in the War of the Pacific—while in Peru the Central Railway, rising to the highest point of any railway in the world, was built to service the new mines of the Sierra.

However, Mexico provided the most striking example of new mineral workings stimulating railway development. The demands of United States industrial expansion encouraged the search for new reserves of raw materials. Between 1897 and 1911 US investments in Mexico increased fivefold, eighty-three per cent of them in railways and mining. Some 15,000 miles of new railways were built, primarily to market this new mineral wealth. In the state of San Luis Potosí, where Guggenheim interests dominated the economy, railways conveyed silver and lead ores to the family smelters. This spate of new railway building was facilitated by not having to cut through the mountain ranges running north to south and thus avoided some of the engineering problems raised by the earlier British-built line between Vera Cruz and Mexico City.

Many US promoters regarded Mexico as an extension of the western frontier; prospectors began moving in immediately after the Mexican War in 1849, and by the 1860s about thirty US companies were working in Mexico. One consequence was the introduction of new technologies; for example, the *patio* process of amalgamating silver which had dominated Mexican mining since the mid-sixteenth century was finally ousted by the cyanide process in the 1880s. Silver continued to attract prospectors; thus the discovery of the Sierra Mojada vein in 1875 sparked off a minor silver rush, attracting perhaps 5,000 North American prospectors. But increasingly the emphasis shifted to base metals as US smelters came to rely on Mexican ores, partly because of lower labour costs. In spite of low wages by American standards, Mexican *hacendados* bitterly resented the newly opened mines as they drew off labour from their own estates by offering higher wages. Another source of friction was the differential payment made to American and Mexican mine employees. This led to the strike at the Cananea copper mines in 1906, the first violent expression of anti-Americanism, which became a legend in Mexican labour history and was another illustration of how tensions caused by US penetration contributed towards making the northern frontier a seed-bed of revolution.

Cattle frontiers

A striking feature of pre-Columbian America was the limited range of its fauna. Horses, sheep, cattle, goats and pigs were all introduced by the

Spaniards. Under New World conditions European animals increased at a remarkable rate: in fifteen months a herd of cattle doubled. Cattle were a weapon in the armoury of conquest. The agricultural basis of sedentary Indian civilizations was virtually destroyed by droves of swine and herds of cows, and the legislation to protect Indians from the depredations of European cattle remained a dead letter. Indian fields were converted into pasture and their owners forced on to steep slopes and into inaccessible places. The age-old conflict between agriculturists and pastoralists was an unequal one in America for the Spaniards, with their experience of peninsular cattle-ranching, gave the 'lazy industry of stock raising' a central place in the economy.

There were good reasons for this. As Indian population declined in the sixteenth century and as Spanish population remained static in the seventeenth century, slowing up the flow of immigrants, labour shortages made pastoralism a rational choice. But in addition it became a mainstay of everyday life not only for meat but also for a whole range of necessities which leather could provide. Leather was an alternative for high-cost imported iron; thonging could be substituted for nails. Leather flaps served as windows and doors, and leather was in constant demand for the harnesses of the mules and horses on which the whole transportation system depended. The wheels of carts were bound in leather and it provided the basis for beds and chairs. The fat of cattle, rendered as tallow, served as candles for domestic use and underground, and was used to grease the wooden machinery in sugar mills and mines; cattle horn was used for a wide variety of domestic utensils.

Cattle frontiers expanded in the search for wider pastures to satisfy an inexhaustible internal demand. At first, few cattle products were exported. Cattle were bred in Cuba to provide dried beef for the transatlantic crossing, but it was not until the late eighteenth century when wars increased the demand of European armies for leather that hides became a major export item, and even then mainly from the La Plata region where, since 1778, Buenos Aires had been permitted to trade directly with Spain.

An expanding cattle frontier became a necessity for the future prosperity of Buenos Aires after the viceroyalty of La Plata broke up on independence. Upper Peru became Bolivia, Paraguay broke away, the rich cattle country of the Banda Oriental became Uruguay in 1828 and endemic disturbances kept the littoral provinces in turmoil. Labour shortages and the threat from Indians constantly frustrated attempts to stimulate agriculture but, in any case, the high cost of wood for fences on the treeless pampas and the absence of barbed wire until the 1870s made agriculture as well as selective breeding impossible. Lean and stringy wild cattle were valuable as hides and for salted beef. With salt from the salt pans south of Buenos Aires, the *saladero* provided the basis for a flourishing triangular trade in dried beef—to the slave plantations of northeast Brazil or Cuba, whence sugar and molasses were exported to the United States, whence wheat was then exported back to Buenos Aires. This and the European demand for hides gave the incentive to push the frontier into Indian territory.

In the 1820s, twenty-one million acres of public land came into the hands of some five hundred individuals. Land was distributed as a reward instead of money for salaries. In 1833 Rosas, the spokesman of *saladero* and *estanciero* interests and the holder of some half a million acres himself, led a military expedition which opened up large tracts of land south of Buenos Aires. From then on the cattle frontier was to push westwards and southwest under Rosas's direction until he was toppled from power in 1853.

When Rosas fell, the *estanciero–saladero* complex gave way to a pastoral sheep economy. Cattle grazing had prepared the pampas grasslands for sheep-grazing which brought more intensive land-use and with the subsequent rise in land values pushed cattle further into the pampas. Bulls and gauchos were now replaced by sheep and by Irish, Basque and Scottish shepherds who were prepared to accept the monotonous life which more volatile creoles rejected. The reduced mobility of sheep-grazing encouraged a more sedentary type of settlement. Shepherds stayed on the land and, by a system of payment whereby they kept between one third and a half of the increase of the flock they were tending, many were able to become sheep farmers in their own right, thus laying the fortunes of some of Argentina's richest families. The spread of sheep-grazing, by pushing cattle out to the periphery, was an important factor in frontier expansion and also in attracting European immigrants who were no longer necessarily condemned to become peons.

Until the disastrous floods of 1902 carried away about fourteen million sheep, they were to be more important than cattle. By the 1880s wool contributed between 50 and 60 per cent of Argentina's exports. From a quarter of a million sheep in 1810 in Buenos Aires province, the number had expanded to forty-six millions by 1875.

Cattle remained important for the export of hides until ways could be found of making the meat acceptable to the European palate, although there had always been an internal trans-frontier trade in live cattle to Chile and Upper Peru where taste was not so fastidious. Quality improved with the introduction of pedigree cattle, and the importation of barbed wire (from 5,000 tons in 1876 to 39,000 tons in 1889) which made selective breeding possible by separating bulls and cows. By 1893 the export of refrigerated meat—mainly mutton until 1904—was greater than all live animal exports and in 1905 Argentina surpassed the United States as the world's major beef exporter. Per capita consumption ran at 170 pounds annually in comparison with only 110 pounds in the United States. The final factor which made such expansion possible was the release of vast new tracts of grazing land liberated by the annihilation of the pampas Indians after the War of the Desert of 1879–83.

In Brazil, the cattle frontier was even more extensive than in Argentina. But, in spite of its importance in the domestic economy, cattle never constituted the basis of an export boom comparable to cotton, sugar or coffee, but was essentially a satellite economy supplying the sugar and cotton plantations of the northeast, Maranhão and the mining camps. The first deep penetration of the vast hinterland was made by cowboys moving further and further afield in their search for new pastures.

Unlike New Spain or Upper Peru where mules were used as draft animals, the Brazilian sugar industry tended to rely on slow moving oxen; they hauled firewood for the sugar boilers and powered the sugar rollers of the mills. Meat was a staple diet of the coastal region—20,000 head of cattle were consumed yearly in Bahia, and in the 1820s Belém with a population of only 13,000 consumed 11,000 head a year. Tallow served for grease, and leather for many essentials.

Like the pampas, the *sertão* was a 'leather culture'. At first planters and mill-owners raised their own herds but by the end of the sixteenth century rising demand for sugar made it unprofitable to waste valuable land for pasturage, and so cattle were purchased from ranches in the interior which specialized in cattle raising. From the early years of the seventeenth century the hinterland of Bahia and Pernambuco was the scene of conflicts between pastoralists and agriculturists. In this struggle the planters, linked to the export economy, won: ranchers were forced to accept decrees legislating in the planters' interests. Cattlemen in sugar areas were first compelled by law to fence their pasture, which was an expensive undertaking, and then by a decree in 1701 they were finally forbidden to graze within forty miles of the coast.

By the early seventeenth century the *sertão* had been converted into a vast cattle range, after *vaqueiros* moved inland up the São Francisco River and beyond the Paulo Affonso Falls. The Dutch occupation interrupted this process as plantations were destroyed and herds scattered, but in the 1640s graziers, forced inland, began to realize the potential of the new pastures. Penetration and settlement were continuous but erratic. In the same way as the northern Mexican cattle lands, the *sertão* became an area of endemic turbulence, one in which the few missionaries had less success than in Mexico and were unable to curb the violent hostility between *vaqueiros* and Indians.

The origins of the huge cattle ranches can be found in the *sesmaria* grants made to cattlemen who were then responsible for enforcing order. Other grants were also made to pioneer cattlemen and Indian fighters among whom were many *paulistas*. But once grants had been made, land-hungry cattle barons recruited their own private armies so that the Crown's writ scarcely ran in the backlands. After independence these men became the *coroneis*—local political bosses, who often resorted to using bands of ruffians (*capangas*) to enforce their will.

The major problem lay in the periodic droughts, usually recurring in a seven-year cycle, to which the *sertão* was exposed, when water holes dried up, pastures withered and herds were decimated. The worst drought occurred in 1791–3 when an estimated seven eighths of the animals died. It was this disaster which finally turned the tide in favour of Rio Grande do Sul which now became the major beef producer. The *sertão*, opened up by the cattlemen, was to remain an economic cul-de-sac, bequeathing a legacy of turbulence and desperation.

The endless grasslands of Rio Grande do Sul invite comparison with the Argentinian pampas or the Banda Oriental of which it is a northerly extension. Described in glowing terms by foreign travellers, it stands in complete contrast to the arid *sertão*. It had been disputed territory between Spaniard and Portuguese; but although the Treaty of Ildefonso of 1777 had demarcated the claims which had been in dispute since the Treaty of Tordesillas of 1494, it was not until the Banda Oriental became the buffer state of Uruguay in 1828 that the political frontier finally crystallized. Until then it had been a disputed region of marauding cattle raiders and smugglers and tended to retain this character until the latter years of the nineteenth century.

Cattle had originally been introduced from the north by the *paulistas*, and by Jesuits from their missions in the west and also by small groups of Spanish settlers moving from Paraguay. During the eighteenth century Rio Grande do Sul began to be integrated into the Brazilian economy with the breeding of mules which were driven north to the great annual fair at Sorocaba. The wayside halts were the nuclei of settlements much as the *fazendas* on the São Francisco trail in the northeast.

It was in the interests of the Portuguese Crown to people the empty spaces and to establish its claim by possession and with this in view the immigration of families from the overpopulated Azores and Madeira was subsidized to Santa Catarina. These small coastal settlements provided a market for meat, but the demand for draught animals in the far-off mining region of Minas Gerais was more important.

Export trade was inhibited by the lack of port outlets—Porto Alegre could not be developed until the dredging of the early twentieth century. Hence the great interest of Portuguese and later of Brazilians in the Banda Oriental with its port of Montevideo. Hides provided the first staple export, stimulated by the demand in the Napoleonic Wars, and this was supplemented by the *charqueada*, producing dried beef, cut in strips and sun-baked, which was a staple food of the slave population in the north-east and also in demand for sailors on transatlantic shipping.

Venezuela, like Brazil, had a mixed plantation and cattle economy but had languished until the early eighteenth century. Then the Caracas Company had laid the basis of its prosperity by trading in cacao produced on the slave-run coastal plantations.

Inland, the *llanos* of the Orinoco valley was one of the great cattle areas of South America. In common with the *sertão*, the *llanos* was a hinterland area of a plantation society, and so a refuge for runaway slaves—hence its varied population of mixed-bloods (*pardos*) and free-coloureds. Both were branded by their origin and were frustrated in their attempts to buy certificates of whiteness by the creoles, anxious to keep them in a subordinate position—even Bolívar dreaded the prospect of rule by a *pardocracia*. The cattle economy was still at a primitive stage at the end of the colonial period. There were few established *estancias*, and *llaneros*, like gauchos, were free-ranging cowboys, chasing half-wild herds. There was little export trade in cattle products and meat and hides supplied mainly the coastal towns and plantations, but what was exported was controlled by merchants who bought cheap and sold dear.

Attempts to whittle down the cowboys' free-range grazing rights threatened to disturb traditional customs, roused their anger and made them a formidable force during the wars of independence and also invaluable allies with their superb horsemanship. At first, it had been comparatively easy for the Spaniards to mobilize them against the creole landowners leading the revolt from Spain and it was only after Bolívar won over their leader Paéz that the tide of war turned, with the *llanero* cavalry playing a similar role to that of the *gauchos montoneros* in north-west Argentina. The hope of booty offered by Paéz was one immediate attraction as was also the promise of the lands of expropriated Spaniards. By a law of 1817 these lands were distributed to veterans on a sliding scale but it was easy for Paéz and other officers to buy up the lots of ordinary soldiers and thus to lay the basis for a new landowning class.

The *llanos* of Colombia are similar in many ways, except that they have been cut off from the major highland settlements by precipitous mountains and have remained a 'perpetually static frontier',[8] supporting a scattered population of herders tending high-cost, low quality cattle. The Casanare has remained backward in spite of what has been called the 'El Dorado complex' of successive Colombian governments who see the future of the nation there, but in no sense can it be compared with the Oriente of Bolivia where a shift from the highlands to lowlands has been occurring since the 'unfreezing' of the rural population by the Revolution of 1952.

In Mexico, mining towns in the north stimulated growth in agriculture and cattle herding. Poor irrigation facilities forced Zacatecas to depend on the Bajío and Michoacán for its wheat supplies but good cattle country in the vicinity of Zacatecas stimulated ranching and it was common for herds of up to 40,000 to be branded yearly and so send as many as 20,000 head annually to Mexico City. The herds were controlled by the highly organized Mexican Mesta, a guild inspired by the powerful sheep Mesta of medieval Spain. New Spain was, in fact, the only region where the Mesta was introduced; hence the administration of ranching was more efficient there than elsewhere. The Ordinances of 1574 prescribed high property qualifications for membership although this does not seem to have deterred the rise of the small stockman. Many cattle haciendas were run by mine-owners who had accumulated estates by grants, purchase, marriage and simple occupation of empty lands. These estates were sometimes entailed in *mayorazgos* to prevent them being broken up on death. The 'rich and powerful men of the north', the Ibarras, Urdiñolas and Velascos, accumulated estates of hundreds of thousands of acres.

In spite of the early expansion of cattle in New Spain, the distance of grazing lands from Vera Cruz prevented cattle from challenging the dominance of silver and tropical products in the export trade. Nevertheless, cattle haciendas in the northern cactus deserts continued to increase in order to monopolize all available land and secure further pastures. After independence, many of these haciendas lay exposed to raids by Indians from over the border, a threat which tended to depress land values. American cattle companies, taking advantage of cheaper Mexican prices, bought up large tracts and established haciendas on them. Cattle were then driven over the border to railheads in the United States for onward shipment to Chicago. Few Mexican haciendas were able to compete with heavily capitalized American cattle companies and this created resentment among the landowning elite against Porfirio Díaz, who had deliberately encouraged foreigners to invest in land.

The *vaquero* of the huge ranches of northern Mexico transmitted the values of Spanish cattle culture to Texas and beyond. Thus the North American cowboy ethos can be traced back to Spanish peninsular precedents. In Mexico itself, the *vaqueros* on exposed haciendas had to fulfil the role of Indian fighters there. Frontier turbulence and a system of inequitable tenancies made the border region one of endemic banditry. The Mexican bandit is a figure of legend, a defender of the rights of poor *rancheros* and peons against rapacious landlords and a symbol of nationality in resistance to the hated gringo. These attitudes crystallize round the figure of Pancho Villa during the Mexican Revolution whose outlaw career was transformed by the fighting in which he became one of the leading protagonists. The crack cavalry of his División del Norte was recruited from among itinerant cattlemen of the big estates and formed the backbone of his army until decimated by Obregón's machine guns at the Battle of Celaya in 1915. The exploits of Villa's *dorados* as well as the legendary doings of Pancho himself are celebrated in *corridos*, popular ballads, and the values of the Mexican cattle culture recalled in the *charreada*, a formalized *rodeo* in which the exaggerated dress of the *charro*, the affluent rancher, recalls bygone days.

Agricultural frontiers

It was an intention of the Spanish Crown to encourage Spaniards to settle down and farm their own lands. Clerics such as Las Casas and Vasco de Quiroga also argued for the Indies to be settled by farmers who would be given land rather than *encomiendas*, which they could then farm as family units. But most Spaniards did not emigrate to the New World to become farmers. The small farms which quickly became the economic basis for much North American settlement had scarcely any parallel in Latin America until the wave of European immigration in the nineteenth century and then they tended to be concentrated in specific areas such as southern Brazil, Santa Fe and Corrientes in Argentina, and southern Chile.

In the early years of settlement, land was subordinated to labour, and the major social differentiation between Spaniards lay between those who had *encomiendas* and those who had not. With the decline of the *encomienda* and the rising importance of land, economic distinctions were based on landownership. Apart from the basic juxtaposition between private landed estates of Spaniards and communally held Indian lands, there was now a further conflict between big landowners and small proprietors. Merchants were attracted to invest in land through the application of the Spanish law of inheritance. By this, capital acquired during a marriage belonged equally to the partner so that on the death of one partner the other's share was divided among all the children; but as no such discrimination applied to landed wealth where entail could preserve it intact, the attractions of landownership were obvious.

The *latifundio*, the general term for a large estate worked by landless labourers, became the backbone of Latin American agriculture and the export of its products, cattle or grains, determined the structure of the economic system. Where land was distributed by *cabildos* dominated by landowners, the pattern of ownership remained unbalanced. Grants made by the bureaucracy could restore the balance but with the eighteenth-century increase in population the number of poor Spaniards and mestizos, squatting or renting increased. These peasants either farmed their *minifundios* for subsistence or were forced to sell their products to the local *latifundista* to whom many owed labour services as part of their rent. It was as difficult to attract European peasants avid for land ownership to migrate into such a social system as it would have been to expect them to migrate to a slave society. It was not until the latter half of the nineteenth century that governments encouraged small-scale proprietorship in order to people empty spaces.

Concentration of ownership was not so much a legacy of the colonial period as a consequence of redistribution in the first decades of independence. Where there was no strict policy for occupation it was possible for individuals to buy up huge expanses of public domain at knock-down prices. Although this was often made conditional on effective use, there was in fact no method of enforcement. The attempts of governments dominated by landowners to control frontier lands were designed to head off colonization and to discourage the flight of labour from poorly paid sharecropping.

During the first forty or so years of Argentinian independence small proprietors were conspicuously absent. Early attempts in the 1820s to attract European immigrants to establish agricultural colonies petered out. Pre-emption of the best land by cattlemen, difficulties in obtaining title, vulnerability to Indian raids, the general absence of amenities and the high wages to be gained in Buenos Aires where there was always an acute shortage of labour, discouraged agriculture. Rivadavia had attempted to use public lands and a system of emphyteutic tenure to settle European immigrants and make Argentina self-sufficient in cereals, but the cattle interests overrode him. During the dictatorship of Rosas between 1829 and 1853 these remained dominant and wheat had to be imported from the United States. By 1865 there was only 373 square miles of tilled land (in comparison with nearly 200,000 in the United States). However, in the latter decades of the nineteenth century the picture changed and Argentina became one of the world's granaries. From 1.3 acres per capita of tilled land in 1865 the figure rose to 7.7 in 1914 (comparable figures for the United States and Canada are 4.8 and 6.0 respectively). This increase was due to huge areas of new land opened up to grain production and to massive immigration from Europe. Between 1870, when Argentina's population was under two millions, and 1914, some two and a half million immigrants came to Argentina, and by 1914 three quarters of the inhabitants of Buenos Aires were foreign born. Immigrants were late-comers to farming and those who did become farmers were not home-steaders. Homesteading acts such as the Land Law of 1876 remained a dead letter as over two hundred speculative land companies bought up lands as the frontier pushed further into Indian territory. The littoral provinces of Santa Fe and Entre Ríos were exceptional.

Santa Fe was the region first developed for wheat growing as a result, initially, of the efforts of Aron Castellanos, an Argentinian landowner. An agricultural colony, predominantly German-Swiss, was established at

Esperanza in 1852 which, after some vicissitudes, became a pattern for later developments, the number of colonies there rising from 32 in 1872 to 365 thirty years later. In neighbouring Entre Rios there was a comparable growth from 3 in 1875 to 200 twenty years later. Railway-building stimulated colonization and crop-farming. As the price of its concession the English company building the Rosario-Córdoba railway line in the late 1860s had to reserve a three-mile strip on either side of the track for colonization. The success of these colonies encouraged private land companies to follow suit and landowners, recognizing that the value of their land would increase with crop-farming, provided the facilities. A spur to land-hungry peasants from Italy and Spain was the prospect of owning land and this was possible in Santa Fe where it could be bought by an industrious peasant in four or five years.

In Buenos Aires province where land was at least four times as expensive, immigrants could not afford to buy, nor were *estancieros* willing to sell at a time when European demand for meat opened up dazzling prospects. But the immigrant could become a sharecropper. Prohibitive labour costs and the reluctance of gauchos to till the soil made immigrants doubly welcome. Selective breeding required sophisticated forage, and land for alfalfa was rented to Italian peasants on a three year sharecropping basis. In return for tools and food, the sharecropper had to hand over half the harvest in payment. Tenuous though this might appear, it often suited the immigrant who could either raise himself to a tenant farmer or return to the city with his small stock of capital and set up as a storekeeper.

Tenant farmers had to supply their own equipment while the owner provided land which had previously lain idle. These tenancies were precarious: contracts tended to be verbal and if the tenant moved on after the tenancy expired, usually after six years, he received nothing for improvements. So long as *estancieros* dominated government there was little chance that sharecroppers or tenant farmers could gain security of tenure. As cattle led the frontier expansion into the interior, few immigrants shared the frontier experience—except in the case of Santa Fe. Efforts were made during the Peronist period to control rents but the rising value of cattle and wheat in the post-war years made it worthwhile for owners to buy out their tenants. Labour was provided increasingly by a landless proletariat using machinery instead of sharecroppers and tenant farmers working with family labour.

In contrast to the experience of the United States, the expansion of wheat lands and the huge increases in productivity which made Argentina one of the world's granaries and Rosario for some years the world's largest grain port, was not a consequence of the family farm but of a combination of settlers, tenant farmers, sharecroppers and migrant labour—the *golondrinas* (swallows) who were peasants, mostly from southern Spain, and crossed the South Atlantic in the off-season at home to work in the Argentinian wheat harvest where they could earn their return fare in a fortnight. Thus we find 'pampas without settlers . . . a frontier filled with migrants'. The endless, monotonous, flat plains were as empty in 1914 as they had been fifty years earlier when immigrants first began to arrive in force. There were few houses, no schools, no churches, roads or villages, and the railway system, the densest in Latin America, radiated like spokes from a wheel from Buenos Aires and contributed little to knitting together isolated settlements. The railway led back to the city where real opportunities existed for tenant and sharecropper alike, and did not beckon the land-hungry peasant into land of limitless promise.

Colonization schemes

Colonization was seen by both government and private companies as a way of filling in empty spaces—'gobernar es poblar', in the words of the Argentinian, Alberdi. Colonization schemes, designed to settle farmers on vacant public land, took various forms. They could be official, government sponsored (either state, as in the case of São Paulo, or national) or they could be based on commercial speculation; they could be utopian, either secular or religious. In the nineteenth and early twentieth centuries most colonization schemes were designed to attract foreign immigrants, mostly from Europe but also from Japan. More recently, emphasis has been placed on using internal colonization as part of overall agrarian reform programmes, to move surplus people from overpopulated regions, as is happening with both spontaneous and sponsored colonization from the Bolivian *altiplano*. In the unusual case of French Guyana the metropolitan government has tried in recent years to sponsor immigration but with conspicuous lack of success.

The support for colonization schemes was not always wholehearted. In the nineteenth century under the influence of racialist ideas, Europeans (especially northern Europeans) were regarded as the key to economic development through their racial superiority and because of their education and skills. They would also help to whiten populations which were felt to have been incurably corrupted by miscegenation, as well as to counterbalance Indian and negro groups. Colonization was synonymous with agriculture, and the settling of farmers on land was considered one way to create a stable society and remedy the instability inherent in pastoralism. These views were not necessarily shared by all planters and *estancieros* who feared possible political challenges from independent rural proprietors: they tended to see European immigrants as a pool of cheap labour which could replace slaves or populate the pampas as sharecroppers or tenant farmers. This provides one explanation why many governments, dominated by landowners, failed to give adequate support to colonization projects except for strategic reasons in border regions such as Rio Grande do Sul or northern Mexico. In the latter, colonization schemes were canvassed as a means of preventing further United States incursions, Apache raids and Indian rebellions. Military colonies were established to pay off veterans after the 1848–9 war but they were only partially successful, and reluctance to allow religious liberty remained a major obstacle to attracting foreigners.

The failure of early colonization schemes in Argentina showed that success was unlikely even with government support and impossible without it.[9] When Rosas, the representative of the cattle interest, abolished the Immigration Commission set up by Rivadavia, he tried to establish military colonies on the Indian frontier, similar in some respects to the *presidios* of northern Mexico. These were not successful, however, because of the reluctance of soldiers to serve in them voluntarily. Slightly more successful were the few colonies in Chihuahua to settle veterans of Pancho Villa's army.

Religious communities such as the Russian Old Believers in southern Brazil and Mennonites in Paraguay regarded the absence of markets and physical hardships as a challenge and an opportunity to develop a self-sufficient community where their customs and beliefs could survive untainted by outside influences. They have flourished in environments like the Chaco desert which have daunted less highly motivated farmers. The common religious bond has clearly been an important factor in the success of these colonies, inviting comparison with the Mormons and similar groups in North America. Without the drive to preserve their language and nonconformist religion, the Welsh colonies in isolated Patagonia would almost certainly have collapsed. Similarly, the Baron Hirsch colony in Argentina, founded as a refuge for Jews fleeing Russian pogroms, owed its success (which involved the transformation of professional men into pampas herders) to the cohesion provided by religious faith, although in this case the large injection of capital by Baron Hirsch was an important contributory factor. Projects by secular utopians, which flourished in the United States but which were rarer in Latin America, do not seem to have been so successful as religious colonies to judge by the failure of the curious Australian socialist colony in Paraguay. One serious problem here, which is an important factor in accounting for successful colonization was the isolation of the womenfolk who did not share their men's enthusiastic but unrealistic ideas.

In contrast to colonization schemes in temperate climates—Argentina, southern Brazil, Chile—attempts to establish colonies in tropical areas tended to be failures. For example, the Nueva Liverpool experiment in Guatemala in the 1830s was originally conceived by Manuel Gálvez as a means of utilizing the technical expertise of British settlers to develop the eastern jungle provinces. But temperate agriculturalists do not necessarily make good tropical frontiersmen and the scheme collapsed as did the Belgian colony to whom the British concessionaires sold out. The much earlier Scottish attempt to set up a colony at Darien in 1699 was a similar fiasco. Attempts by British colonists to farm jungle land in southern Brazil were equally unsuccessful and Angel Clare's experience in *Tess of the d'Urbervilles* accurately reflects what Hardy had heard of the failures of the brief Brazil craze which sent groups of British colonists to Brazil in the 1870s.

In any case, the United States and the British Empire were more attractive to British emigrants. Few who went to Latin America were successful, hampered by prejudices against Catholicism and against 'inferior races', unable to cope with the climate and prone to drink. Their dislike for Latin Americans was reciprocated except in elite circles. A few family dynasties were of British, or rather, Irish origin—soldiers of fortune who had risen in Bolívar's armies or shepherds on the pampas from the 1850s. However, many British, such as Scots engineers or textile technicians from the north of England, went out on short-term contracts. One of the largest communities of this kind were the sheep-managers of Patagonia and Tierra del Fuego, site of some of the world's largest and most desolate sheep runs.

The success of a colonization scheme wherever it was founded depended on it being well capitalized at the outset together with subsequent easy access to credit, as well as on being able to get round inheritance laws which subdivided plots on the death of the head of the family. Colonists also had little chance of achievement unless they had some previous farming experience. Thus the self-sufficient German colonies of southern Brazil transplanted European mixed-farming techniques into a fertile area and were sufficiently flexible to adapt themselves to a horse-culture. When export opportunities did present themselves in the early 1900s with the opening up of Porto Alegre, they were well prepared to take advantage of them. Colonization by German settlers in forested areas in Entre Rios in northeast Argentina, unsuitable for Spanish colonization practices, illustrates the transference of traditional settlement patterns; in this case the *Waldhufendörfer*, or series of individual forest farms, were spaced along forest trails to give the appearance of a village. This had been a traditional method of colonizing forest land in central Germany.

Similar methods were used in southern Chile where German colonists started clearing the rain forests from the 1840s. In both the Brazilian and Chilean cases the Germans in frontier regions almost became a state within a state. In Chile it had been deliberate policy to encourage

Germans to colonize the southern frontier even to the extent of excluding Chileans from colonization projects in a law of 1874, for fear of draining off labour from the estates of central Chile. It also served later to ensure that any surplus labour would be available for the nitrate working in the far north.

In many cases failure can be attributed to inflated expectations, raised by the glowing accounts of unscrupulous recruiting agencies. Some idea of the excessive optimism bred by the potentialities of the Amazon, notoriously the most intractable pioneering area in the whole of Latin America, may be gained from this description by Alfred Wallace, a colleague of Charles Darwin, who wrote:

> When I consider the excessively small amount of labour required in this country, to convert virgin forest into green meadows and fertile plantations, I almost long to come over with half-a-dozen friends, disposed to work, and enjoy the country; and show the inhabitants how soon an earthly paradise might be created, which they had never conceived capable of existing. . . . I fearlessly assert that here the primeval forest can be converted into rich pasture and meadow land, into cultivated fields, gardens, and orchards containing every variety of produce, with half the labour, and what is more in half the time that would be required at home.[10]

Wallace believed that three or four families with only £50 of capital could create a paradise on earth in a few years. Behind such uninformed, optimistic assertions lay unspoken assumptions about the moral turpitude and lack of entrepreneurial drive of the local inhabitants. Wallace had obviously not lingered long enough to experience the enervating effects of humidity, and all the other problems of jungle colonization which do not daunt the armchair enthusiast. Among the few colonists who have ventured into the Amazon the Japanese have been among the most successful.

The Japanese have, in fact, provided some of the most dynamic frontier colonists in Latin America, especially in Brazil and the Bolivian Oriente. Part of this success can be explained by the meticulous organization and preparation by government agencies in Japan anxious to encourage emigration to ease population pressure. The first Japanese immigrants arrived in 1908 but the main expansion came after the establishment of the Overseas Development Company in 1917. Japanese immigrants brought with them many agricultural techniques which enabled them to rise quickly from *colonos* to tenant farmers and owners. The Japanese case illustrated the influence of a high man-to-land ratio for in Japan population density has forced the Japanese to husband their resources and farm meticulously in contrast to Brazil where abundance of land has encouraged prodigality. A further factor in their success has been their close links with Japanese banks and merchants in the cities.

The case of coffee

Coffee can be grown in a variety of conditions and with differing degrees of labour intensity, and this produces distinctive societies as can be seen by comparing coffee frontiers in Guatemala, Cuba, Colombia and Brazil.

In Guatemala, coffee production expanded in response to market opportunities in the 1870s. Early attempts by development-conscious governments to stimulate colonization in eastern jungles failed with the collapse of the Nueva Liverpool experiment in the 1830s, after which attention switched to the west and northern highlands. Here, the success of German planters, who as merchants had been impressed by the possibilities of coffee cultivation, was largely due to the availability of cheap labour from Indians who had been dispossessed of their communal lands by successive Liberal governments. The Guatemalan coffee plantation, based on peon labour, therefore, shared features of the traditional hacienda.

The initial impetus to coffee production in Cuba came from French colonists fleeing from the Haitian slave revolt of 1790. They established coffee estates (*cafetales*) in Oriente, some of which expanded westward into land not already pre-empted by sugar plantations, which would move eastwards as the sugar revolution of the early nineteenth century gathered momentum. Short of capital, *cafetales* were limited in size and worked by small numbers of slaves. It was from these planters that leaders of the revolution against Spanish rule in 1868 were drawn. Working on narrow profit margins in common with the smaller sugar planters of Oriente, they were unable to bear the increased fiscal burdens of new tax reforms. Cuban coffee was, therefore, a small-scale, marginal slave economy. It did not generate dynamic frontier expansion into empty lands, and Oriente remained a backward province and breeding ground for every subsequent revolt in Cuban history. When capital had started to flow into Cuba in the 1820s—expatriate capital from the mainland, from Spain itself and from foreigners—it was attracted to big plantations. Here an expanding sugar frontier pushed into rich uncultivated lands of the central provinces giving Cuban sugar a clear lead over other Caribbean producers and those of northeast Brazil where all available sugar land was already under cultivation. These huge plantations, with their economies of scale and reserves of good land and rising profits, could shoulder the high costs of African slaves which had risen with the introduction of the British blockade, unlike the smaller planters of Oriente, one of whose first acts in the War of Independence in 1868 was to free their slaves.

The case of Colombia, or more particularly, of the department of

Antioquia, is a marked contrast. Antioquia provides one of the most dynamic expanding frontiers in Latin America. From the 1830s the coffee frontier pushed into the southern part of Antioquia as a consequence of initiatives by Medellín merchants, whose purpose in acquiring land was to encourage migration and settlement. New towns such as Fredonia and Valparaíso were founded under merchant patronage. This was a policy of enlightened self-interest. Merchants required a settled labour force on which they could draw for their own speculative ventures. They also needed labour to build mountain roads. This not only facilitated future development of their own coffee estates but assisted the emergence of a sizable class of smallholders who turned to pig-breeding and growing coffee themselves when the economy expanded. In its early stages, therefore, the coffee market was dominated by big estates but later these were overtaken by production on smallholdings. Population pressure provided a push for the southward movement of smallholders into empty lands at the same time as merchants began to invest their surplus capital in industry, the internal market for which was provided by an increasingly prosperous class of coffee homesteaders. Thus the small man frontier of coffee farmers and Medellín industry grew together in a mutual but not always peaceful relationship.

The reason for Antioquia's remarkable economic growth which has earned for *antioqueños* the sobriquet, 'yankees of South America', has long puzzled historians, for many of the normal prerequisites of economic growth were absent. The hypothesis which seeks the explanation in terms of status deprivation of *antioqueños* who were unable to break into the Bogotá elite and so channelled their energies into entreprenurial activities, is not sufficient.[11] More important was the legacy of the mining economy of the colonial period. The absence of an Indian population which could be impressed for mining, combined with the high price of slaves owing to transportation costs from the slave markets of Cartagena, had forced prospectors and their families to work the mines themselves and to acquire entreprenurial skills which gave them expertise to exploit commercial opportunities when these occurred. With no traditions of labour intensive agriculture, and lacking a landowning tradition, the miner-merchant elite had little incentive to try to close off the frontier to settlement. On the contrary, settlement was encouraged in order to establish cattle and coffee farms. The merchant elite acted as midwife to the birth of a rural middle class which provided a basis for growing internal markets. Antioquia was a rare case in Latin America of a frontier producing a rural middle class; it was an exception even in Colombia where the neighbouring department of Cauca was torn apart by social conflict after slavery had been finally abolished in the mid-nineteenth century, and estates were deserted after the flight from them of ex-slaves.

Unlike Colombia, the existence of a slave economy in Brazil required that the frontier be sealed off in order to check the growth of squatters (*posseiros*). This was partially achieved by the Land Law of 1850, which ensured that the plantocracy had monopoly of access to the virgin land increasingly needed for coffee cultivation. Coffee first became an important crop in the 1830s and was originally confined to the Paraíba Valley and based on slave labour imported through Rio. Many planters were drawn from Minas Gerais where mining had been in decline since the 1780s. Reckless farming methods and prodigal land-use pushed the frontier westwards into the rich *terra roxa* of São Paulo. Here a combination of local capital and British expertise achieved the difficult engineering task of linking São Paulo with the port of Santos, thus contributing from the 1870s to one of the most spectacular cases of frontier expansion in the whole of Latin America. At first, this relied on slave labour recruited via the interprovincial slave trade from the declining northeast where shortage of land had made it impossible to meet the challenge for Cuban sugar. Coffee planters became seriously interested in recruiting labour from Europe only when the town-based abolitionist movement assisted slaves to desert plantations.

With European labour, mostly recruited from Italy on short-term contracts, the coffee frontier pushed west and north of São Paulo. Plentiful land and massive immigration encouraged prodigality as it had before in the Paraíba valley. As soon as productivity began to fall planters would sell out at high prices and move on into new land which had earlier been bought up as a speculation. The speculators' frontier might precede actual occupation by as much as a hundred miles or twenty years.

This type of frontier expansion gave rise to a 'hollow frontier' where the exhausted lands were occupied by immigrants, either moving off the plantations after their contract had expired or moving out from the city. This second wave of settlers grazed cattle or grew cash crops for the rapidly expanding urban centres. The São Paulo frontier thus produced a speculative entrepreneurial coffee plantocracy whose profits were based on a near monopoly of the world market, on a limitless supply of cheap rich land and on cheap contracted south European labour, and much of which was to be invested in industrial development.

The north Paraná coffee frontier provides yet a different case, this time of successful frontier expansion by colonization companies. The Paraná Plantations Ltd, an English company founded in 1924, established a successful pioneer zone of small independent farmers based in Londrina (although English-financed it was not intended for English settlers). In 1944 it was sold to a consortium of São Paulo banks which continued the original policy as well as running their own fazendas to provide a model of modern farming techniques for new arrivals. In 1951 another land company began opening up the frontier further west on the borders of São Paulo state. The coffee frontier has been beset by difficulties because of soil depletion, falling prices and recurrent frosts. Another factor has been the proximity of cheap frontier land one hundred and fifty kilometres to the west which has siphoned off the small and medium farmers who prefer to try their luck on a new frontier rather than switch to cattle or use expensive fertilizers. The moving on of the rural middle class has left behind an increasingly stratified two-class society and reduced the possibilities for social mobility as the number of share-croppers (the most socially mobile group who could normally have expected to buy a small farm after two or three years' good crops), are being squeezed out by cattle farms. The Paraná coffee frontier, in 1959 surpassing even São Paulo's production, illustrates again the mobile nature of frontier expansion which has been a constant feature of Brazilian history.

The expansion of the coffee frontier into western Paraná has not stopped at the political frontier but has moved over into Paraguay where plantations have been bought up for speculative purposes. As the Brazilian frontier in the southwest begins to close, so the experience of the United States in the 1890s in northern Mexico is being repeated, this time with Brazilian investors and speculators turning smaller neighbours into economic satellites.

The rubber frontier

The Amazonian rubber boom before 1914 was a caricature of boom frontier expansion. The forty years of frenetic activity made scarcely any impression on the vast rain forests except for a few isolated settlements and the jungle emporium of Manaus with its stuccoed villas, ornate cemeteries and the great opera house built at a cost of 10 million dollars, its sparkling coloured roof and lavish interior rivalling anything in Europe. Nothing could be more anomalous than an opera house, the grandiloquent symbol of the nineteenth century *bourgeois conquérant*, transported brick by brick from Europe to a riverside flood-site hemmed in by impenetrable forest.

Charles Goodyear's invention of the vulcanization of rubber in 1839 turned rubber from being a curiosity into one of the boom products of the pre-1914 era. With its promise of wealth, rubber was the major factor in attracting the attention of governments to the rain forests in which their writ scarcely ran. As a result, territorial borders which had remained in dispute since independence had to be firmly delineated. Bolivia and Brazil were the two countries primarily affected although Venezuela, Colombia and Peru were also involved in frontier disputes.

The Treaty of San Ildefonso of 1777 had in theory marked out the borders between Portuguese and Spanish America but in practice obstacles prevented the projected joint boundary commission from surveying the borders on the ground. At independence, therefore, the new states were heirs to a confused situation and in the absence of agreement the Brazilians insisted on the *uti possidetis de facto* principle by which sovereignty would be determined by physical occupation—a principle which underpinned the boundary arrangements between the states of Spanish America as well.

Poor communications, intractable geography, an empty treasury and Brazilian intransigence blocked Bolivian attempts to settle the virtually uninhabited border regions. A Bolivian concession in 1832 to Major Oliden, an Argentinian, produced little as he failed to interest either the British ambassador, Rosas, or Hamburg merchants in his colonization scheme. A Belgian project similarly failed and it was not until 1867 that Bolivia, under the dictator Melgarejo, succeeded in gaining a much coveted outlet to the Atlantic by securing title to five ports on the River Paraguay and free navigation rights through Brazilian territory via the Amazon. To consolidate this achievement it was necessary to colonize the unsettled northern region and to construct a railway past the impassible falls on the Madeira River. Major Church, a retired US army engineer, accepted the challenge and another North American chartered a company to colonize the wild Acre province. These schemes lapsed on Melgarejo's fall in 1874 but the rise in the value of rubber and the exploration of the River Beni by another North American, Edwin Heath, in 1880, sparked off the rubber rush in northern Bolivia. These were good enough reasons for the Bolivian government to think of developing the northeastern border regions in order to anticipate possible Brazilian moves. Unable to bear the costs of this development itself, the government granted concessions in which, as in the Brabo concession of 1880, virtual rights of sovereignty were alienated over an area of almost 750,000 square miles. The loss of an outlet on the Pacific after the war with Chile in 1883 was an additional reason for Bolivian interest in trying to find an outlet via the Amazon to the Atlantic.

By 1900 rubber had become an important item in the Bolivian economy, providing nearly half the national income. Much of this achievement had been due to the remarkable work of the Suárez brothers, 'the Rockefellers of the rubber trade', who had built up a huge commercial empire from the early 1870s and which at one time had 10,000 men on its payroll and was worth some £10,000,000. Nicolas Suárez's success was largely a result of his being able to tap the London money market as well as to a strong sense of family solidarity and his own talent and drive. A major problem had been shortage of labour but this was overcome by impressment of jungle Indians (their ill-treatment by one of Suárez's rivals, the Peruvian rubber company, had provoked an international inquiry headed by Sir Roger Casement which created a scandal when its report was published in 1909). At the same time Brazilian *seringueiros*, as many as 60,000 of whom may have moved up the Amazon's tributaries since the great Ceará drought of 1878, had been driven to seek a living from rubber tapping. The boom built on this labour lasted until the First World War when East Indian rubber plantations, developed from seedlings originally smuggled out of Brazil in 1876, undercut Brazilian rubber. High transport and labour costs which in 1914 were estimated at 8s 8d a day in comparison with less than a shilling in the Far East doomed the Amazonian industry.[12]

Unlike other rubber barons, Suárez survived the collapse of the boom because of his diversified interests, which included ranches with a quarter of a million head of cattle in the adjacent savannah country of the Beni, sugar mills in Santa Cruz and the virtual monopoly of provisioning the whole area. But, except for the liana-covered ruins of the storage sheds at the company's headquarters in Cachuela Esperanza, little remains today to remind us of this huge commercial empire, whose assets when the company was finally wound up in 1961 were valued at £1,500.

Nearly sixty per cent of all Amazonian rubber was produced in Bolivian Acre but most of the rubber gatherers were Brazilians who resented the attempts of the Bolivians to tax them. Resentment flared into the open and, with the tacit support of Brazilian authorities, an independent republic of Acre was declared in 1899 under the leadership of a Spanish adventurer. A Bolivian military expedition restored the situation but its victory was nullified by the subsequent signing of an agreement by the Bolivian government with an international consortium. This alerted Brazil, who accused Bolivia of introducing into South America the chartered company idea which in Africa had been a prelude to full-scale European control. Threatened by a Brazilian force, the Bolivians agreed to withdraw and by the 1903 treaty Acre was handed over in return for a monetary compensation and the promise of a railway which would bypass the Madeira River Falls and give Bolivia the much desired access to the Amazon. Ultimately, Bolivia was defeated by geography as Brazil had access to the heart of Acre via the tributaries of the Amazon whereas communications from Bolivia posed almost insuperable problems.

The rubber boom not only illustrates the way in which an expanding economic frontier caused a readjustment of a political frontier, much as nitrates had already done in the case of the frontiers between Chile, Bolivia and Peru, but it also shows the haphazard exploitative attitude of the Brazilians to a potentially valuable crop. The government's interest was mainly fiscal. Some rather desultory attempts to organize plantations failed and a valorization scheme, by which the government bought up rubber to keep it off the world market until prices rose, came too late. The lure of a cash crop led to a disastrous decline in agriculture and resulted in dependence on high-cost imported food; this was beyond the pockets of most rubber gatherers who through malnutrition became even more liable to diseases like beri-beri. The failure to develop any viable alternative to rubber meant that once the boom burst the jungle reverted to its former state and most tappers moved out or became subsistence farmers.

The Anglo-Hispanic frontier

Two great frontier movements clashed and intermingled in what are now the southwestern states of the United States—California, New Mexico, Arizona, Texas, Colorado and Nevada. As this is the area where Anglo and Hispanic culture were compelled to coexist, it deserves separate treatment. In addition, however, the process of expansion into the Great Plains and the Far West—which Turner virtually ignored—cannot be fully appreciated without realizing the contributions made by the Hispanic legacy in mining, sheep-rearing, cattle-breeding, irrigation, dry-farming, and Texas land-law. The conquest of the West was not simply the triumph of Anglo courage and determination against intractable nature, as Theodore Roosevelt liked to believe, but a process of adopting and adapting techniques which had been pioneered on the Hispanic frontiers over previous centuries, as earlier frontiers in the Thirteen Colonies had benefited from Indian example.

In geographical terms this area was a natural extension of the northward moving Mexican frontier but because of the shortage of potential settlers both Spaniards and Mexicans failed to sustain the momentum of expansion. Their frontier was essentially strategic-defensive—strategic in the sense of pre-empting territory which might otherwise have been occupied by rivals, such as Russia, Britain, France, or the United States; defensive against Indian raiders, who in New Mexico and Texas kept the frontier in a state of turmoil. The northward push took three distinct forms in New Mexico, California and Texas and left legacies which can be seen in the different structures of Mexican-American society in the border states today. Different though their social and economic situation may be, most Mexican-Americans continue to adhere to Hispanic values. They, and more particularly those who prefer the self-description Chicanos, have refused to melt in the melting pot.

The earliest thrust was into what is now New Mexico. In 1599 Juan de Oñate led an expedition of less than two hundred soldier-settlers (which possibly included more Tlaxcalan Indians than Spaniards) attracted by the Crown's offer of *hidalgo* status. Oñate's motivation, very much in the tradition of the early *pobladores*, was the desire of a rich miner to found a colony. At first traditional methods of colonization were based on the *encomienda*, but the thinness of native population made the system unworkable. Attempts to levy service from the Pueblo Indians, who had originally accepted Spanish rule as a protection against Apache raiding, and resentment at Franciscan attempts to destroy their religion, goaded the Pueblos to revolt in 1680. When an expedition reconquered the lost province the *encomienda* was not reestablished, instead settlers and villages were given grants of land. Thus a distinctive settlement pattern emerged on this frontier, with smallholding, village-oriented farmers and shepherds working a pastoral-mercantile economy and living in a symbiotic relationship with surrounding Indians. This economy was based on the hardy *churro* sheep whose coarse, light wool was used by Navajo Indians in weaving textiles (the techniques of which had been introduced by the settlers) with their own designs and dyes.

Conquest by the United States in the Mexican War did not disrupt this traditional community as it did those of the *tejanos* or *californios*. Hispanos outnumbered Anglos until late into the nineteenth century—one reason for statehood being delayed until 1912—and the *ricos*, or the upper class, came to mutual understandings with Anglo politicians in the 'Santa Fe ring'. The *patrón* relationship which underpinned social relationships in the Hispano community became a feature of New Mexico politics as well. From the 1880s, after the arrival of railroads speeded up immigration by Anglo settlers, the Hispano villages became increasingly isolated, and community ties were threatened as land was sold for ready cash and men went further and further afield in search of seasonal employment. The threat which this social mobility posed to traditional Hispano cultural values has been one of the motives behind the Alianza Federal de Pueblos Libres movement, founded in 1963 by Reies López Tijerina; the subsequent 'land-grant' war has focused attention on the erosion of the original Spanish land grants, guaranteed by the Treaty of Guadalupe Hidalgo of 1848, by real estate speculation.

The contrast in California could scarcely have been greater. The motivation behind the first colonization was strategic and missionary, with the Franciscans as the vanguard of empire. Settlement was thin and confined to the coast; the climate was benign and the Indians peaceful and pliable. Surprisingly, in view of later discoveries, hills inland were not scoured by gold hunters. Nevertheless, when gold was discovered, some 5,000 Mexican miners, the *gambusinos* or professional prospectors from Sonora, moved north, bringing with them their mining skills, the batey, the dry-wash method for gold panning and the *arrastra* used in quartz mining. The discovery of mercury in New Almadén in 1845 which had been the basis of Spanish-American silver mining technology since the invention of the amalgamation process in the 1550s, came at exactly the right time. Apart from these technical contributions to a non-Hispanic mining community, largely ignorant of mining techniques, Mexican labour was important to the development of Western mining generally especially in the copper mines of Arizona, where Mexicans were employed both as *barrateros*, rock face miners, and as *tanateros* or carriers. Thus California mining in its early days was indebted to Mexican expertise and Mexican labour, as well as to Peruvians and Chileans.

The other main activity in California was ranching which had expanded faster than in Texas because of the absence of Indian raiding. Ranching had been pioneered by the missions but was given a fillip by the Colonization Law of 1824, awarding land grants to Mexicans which swelled to over seven hundred after the secularization of the missions in 1834. The flourishing trade in hides and tallow was largely managed by Yankee traders who comprised a small but crucial element in Mexican California's population. At first, ranchers benefited from the opening of the mines but the *californios* lacked the capital to improve stock for consumption, as well as having to compete with cattle driven from Texan pastures. However, the main threat to their livelihood came from overland immigrants seduced by Dana's image of idyllic California and from those frustrated miners who looked enviously to the uncultivated estates of the ranchers, once their hopes of striking gold had vanished. As land-hungry immigrants and ex-miners began squatting, the ranches were sold up to pay debts incurred in litigation, to pay land taxes and in labour costs. By the 1860s the *californios* had been largely dispossessed or their estates. What early squatters, litigation and land taxes had failed to achieve was finally completed in the course of the real estate boom in the 1880s which followed the completion of the Southern Pacific railroad. Now irrigated orchards and farms could produce for eastern markets, drawing on cheap oriental labour; increasingly those of Mexican descent would be either *barrio* dwellers in the Mex-towns of urban sprawls or migrant, seasonal workers in the booming agri-businesses of fruit and vegetable farms.

It was in Texas, however, the third prong of the Spanish advance northwards, that the clash of cultures was most sharp and prolonged. Resentment on both sides fed on the bitter memories of conflict during the Texas Republic and the Mexican War. The victory of the Anglos justified, in their eyes, their scornful views of Mexicans who were treated with the contempt reserved for the conquered. It is a region about which it has been difficult to write objectively. Early attitudes can be explained by the high proportion of lawless men attracted to Texas in the 1820s and 1830s who had no interest in observing the conditions on which Anglos were permitted to settle. Later attitudes derived from the frontier atmosphere of the post-Mexican war boom and the flood of southern immigrants.

Texan attitudes to non-Anglos were a reflection of those of the Deep South, often the more violently expressed because of the anti-Catholic bias of Protestant fundamentalism. Slaves constituted a third of the population and until slavery was abolished the escape of slaves to the freedom of Mexico was an added irritant as, conversely and paradoxically, was the escape of peons from Mexico to the freedom of Texas.

Three cultures met in Texas; a slave plantation culture expanding from the Deep South; the mixed-farming of German immigrants; and the Hispano open-range cattle culture. By the 1860s most of the best ranches had come into the hands of Anglos. Those Mexicans who had still not got their own *rancherías*, now comprised the *vaqueros*, packers, and drovers on Anglo-owned ranches. Although Mexicans had perfected the management of half-wild cattle on the open range, Anglos introduced new breeds to improve stock for the urban markets of the north. The cattle industry, as it developed in its heyday after the Civil War, was a blend of Hispano and Anglo skills; it was also a cause of cross-border raiding and raiding by Indians in west Texas.

Undamaged during the Civil War, Texas became the great post-bellum Southern frontier where the defeated could work out their resentment on 'natural inferiors'. Many immigrants from the north seem to have adopted the Texas tone of superiority wishing to identify with the distinctive Texan self-image which owed part of its inflation to being contrasted with the alien culture of the defeated Mexicans.

The southern counties of Texas have been the strongholds of Hispano culture—in some places as many as three quarters of the population are Mexicans. This is a bi-cultural region, economically interdependent but socially segregated with towns having Mexican *barrios* 'across the tracks' and each group having its own shops, churches and schools, and where violence readily flares up. A particularly savage example of this was during the Mexican Revolution after the Plan of San Diego (Texas) of January 1915 had called for the creation of an independent Mexican-American republic. In the next year in order to force the withdrawal of the Pershing expedition (which had invaded Mexico in March in response to Pancho Villa's raid on Columbus), Carranza planned an invasion of Texas in support of the Mexican-Americans. Raids by Mexican-Americans with Mexican support provoked violent Anglo reprisals, in the course of which over 300 Mexican-Americans were killed, and which led to a flood of refugees crossing over into war-torn Mexico.[13]

The Chicano movement is the expression of a minority which has failed to be assimilated and feels itself to be discriminated against by the dominant culture. The complexities of the upsurge of Mexican-American consciousness as well as the reasons for its slow growth are beyond the scope of this book but it is relevant to observe that it is a direct consequence of two very different frontier experiences, both of which have perpetuated the values which their respective societies took to the frontier. The residual tensions between these two value systems is a unique feature of the American frontier heritage and one which deserves more sympathetic attention than has habitually been given to it apart from those professionally concerned with the Mexican-American problem.

Political frontiers

The cultural clash of the Mexican-United States borderlands has been unique. In the rest of Latin America, however, there has been ample scope for another type of conflict—that over territorial sovereignty on thirty-six political frontiers.

Early hopes that the unity of the Spanish Empire would survive independence were soon shattered by geographical intractability, sparseness of population, breakdown of integrating economies, intense personal rivalries and a particularist spirit which emphasized loyalty to regions and towns rather than to Bolivarian confederal ideals. The *uti possidetis* principle of 1810, by which boundaries between the new states should coincide with those of former Spanish administrative divisions, became the accepted basis of the new nations. But faulty maps and inadequate cadastral surveys of unexplored territory left a tangle of disputes in the resolution of which colonial archives were ransacked in justification of claims.

Once Spanish America had been balkanized after the break up of the Viceroyalty of La Plata, the collapse of Gran Colombia and of the Central American Federation, any further attempts to create larger units were frustrated in the interests of preserving a balance of power. This can be seen very early in the opposition of Argentina and Chile to the Peruvian-Bolivian Confederation which collapsed in 1839 after only three years' existence.

The longest dispute was that between the Spanish and Portuguese empires, with precedents stretching back to the Treaty of Tordesillas of 1494 in which the pope, by virtue of the claimed right vested in him by the Donation of Constantine, disposed of all newly found territories. By this treaty, Portugal was given all land in South America east of the twenty-third parallel and Spain all land to the west of it. Whereas Spanish claims were based on this juridical precedent, the Portuguese pragmatically applied the *uti possidetis* principle of prior occupation. Throughout the seventeenth and eighteenth centuries, therefore, the heartland of South America was disputed territory in which *bandeirantes*, missionaries and settlers were protagonists in a geo-political conflict which finally resulted in establishing Brazil's hegemony over this vast area. Indeed, one of the most striking features of South American history has been the success of Brazilian expansion at the expense of its Spanish-speaking neighbours. The one outstanding exception was Brazil's failure to absorb the Banda Oriental with its valuable port of Montevideo. After a three year war with Argentina, Uruguay was created as a buffer state in 1828 under the prompting of the British, anxious to ensure stability for their commerce.

Two other major territorial disputes involving Brazil were to be resolved by force. Paraguayan ambitions to dominate the upper reaches of the River Plate system led to the War of the Triple Alliance of 1865–70 in which Paraguay was finally crushed by the combined forces of Brazil, Argentina and Uruguay. This war was fought over the same ground as the conflict between Jesuits and *paulistas* in the seventeenth century and finally confirmed Brazilian hegemony in that region. The second conflict arose when Brazilian rubber gatherers moved into sparsely settled rubber-rich Acre, a territory of northern Bolivia. After a short desultory war Bolivia yielded almost a third of its land to Brazil in return for meagre financial compensation.

Turbulent frontiers with freebooters indulging in cross-border raiding gave an added sensitivity to Brazil's relationship with all those states with which she shared ill-defined jungle frontiers. Nomadic Indians, oblivious of national boundaries which might run through their hunting grounds, similarly were a potential source of conflict as well.

Political frontiers also cut through sedentary Indian communities sharing a common language and culture—as on the Peruvian–Bolivian border. Trans-border smuggling is a common phenomenon here and a submerged nationality situation is not beyond the bounds of possibility whereby a roused Quechua or Aymara Indian consciousness could conflict with weaker loyalties to the national states of Peru and Bolivia.

Although there were enough interior frontiers of settlement to engage the energies of the new states, some began to covet territory beyond their political frontiers once the discovery of new mineral resources opened up the potentialities of hitherto neglected and unsettled regions. The demands of industrialized powers for raw materials brought the added complication of Great Power interests. Conflicts over these regions were indicative of the increasing integration of Latin America into the world economy. Chile illustrates this process most graphically. The founding in 1840 of the Pacific Steam Navigation Company based in Liverpool heralded the quickening of European interest in Pacific coast commerce to which the California gold rush in 1848 gave an enormous impetus. After losing its colonial market for wheat in Peru, new export opportunities opened with the stimulus of mining in California and Australia. These developments underlined the strategic importance of the

Cape Horn route to Chilean interests, anxious to ensure commercial hegemony on the Pacific coast. In the 1840s, therefore, Chile established settlements on the Magellan Straits, the most important of which was Punta Arenas, the world's southernmost town, an isolated frontier outpost linked to the rest of Chile by sea and peopled largely by immigrants of Jugoslav descent.

In the far north of Chile, the growing demands of European agriculture for fertilizer focused attention on the hitherto-despised *guano* (seabird droppings) in the waterless and unsettled Atacama desert which was part of Bolivia, although Chile claimed up to the twenty-third parallel. When nitrate deposits were discovered in the same region, this conflict was only resolved by the War of the Pacific (1879–83) in which Chile defeated both Peru and Bolivia. As a result of this victory Chile's desert frontier expanded to include Antofagasta as a desert emporium and outlet for nitrate exports; new settlements stimulated a trans-Andine cattle trade but the war's most pervasive legacy was Bolivian bitterness at being excluded from the sea. Obsession with being a maritime power motivated Bolivia's later unsuccessful attempts to find an outlet to the Atlantic via the Amazon or the Platine river system. The *rumbo al mar* can always serve to provide Bolivian governments and opposition parties with a rallying nationalist cause.

Peru was similarly resentful at the loss of Tacna and Arica and, in order to be free to pursue the recovery of the two towns, acceded in 1890 to Ecuadorian claims to a substantial area of Peruvian Amazonia, thus satisfying Ecuador's frustrated historical claims to be an Amazonian power (early exploratory expeditions had set out from Quito as had Jesuit missionaries). Failure to recover Tacna and Arica and suspicion that the lost Amazonian territory was rich in minerals underlay the conflict which broke out into war in 1942, as a result of which Peru regained her Amazonian possessions—a loss to which Ecuador has never been reconciled; it is doubtful if a booming trans-Andine oil frontier will serve to assuage Ecuador's irridentist claims to the lost provinces.

Economic interests might be additional provocation for border conflicts, as in the case of the Venezuela–Guyana dispute over territory thought to be rich in diamonds or between Bolivia and Paraguay over the supposedly oil-rich Chaco desert; but disputes need not necessarily be economically motivated. Hypersensitivity towards any violation of national integrity, a fierce territorial imperative—caused by fear of a smaller power at the ambitions of its larger neighbour as in the case of Chile, sharing a two thousand mile long frontier with Argentina or a historical grievance as with Guatemala's claim to Belize—turns frontier conflict into an inflammable issue which can be exploited for political purposes.

Demographic pressure provides another source of friction. Wherever there is substantial cross-border migration from an overpopulated to an underpopulated country, there is potential for conflict as in the case of Salvadorians migrating to Honduras and Haitians to the Dominican Republic.

Many frontiers rest on rivers—the Putumayo between Colombia and Peru, the Paraguay and Paraná between Brazil, Paraguay and Argentina, the Uruguay between Argentina, Brazil and Uruguay and the Pilcomayo between Argentina and Paraguay. Even such clearly demarcated frontiers can still give rise to disputes as when the Rio Grande between Mexico and the United States changed its course in 1864 at Chamizal, leaving six hundred acres on the American side. Although a minor dispute it left a legacy of bitterness and was not solved until handed back to Mexico in 1963. Where rivers flow from one country into another the use made of their upper reaches may have profound effects on its neighbour. In Mexico, the salinity of the Colorado River caused by irrigation in the United States has had adverse effects on Mexican agriculture in the border region. In the case of the River Lauca which rises in Chile and flows into Lake Coipasa in Bolivia, Chilean use of its waters to irrigate infertile desert roused Bolivian anger at the threat which this action posed to irridentist claims. A potentially more serious dispute has arisen with Brazil's exploitation of the hydroelectric potential of the upper reaches of the Paraná which Argentina claims has adversely effected them.

Although Spanish Americans share a common cultural heritage, religion and experience of economic dependence, a hundred years of independence have created a complex web of nationalist loyalties which has proved difficult to erase. In the process of nation-building, each state elaborated nationalist symbols which commanded primary loyalties in comparison with which the pull of wider Latin American heroes and symbols is attenuated. As internal frontiers of settlement move closer to political frontiers with the filling in of empty spaces and as new issues arise, like the exploitation of maritime resources or rival claims in Antarctica, disputes over territorial sovereignty will come to assume an even greater importance; these underline the urgent need for international cooperation and regional integration before it is too late.

4
Frontier Society and Culture

Frontier types

In general, frontiers attract the restless and adventurous. There is, there-fore, a sense in which frontier environments confirm traits already implanted rather than originate new ones, but whether the frontiersman makes a success or failure of his life depends on a wide range of factors; there are the nature of the opportunities offered and the means available to achieve them, the ability to adapt to the often harsh climate and the question whether his attitude towards the natives is one of hostility or of friendship in the attempt to ease his adaptation to a strange environment. These attitudes will be conditioned in turn by the aspirations and expectations of the frontiersman.

For some—communers with nature, marital misfits or debtors—the frontier is an escape from the restraints of urban civilization, for others a purgatory to be endured until the windfall which will make possible a return to civilization; for a few, like Yannis, the Greek prospector in Carpentier's *The Lost Steps*, frontier life is an odyssey while for many, perhaps the majority, necessity traps them in an economic system from which there is no escape like the hero in Ferreira de Castro's novel *The Emigrants* trapped as a contract labourer on a São Paulo coffee plantation or the Brazilian *seringueiros*, emigrants from the drought-stricken back-lands of the northeast in the 1870s who became stranded in the Amazonian rain forests, racked by disease, enervated by humidity and unable to raise the cash to buy their way out. To yet others, the escaped slaves, *cima-rrones*, maroons and bush-negroes, the frontier is a haven where dimly remembered rituals can be reenacted and traditional African social organization revived; the 'Republic of Palmares', for instance, the seventeenth-century *quilombo* in the Brazilian *sertão*, defied the attempts of Portuguese and Dutch to suppress it for almost a century.

In primitive regions the person who has a wide range of skills will have the best chance of survival but, as the density of settlement increases, so diversification and specialization will also increase; the division of labour will become more complex and as the frontier becomes locked into the wider national economy, making the changeover from subsistence to market exchange, there will be a need for brokers and middlemen who can mediate between the frontier and national or regional centres of economic and political power. There will also be a range of occupations linking the periphery with the centre, lawyers, government officials, merchants, land-speculators and especially those involved in transportation—railwaymen where railways exist or muleteers of the pre-railway age, the *arrieros* of Spanish America and the *tropeiros* of Brazil, groups who played an important role in integrating the colonial economies and, in more recent times, bus and lorry drivers and itinerant peddlers often *turcos*—Syrians or Lebanese. These people have contacts with the frontier but do not necessarily identify with it. But even in its primitive stage frontier society will produce its specialists, those with a particular skill or technique which is needed for survival. Sarmiento and da Cunha in their analyses of pampas and *sertão* society emphasize the importance attached to certain skills, such as pathfinding and tracking in the pampas— the *baqueano* and the *rastreador*.[1] Similarly, exposed Indian frontiers will produce their professional Indian fighters, the *bugreiros* of the *sertão* while the hinterlands of slave plantations will have their *capitãos do mato*, bushwacking captains with squads of slave catchers.

The most isolated of all frontier types were those who worked as gatherers in jungles—the *chicleros* (chicle is the basis of chewing gum) in the jungles of Yucatán and the *seringueiros* of Amazonia. Amazon rubber grew wild, not in plantations as in Malaya, and required large numbers of gatherers working on their own over vast areas. Recruitment of labour was difficult; no European immigrant could be attracted (one of the most unusual, and unsuccessful, examples of immigrants was a group of Confederate exiles who finally decided that the rigours of Reconstruction were preferable to dying of jungle fever). Without the savage drought in Ceará of 1877–9 which drove 60,000 Cearenses to search for work, it is doubtful if there would have been a rubber boom at all, for jungle Indians were hard to recruit. Those that were employed were so badly treated as to provoke an international scandal in 1909.

The system of rubber gathering has changed little. The exploitation of the wild rubber trees is done by individual collectors who gather the latex in paths cut into the jungle. The *seringueiro* lives in his isolated hut on the river bank. He does not own his trees which are usually the property of the *seringalista*, either an individual trader or a company based in Manaus or Belém. These operate through a network of traders who are paid on a commission basis. The trader-middleman may have up to fifty trappers selling him their rubber. By advancing credit to the trapper, the latter becomes dependent on him for necessities and hence is nearly always in debt. Unlike the fur-trappers of North America the relationship between *seringueiros* and Indians tends to be one of mutual fear and hostility.

An important and ubiquitous figure on many Latin American frontiers as in the United States was the land speculator. Often uninterested in land for social prestige or for development purposes, the speculator was more concerned with its potential as a realizable asset, appreciating in value as areas were opened up for settlement and exploitation. The speculators' opportunity came with the sale of communal lands in the nineteenth century. Liberal governments regarded any form of communal property—whether Indian or Church lands—as a barrier to economic progress because it frustrated the individual's profit drive. In Mexico, for example, companies surveying the public domain were entitled to keep a third of the land surveyed as payment, and by the end of the Porfirian period as much as one fifth of the total land area had been alienated, much of it to foreigners, mainly North Americans. Although the object of Liberal land legislation had been to create an independent peasantry, the Indians' lack of capital forced them to become a landless agrarian proletariat at the same time as landed property became even more highly concentrated.

Similarly, in Argentina, land companies speculated in the 150 million acres thrown open after the Desert War of 1879–80 against the Indians. Frontier land did not become available to independent settlers; homesteading acts remained a dead letter. In São Paulo, where there was considerable confusion over the demarcation of land, the *grileiro* or land speculator was a key figure in the expanding speculators' frontier, moving ahead of the frontier of settlement.

During the colonial period it was the silver mining frontier which produced the most diversified society. This was based on a sophisticated division of labour, far greater than that necessary on cattle or agricultural frontiers because of the level of technology involved, although gold panning, as everywhere, produced individualists like the Brazilian *faisqueiro*, the poor itinerant prospector. Mining societies are highly stratified within themselves as well as differing widely from each other. Labour exploitation ranged from free labour and individual prospecting to forced and slave labour. Coffee was similar in that it could be grown under a variety of conditions both in size of enterprise and in labour intensity. This lack of social homogeneity makes it difficult to talk in any general way of a 'coffee culture' or a 'mining culture'. Each type of labour exploitation engendered its own social relationships and cultural expressions. For example, where there are family smallholdings there are often found variants of the Brazilian *mutirão* in which families assist each other at harvest time.

Miners have a great deal in common and the traits and beliefs in mining communities transcend time and place; but lack of visibility gives mining lore an esoteric quality which it is difficult for the outsider to share. This is one reason why, although the wealth of many Latin American countries derives from their mines, miners as such are not enshrined in national myths.[2] The 'hero' of mining communities tends to be the outsider—the smuggler attempting to evade payment of the royal fifth, the *garimpeiros*, the illicit diamond miners of eighteenth-century Brazil, or those believed to be endowed with supernatural powers in gold divining, particularly negresses who were often taken as mistresses by miners for this putative skill.

Runaway slaves, *calhambolas*, constituted another group. They were in constant danger of recapture and were therefore precluded from earning an honest living and so had to support themselves by banditry, preying on cattle for food.

In contrast, the visibility of the cowboy complex as represented by stirrups, chaps, cattlemen's hats, rodeos, *vaquejadas*, cowboy ballads and other poetic, musical and dancing forms, has helped to impress it on the public consciousness. In this respect cattle herding is different and there is a definite sense in which we can talk of a 'cattle culture' with the cattleman *caudillo* often becoming a national culture hero.

Perhaps the most notable feature common to cattle societies is the restlessness which makes cattlemen reluctant to put down roots and settle in any one place. The fact that the New World produced so many cattle frontiers is not solely a result of climatic or market conditions but also of the availability of so many rootless men to whom cattle herding was temperamentally attractive.

Unlike agriculture, plantations and much of the mining economy, a pastoral economy produced relatively free men. Slavery and forced labour systems were incompatible with open-range ranching. In Argentina, for example, the small slave population, comprising some ten per cent of the population of the viceroyalty of La Plata in 1800, lived in Buenos Aires as domestic servants and had little connection with the pastoral economy on which Argentinian wealth was based. The nature of grazing would have made it impossible to keep them under surveillance. Cowboys had to be armed and in this respect stood on a level with their employers. Where blacks were cowboys they were either runaways or freemen. Mobile and armed, the cowboy became a political force in the nineteenth century as retainers of regional *caudillos* in their mutual feuding or in support of *caudillos* defying the attempts of central government to subdue them.

The distinctive feature of labour control in herding is that it is maintained by internal rather than by external restraints. The cowboy herds because he wants to, not necessarily because he must. His work is defined by himself, and by most others, as carrying prestige in comparison with the farmer or field hand. Cowboy and employer often share and value the same skills and indeed, it is often an employer's talent which rouses the admiration of his cowhands, binding them to him in a way which has few parallels in other activities. The appeal of Rosas, a townsman but the greatest of Argentinian *caudillos*, was partly based on his ability to beat his gauchos at their own game and, in so doing, to control and direct them. Interpersonal relationships are fiercely egalitarian. An effete townsman who cannot ride or compete with the equestrian skills of the cowboy is beneath contempt and if 'mounted on an English saddle would bring ridicule and brutal assault upon himself'. The farmer and townsman rooted to a particular place and job, cannot be free men like the mounted herder. The cowboy had more respect for the Indians with whom he was in conflict than for the merchants whose interest he was indirectly often defending. The shepherd was also scorned by the cattlemen for his sedentary, horseless life and a gaucho would rather be dead than eat mutton. Where the cowboy implicitly takes the bull as a model for his virility, who wants to be a ram? The shepherd as a symbol of gentleness is the antithesis of the masterful domineering cowboy.

From the standpoint of democratic values cattle societies are highly ambivalent. On one side, we can talk of 'pastoral democracy' confined to the in-group of cattlemen. This is essentially a male-dominated society, based on the bond between men united in the face of natural hazards. The scale of values is masculine, the quality most admired is *machismo*, based on physical strength, sexual prowess, loyalty, skill with the knife, ability to break horses and fell cattle, in a society of equals where hierarchy rests on natural ability not on acquired bookish skills and where 'the existence of conscious egalitarian values and practices give rise to an unconscious hierarchical order.' But as far as outsiders are concerned, cattle societies are 'pastoral despotisms' with nomadic cattlemen scorning earth and season-bound agriculturists and others who do not share their values. Agriculturists, for their part, have a different concept of freedom, based on property, legally guaranteed which, in Jeffersonian tradition at least, is regarded as the bedrock of a democratic system. For the cattlemen, liberty is freedom from restraint. These values have gradually been eroded with the decline of the open range and, with the growth of the modern *estancia* and agro-industrial enterprise, a specialized division of labour replaces the previously largely undifferentiated society; but the residual legacy of the strong man ethos can still exercise a potent fascination both in the countryside and among the migrants in the teeming industrial cities who may seek to recapture the simple loyalties of their rural past by surrendering to strong-man rule.

The gaucho

In Argentina, it was at the moment when the gaucho, the most famous of all Latin American cattlemen, was beginning to disappear that he became a romantic figure and a symbol of Argentinian nationality. In origin, gaucho may derive from *gaucho*, an Indian word meaning orphan. At first it was a term of abuse, the *gaucho malo* being no better than a cut-throat but it was nevertheless the gaucho who kept the Indians at bay and made possible the meteoric rise of Buenos Aires as the great meat port of the western hemisphere. Most observers of pampas life shared Charles Darwin's ambivalent attitude to the gaucho:

> Their appearance is very striking; they are generally tall and hand-some, but with a proud and dissolute expression of countenance. They frequently wear their moustaches, and long black hair curling down their backs. With their brightly coloured garments, great spurs clanking about their heels, and knives stuck as daggers (and often so used) at their waists they look a different race of men from what might be expected from their name of Gauchos, or simple country-men. Their politeness is excessive, they never drink their spirits without expecting you to taste it; but whilst making their exceedingly graceful bow, they seem quite as ready, if occasion offered, to cut your throat.[3]

Outsiders deplored the gaucho's love of fighting, addiction to gambling, swiftness to take offence and fecklessness but they admired his sense of honour, love of poetry and song, his hospitality and simplicity, his tough resourcefulness, superb horsemanship and freedom-loving temperament, although this led the gauchos to scorn the frock-coated money conscious *porteños* and the poor immigrants who ventured to the pampas as shepherds, sharecroppers and tenant farmers. These, as well as their unmanly way of life, represented the threat of change—domesticity, encroaching agriculture and sheep-farming pushing the cattlemen farther into the interior.

In contrast to the *bandeirante*, who fulfils a similar role as nationalist culture-hero in Brazil and who moved mostly on foot, the gaucho was inseparable from his horse. 'Babies play with sharp knives and lassos and at four years are able to ride and herd.' Like the *bandeirante* he was a restless wanderer but whereas the *bandeirante* was a social being, the *bandeira* being a tightly knit group with a hierarchical chain of command and bound together by ties of kinship, the gaucho was a solitary figure, an individualist, operating on his own account, uninterested in accumulating anything beyond the requirements of his skill and the satisfaction of immediate needs—lasso, bola, stirrups and *facón*. Originally Spanish malcontents escaping from the river settlements, the gauchos mated with Indian women to sire a mestizo race.

The rapid multiplication of wild cattle and the availability of wild horses made life easy for someone with limited wants and expectations. A rude shack provided shelter for himself and for the women who served several men, while meat, ostrich eggs and *maté*, the Paraguayan tea rich in vitamin content, were a healthy staple diet, and leather could provide for most of the gaucho's needs. His heyday was in the late eighteenth and early nineteenth century when European wars created a limitless demand for hides. The gaucho's skills were required by the *estancieros* and *saladeros* who exported dried beef for the slave plantations of Brazil and for the ships plying the transatlantic routes.

The gauchos also fulfilled other roles. Gaucho armies, the *montoneros* after whom Peronist guerrillas are named, repelled Spanish invasions from Upper Peru during the wars of emancipation. After independence and the breakup of the flourishing mule trade of northwest Argentina, pauperized gauchos became armed retainers of the *caudillos* who wrestled for control of the rural areas. But their major function was to act as a 'soft frontier' in the no-man's-land between the 'civilization' of Buenos Aires and the 'savagery' of the Pampas Indians whose deep raids into settled areas became more frequent as the expanding cattle frontier moved into their traditional hunting grounds. The gauchos now found themselves squeezed between the *estancias* interested in obtaining a tied labour force and the Indians to whom gauchos were competitors for the diminishing herds of cattle and horses. The gauchos' days as free ranging cowboys were numbered as the *estancieros* legislated to force them to be attached to *estancias* by passing vagrancy laws, and the government used infringements of this legislation to impress them for frontier defence. The introduction of barbed wire, railways and the *frigorífico* spelt the end as selective breeding could now produce meat palatable to European taste.

It was at the point when the process of transformation from free-ranging cowboy to hired peon was already far advanced that José Hernández wrote his classic epic poem *Martín Fierro* which idealized the disappearing gaucho. As the pace of European immigration quickened, the cult of the gaucho as a symbol of Argentinian nationality grew both among creoles who saw the invasion by poor Italian peasants as a threat to traditional values and among the Italians themselves who believed that by reliving the gauchos ethos, dressing up, singing their songs and holding *asadas* in the pampas they would be able to identify themselves more thoroughly with their new homeland.

Bandits and messiahs

The open range not only perpetuated restlessness but engendered conflict with Indians, cattle raiders, horse thieves, between big ranchers and their retainers over pastures, water-holes and salt-licks, with the authorities trying to establish order, with farmers trying to protect their crops against herds. Where cattle lands were the hinterlands of slave economies, there was the additional restlessness provided by escaped slaves on the run. The cattleman's life was also spent in constant conflict with the elements and the cattle in his charge.

In this atmosphere banditry was endemic; in northern Mexico, for instance, the border with the United States was a constant invitation to smuggling and cattle raiding, as was the border between Brazil and Uruguay. The problem was exacerbated in Mexico by the difficulties of absorbing guerrillas after the wars of independence in the 1820s, and by the Civil War and French intervention of the 1860s, as well as by the break up of Indian communities which threw many on to the labour market at a time when they could not be absorbed because of rising population and a slow growing economy.

The northeast of Brazil was another region of endemic banditry. Endless disputes over the demarcation of *sesmaria* grants provoked conflicts between landowners who would recruit *capangas* to patrol their border and beat up opponents. These private armies became necessary for the survival of rural clans. In contrast to this 'official' banditry, acting on the orders of a rural clan leader, there was banditry rising from harsh social conditions. This might take the form of anomic desperation or of social banditry—Robin Hood-style action like that of Lampião, the most famous of all the *cangaceiros* who was a legend in his lifetime and after his death in 1938. The *cangaceiro* is a magical figure in the backlands, with his distinctive turned-up cattleman's hat decorated with five-pointed stars, draped with bandoliers and the *cangaço*, the bundle of arms after which he is named, and cluttered with charms and medallions.[4] The word *cangaceiro* carried overtones of social purpose which other words like *jagunço* or *capanga* do not. These latter are ruffians who are paid well for their violence and although it is possible for a *cangaceiro* to become a *capanga* the reverse is unlikely.

Banditry increased as the patriarchal bonds which had been a cohesive force, with mutual obligations, began to weaken under economic pressures and sharpened the basic conflict between landowners and tenants. The problem of banditry became acute from the mid-nineteenth century: population rise and periodic droughts turned *vaqueiros* into highwaymen, especially during the great drought of 1877–9, when dozens of small bands infested the roads. Once the immediate crisis had passed, *cangaceiros* were available for hire as *capangas* for landowners or local political bosses. Unlike Porfirian Mexico where the state had suppressed banditry by organizing a strong Rural Guard, the weakness of the states in Brazil meant that social control was usually enforced by locally recruited bully-boys, acting in the interest of a particular clan.

On occasions the state would be compelled to intervene; in 1897, for instance, a military expedition had to be sent to Canudos. This episode has become deservedly famous through Euclides da Cunha's *Rebellion in the Backlands* which focused attention on religious messianism, one of the most distinctive features of the *sertão*. The leader of the Canudos rising was Anthony the Counsellor, one of the many charismatic preachers who wandered through the backlands promising redemption to the *sertanejos* in times of calamity and social stress. 'When drought comes', comments da Cunha,[5] 'the *sertanejo* resorts to religion—a monotheism which he does not understand, marred by an extravagant mysticism with an incongruous mixture of the Indian and the African. . . . This religion, like himself, is mestizo in character.' The *sertanejo* 'is heir to a multitude of extravagant superstitions, which are no longer found on the sea-board, owing to the modifying influence of other creeds and races, but which in the backlands have remained intact.' The strains of religious mysticism are strengthened by the lack of priests which enables numerous self-appointed religious leaders, *beatos* and *beatas*, to play on the fears of the credulous.

Religious mysticism has its political counterpart in Sebastianism. This is a peculiar persistent version of the redeemer-king myth found in many societies and has flourished for three hundred years in the Brazilian backlands since it first appeared in Portugal at the end of the sixteenth century. The body of the young king Sebastian was never discovered after the disastrous Portuguese defeat by the Moors at the Battle of Alcazar Quiver in 1578 and this gave rise to the notion that he had not died but was in hiding waiting to return at the propitious moment to lead Portugal out of bondage to Spain, and the poor out of bondage to rapacious land-lords and natural calamities. Sebastianism idealizes a golden age in the past and yearns for a future free of care with messianic notions similar to the Fifth Monarchy idea in which a redeemer king will establish a reign of right and justice. The popular versions of the belief were carried over by migrants to Brazil where they were perpetuated in the collective memory in the ballads sung by itinerant singers.

Ballad singers play an important role in illiterate rural societies and nowhere more so than in the Brazilian northeast where one estimate has put their number at 12,000. They are professionals who move from town to town singing *desafios* (challenges) and romances. They reflect the carry-over of a vivid oral popular culture from Portugal, sharing common features with many other Mediterranean countries. The *desafio* is the equivalent of the Argentinian *payada,* common in herding societies where long hours of isolation stimulated competitive singing. The *desafío* became a formalized method of testing poetic skills and often treated of traditional themes as did the *chansons de gestes.* More recently, the songs have tended to relate to current events and especially the exploits of the *cangaceiros.* In this way, the *cantadores* who are literates in a still largely illiterate society, act as mediators between the *sertão* and the outside world as well as being guardians and transmitters of historical memories.

At times of crisis such as the years after the fall of the Empire in 1889, a threat of impending social change gave new life to Sebastianism which merged in with other messianic religious beliefs. Messianic movements are endemic to many societies poised on the edge of disastrous change over which they feel they have no control. When a native culture senses that it is doomed, by military attack or by superior culture, a prophet appears who promises to fulfil suppressed longings of release from travail and from the human impasse by supernatural means. Thus arises a revivalistic movement for a return to the good old days as in the Taqui Ongo movement in Peru in the sixteenth century which looked back to the halcyon days of Inca power. In Yucatán, to take another case, mounting social pressures led to the revivalistic movement of the Little Holy Cross in 1850 which provided the ideological drive behind the great Mayan Indian rebellion of that decade. In Brazil these movements do not flourish exclusively in the *sertão* although they seem to have their origin in stock raising and subsistence farming areas where there is little differentiation between social classes. Largely a response to despair, messianic movements are usually regarded by the authorities as a threat to the established order but they are rarely revolutionary, seeking rather to reestablish order once it has broken down.

The Canudos rising collapsed largely because Anthony the Counsellor failed to form an alliance with a dominant local clan who could have afforded him protection; he preferred to rely on the fanaticism of his followers who were massacred to a man. In contrast, another backlands religious leader, Father Cicero, a Catholic priest but condemned by the Church, was able to exert political power and exploit a local miracle to the benefit of his community. From a struggling hamlet, Joaseiro, the site of the reputed miracle in 1890, rose in a generation to become the commercial emporium of the backlands of Ceará. The influx of thousands of pilgrims transformed the local economy. Scattered settlements were concentrated and a transformation effected from subsistence to commercial farming. Small industries were developed within a paternalistic framework and without causing severe local dislocation.

In the past there has been a tendency to underestimate the rationality of popular revolts but as historians begin to study them from below their rationale becomes clearer as in the case of the Quebra-Quilo revolts of 1874–5 in an area of recent settlement in northeast Brazil.

The bandeirantes

The heyday of the *bandeirantes* was the seventeenth century. The word derives from *bandeira* which in Portugal used to refer to a group of soldiers distinguished by a banner. It came to be applied to the expeditions formed by *paulistas* scouring the inner regions of Brazil in search of Indian slaves, emeralds and gold. São Paulo had been founded in 1554 as a Jesuit mission and had grown slowly because of its isolated situation, cut off from the coast only sixty miles away by forbidding mountain terrain. Nor was there any obvious attraction for settlers: it had no mineral wealth, distance precluded the possibility of exporting cash crops and there was no readily available labour supply. However, it had three advantages—a healthy climate, rich soil, and freedom from close interference by the colonial authorities. It therefore tended to attract malcontents, fugitives from justice and from the rigidities of the coastal slave plantations. Very few women risked the hazardous journey inland, so *paulistas* mated with Indian women and by the seventeenth century a high proportion of them were mixed bloods, most of whom preferred to speak Tupi-Guaraní in preference to Portuguese. The high price of African slaves impelled them to comb the interior for Indians and it became profitable to sell these to plantations cut off from their African sources of supply during the Dutch occupation of the coast between 1634 and 1654. The slave raiding expeditions consisted of groups of around three hundred men often accompanied by women and Amerindian auxiliaries to act as scouts and interpreters. The *bandeiras* were highly organized bands—a 'town on the march'—and would often be on the move for years on end. The majority of them returned to São Paulo without founding new settlements.

By the 1650s they had blazed trails as far as the Peruvian Andes and the Amazon. They also attacked the Jesuit reductions in Paraguay where the policy of congregating Indians facilitated the task of capturing them. Other groups moved into Rio Grande do Sul where they started to breed mules to sell in the great annual fair at Sorocaba near São Paulo. Yet others roamed the highlands of Minas Gerais, searching for precious metals. In the 1690s they were at last rewarded with the discovery of gold, thus sparking off the gold rush and a conflict with the foreigners who by sheer numbers engulfed the original discoverers and compelled many of them to set off on their wanderings again.

The *bandeirantes* are a striking example of adaptation to environment. Their maternal cultural inheritance enabled them to identify with and absorb the mores of nomadic Indians. Unlike the static northeastern plantation society, dependent on economic links with Europe, the *bandeirantes* turned their backs on Europe and identified themselves totally with the Brazilian interior. In the vast unclaimed highlands and jungles of the continent they fulfilled an important geopolitical role by enabling the Portuguese Crown to make claims of prior possession against the Spaniards. Their Indian heritage and repudiation of European influences made them potent symbols of Brazilian nationality while their dynamism and ruthlessness endeared them to twentieth-century *paulistas* who like to think of themselves as modern *bandeirantes*. Not all historians share the optimistic evaluations of their role and some regard them as predators epitomizing values which have impeded the growth of economic stability and political democracy.

The frontier in literature

There is nothing in Latin American popular literature corresponding to the Western novel, the genre which was both perpetuated by and in its turn perpetuates the Western myth. This can be partly explained by the absence of a mass reading public in many Latin American countries and by the way in which the gap has been filled by translations of North American works.

It is a truism that Latin American writers have been fascinated by European and more especially French culture: Paris has been the intellectual capital of the continent, and the crowning pinnacle of a Latin American writers' career is to be appointed ambassador to France.[6] But against this strong cosmopolitan current must be set the three traditions of the *novela de la tierra*, *indigenismo* and *lo real maravilloso*, all of which represent attempts of writers from the 1920s to come to terms with the realities of the continent's rural areas and the people living in them. Although these genres cannot be described exclusively as 'frontier novels', they nevertheless explore the relationship between urban values and those of the untamed and unsettled interior.

The dichotomy between the barbaric interior and civilized cities of the coast was formulated most memorably in Sarmiento's *Facundo* (1845) and da Cunha's, *Rebellion in the Backlands* (1902). *Facundo* was an analysis of pampas society and a political tract against the dictator Rosas whom Sarmiento saw importing the values of the pampas into the city where his political terror was an extension of the brute force of the rural *caudillo*. All civilization, Sarmiento believed, was city-based. Cities represent civil society whereas the pampas was its negation. He believed that the Spaniards, as an urban-oriented people degenerated under the influence of telluric forces. Sarmiento postulated a Latin American *modo de ser* existing in permanent tension between urban civilization and rural barbarism. The city engendered morality, commercial and political organization while the countryside spawned tyrants like Facundo Quiroga. Sarmiento's views did not go unchallenged: his Argentine contemporary Alberdi accused him of being a sterile intellectual, a *caudillo* by temperament whose fulminations against the countryside ignored the fact that the civilization of Buenos Aires was sustained by the wealth produced by the very countryside he was so quick to denigrate. *Facundo* is a complex book and full of ambivalences but Sarmiento's views, perhaps oversimplified by his readers, captured the pessimism that most urban-based intellectuals felt about the rural areas and their inhabitants, a feeling that only by swamping the indigenous peoples with European immigrants would the virtues of entrepreneurial drive and morality be injected into the pampas. Salvation could only come from Europe or, as in his educational ideas, North America. There is no Jeffersonian 'middle ground' in *Facundo*. Sarmiento is at the other end of the spectrum from the European pastoral tradition and indeed, the vision of the shepherd in a Virgilian landscape, in harmony with nature, the inspiration of countless European poets and painters, finds little echo in the Latin American imagination. That particular poetic fantasy was not considered to have much chance of fulfilment; daunting empty spaces precluded sentimental pastoralism and where the landscape could have been the location for a pastoral idyll, such as the Central Valley of Chile, it was pre-empted by *latifundios*. The romantic imagination could not generate a vision of lovers retiring to a sylvan retreat without straining the reader's credulity, although many poets attempted just this, writing in lifeless and artless imitation of European forms.

Da Cunha's book was written to draw the attention of the coastal, urban literate Brazilian public to the vast unknown backlands and to expose the bankruptcy of the new Republic's response to the plight of the *sertanejos*. It was not, as with Sarmiento, a question of the frontier overwhelming the metropolis with its barbaric values, but rather of the metropolis ignoring the existence of the frontier altogether. Da Cunha's attitude towards the *sertanejo* is ambivalent as is Sarmiento's towards the gaucho and even to Facundo himself. His fascination with the various types he analyses is based on his admiration of the way in which they have adapted to the harsh environment. He describes the *sertanejos* as the 'bed-rock of our race' but his views on social evolution, reflecting those of current European social thought and racial theorists, left him no alternative but to predict their disappearance. In describing the various sub-races of the *sertão* he writes:

> These races are destined to be short-lived, soon to disappear before the growing exigencies of civilization and the intensive material

competition offered by the stream of immigrants, that is already beginning to invade our land. The fearless *jagunço*, the ingenious *tabereo*, and the stolid *caipira* are types that will soon be relegated to the realm of evanescent extinct tradition.[7]

Da Cunha never resolves the conflict between his views on the influence of race as against environment but neither he nor Sarmiento saw redemption emanating from the countryside or from the racially mixed population which lived in it. This was not the stuff out of which national mythologies could be constructed.

The domination of literature by European conventions impeded Latin American writers from looking at national realities unclouded by European prejudices, but in the 1920s, as part of a swing against a Europe discredited by the First World War and under the influence of the Mexican Revolution with its revindication of Indians, writers began to explore the realities of their own countries. The *novelas de la tierra* were located in the untamed regions of the interior where the values of city life and bookish learning based on European precepts were useless lumber.

The unrestrained hostility of nature is represented most graphically in the novel, *La vorágine*, by the Colombian Rivera, who wrote from his experience of the Venezuelan and Colombian jungle. The protagonist, a weak ineffectual townsman, passes through the violent cattle country into the rubber forests where he plans to make his fortune. Nature here is the antithesis of romantic literary convention. The jungle is a hostile force—a prison from which there is no escape and where the struggle for survival is reduced to elemental forms. The violent conflict between rubber gatherers echoes the actual violence of the rubber boom years. Civilization is a fragile growth which collapses under armies of ants, man-eating piranha fish and disease. The Uruguayan, Quiroga, was a short-story writer marginal to this tradition whose own failures as a pioneer farmer in Misiones and in the Argentinian Chaco gave a realistic edge to his writings. In these, the weak go to the wall and the doers survive while the talkers die—an oblique criticism of the urban-based writers who dominated the Latin American literary scene.

In Latin America there is a reversal of the romantic convention of flight to the countryside to escape the horrors of industrialization. Intellectuals in underdeveloped and underpopulated countries do not feel the same constraints; claustrophobia is not their obsession. Industry is the key to emancipation and a fuller life. The rural interior conjured up visions of fear, horror, solitude, barbarism and cruelty; yet there also writers were to find the sources of energy and perhaps even of eventual redemption from a weak, effeminate and cosmopolitan society emasculated by dependence on Europe. To the fragility of civilized life as in Carpentier's *The Lost*

Steps where 'a few hours of neglect, of man's vigilance relaxed had sufficed in this climate for the denizens of the slime to take over the beleagured stronghold,'[8] one might juxtapose the figure of Gallegos' *Doña Bárbara*, the virago personification of the *llanos* who can dominate men and whose natural daughter marries the townsman Santos Luzardo, thus bringing to their offspring the strength of the *llanos*.

Regeneration comes from an acceptance of frontier values, not from the imposition of foreign ideas in the conquest of nature by technology. The engineer is not a hero figure in Latin American fiction. He is more likely to be a foreigner, like the real-life North Americans, Henry Meiggs, the builder of the Peruvian Central Railway, and Major Church, builder of the Madeira-Marmoré Railway, intruders importing the values of an alien materialism.

The regionalist novelists stressed the virtue of spontaneity in rural life against the artificiality of Europeanized cities, dominated by penny-pinching and small-minded immigrants intent on making their fortunes, and uninterested in settling in the country. It is not surprising that Argentina, with its huge immigrant population, exemplifies this approach most graphically. José Hernández's *Martín Fierro* (1872) idealizes the fast disappearing gaucho who was adopted as the symbol of Argentinidad, and in Ricardo Güiraldes's *Don Segundo Sombra* (1926) the values of the vanished gaucho society, evoked nostalgically by the author, are transmitted to a young orphan. The point made by Güiraldes is that the values of Sarmiento's urban civil society detract from the real spiritual virtues represented by the society of the pampas which obeys its own imperatives. But when the orphan becomes an *estanciero* by coming into an inheritance, there is a happy ending and all is well with the *estanciero's* world which will now survive thanks to the gaucho virtues he has assimilated.

In contrast to the transitory immigrant, the Indians' telluric attachment to the soil now comes to be hailed as a virtue worth emulating; hence the vogue of the *indigenista* novel of the 1920s and 1930s which draws much of its inspiration from the Mexican Revolution's revindication of Indians' rights.

These novels vary widely between the early Mexican models like Gregorio López y Fuentes's *El Indio* (1935), the social realism of the Ecuadorian Jorge Icaza's *Huasipungo* with its stark but unrealistic confrontations and the Peruvian José María Arguedas's *Yawar Fiesta* or *Los Ríos Profundos*, in which the author's knowledge of Quechua and experience of childhood among Indians gives him insights lacking in other *indigenista* novels. In many of these, experience is too often externally observed, as in the Peruvian Ciro Alegría's *Broad and Alien is the World*, or used to argue a thesis as in the Bolivian Alcides Arguedas's *Raza de Bronce*. The *indigenista* novel for all its imperfections, such as lapses into exoticism and exaggerating what an Indian would take for granted, nevertheless attempted to come to terms with social realities; it introduced Indian society to a non-Indian urban audience, in ways which indianist novels, pastiches of Rousseauesque sentimentalism, did not.

Finally, in writers such as Miguel Angel Asturias, Augusto Roa Bastos and, most notably Alejo Carpentier, an attempt is made to explore the myths of Latin American history—myths which are rooted in man's attempt to come to terms with a luxuriant and forbidding environment. Carpentier's *The Lost Steps* is the odyssey of a jaded urban intellectual who journeys into the jungle and through it into the past to discover his roots and forge his identity. It is a complex and subtle work but a major theme is his repudiation of the European values which have been accepted by the cities. It is an exploration of the myths which provided the dynamic behind the real as distinct from the artificial history of the continent and which grew out of the untamed jungles, unconquered mountains, irresistible rivers, and the indigenous inhabitants.

5
The Contracting Frontier

The rural crisis

Latin America's rural crisis has economic, social and political dimensions. Because expanding frontiers failed to develop a rural middle class which could both increase food production by efficient farming as well as provide a market for industrial goods, and because of the perpetuation of a two-class system in the countryside, old social and economic structures have remained largely unreformed. Agriculture is inefficient, barely able or even unable in some cases, to meet the food requirements of a population which is growing at double the rate of European countries at the comparable period of their development. But even where efficient farming (as in post-revolutionary Mexico or in Brazil where frontier lands are being brought under cultivation) is meeting food requirements, these economic achievements are not matched by social equality.

The roots of the rural crisis lie in the landholding pattern bequeathed by the colonial period and reinforced by the nineteenth-century land policies of the newly independent states. Land was bought for prestige (and in order to monopolize labour which continued to be scarce in relation to land), and increasingly now as a hedge against inflation which rarely drops below double figures and may even rise to treble figures. Land concentration—by which out of some 110 million rural dwellers as many as 80 millions might be smallholders with insufficient land for subsistence, or landless labourers, and where perhaps as few as 100,000 own sixty per cent of all agricultural land—encourages inefficient use of land and labour. There is little incentive for the landowner to improve technology or increase output. Personal income, social prestige and political power rather than agricultural productivity are the motives for landownership. Absenteeism and speculative buying are common and as landowners exercise political power at the national level they are able to gain access to public domain and to block land-tax legislation or make it inoperative.

On the big estate there is constant underemployment and much land is kept fallow. Farming is extensive rather than intensive as large landowners can make their profits with minimal capital outlay and an unorganized labour supply. Labour may not be paid in cash at all but with concessions such as private plots or grazing rights. The landowner, therefore, does not need much working capital and, by threatening his workers with expulsion and playing on dependency ties, he can dominate his work force politically.

In the main, the mass of rural dwellers are landless labourers—known variously as *huasipungueros* in Ecuador, *conuqueros* in Venezuela, *peones* in Argentina and *colonos* in Brazil. While vertical social mobility is virtually impossible, there is high geographical mobility as younger sons migrate to the cities to seek opportunities which do not, and in most cases cannot, exist in rural areas. There is no incentive to foment educational programmes and most rural schools fail unless there is an obvious spin-off. It is pointless teaching peasant children to read unless it serves a useful purpose, or teaching farming methods if they benefit only the employer. In such a stagnant situation traditional prejudices, such as those against manual labour, are reinforced and with no incentive to save (and what is saved is often spent in the conspicuous consumption of religious fiestas), the stereotype of the lazy feckless peasant is perpetuated. There is no spur to invention or innovation, and work is routinized.

In Indian areas the situation is exacerbated by the divisions between mestizos or *ladinos* and Indians. Where communal landholding has declined, social solidarity is weakened and often is not replaced by other forms of organization; this leaves the Indian open to exploitation by the *ladino* middlemen who dominate the local distribution and market centres. As commerce is often the major source of capital accumulation, *ladino* merchants carry the highest prestige. They act as moneylenders, as middlemen and cultural brokers between the local Indian community and the wider national society.

Socially, an inequitable tenure system has perpetuated small plots, compulsory labour obligations, crop-sharing, privilege and inequality while economically it has encouraged inefficiency and slow growth, underutilization of land and underemployment of labour.

The rural crisis has implications which reach beyond the rural areas. Before 1929 the Latin American economy was geared to the export of primary products to the United States and Europe. The Great Depression disturbed this pattern. To meet the decline of traditional markets for agricultural products which had previously paid for manufactured imports, the larger Latin American countries embarked on a policy of import-substitute industrialization. However, there was not only a limit on what could be easily and competitively produced but, with a pauperized peasantry, internal markets were too small to absorb the new manufactured products. In simple terms, Latin America was attempting to carry out an industrial revolution without an agricultural revolution.

By the 1960s it had been generally recognized that there could be no way out of the impasse except by a radical reform of agrarian structures in which land would be expropriated and redistributed, cooperatives founded, family holdings bolstered, rural syndicates set up and a whole network of supportive organizations established offering technical advice and facilities, easy credit, improved marketing, storage and transport facilities together with an imaginative rural education policy. Such policies depended on political will but, because of the interlocking of economic and political interests, this was largely lacking.

Frontier versus metropolis

The crucial factor in the historical development of Spanish America after the breakaway from Spain has been its political and economic fragmentation. Intractable geography, poor communications, restricted population, administrative disorganization, political particularism, the dislocating effects of war and the breakup of integrated economies resulted in the collapse of Bolívar's dream of a Spanish American confederation and destroyed the possibility of the political unity of the newly liberated continent. The crystallization of political frontiers between the new states —as effective in their exclusivity as the frontiers between European powers when each began to elaborate its own nationalist ideology— prevented closer ties between them. Each new state tended to be bound closer to Europe than to its immediate neighbour. Even today, only eleven per cent of Latin America's trade is carried on between Latin American nations. Capitals of the old administrative units which previously had been subordinate to the Spanish metropolis now in their turn became the metropolises of the new states and the mediating links between their hinterlands and Europe. Where during the colonial period settlement had tended to be centrifugal, now there was a growing centripetal tendency for the national metropolises to draw in the politically ambitious and economically aspiring—the phenomena of a contracting frontier. By the beginning of the twentieth century every capital except Havana was growing faster than its nation, a trend accelerated in many cases by the in-flow of European immigrants who found opportunities for advancement in the capital and not in the countryside.

With the economic growth which followed political stability in the latter half of the nineteenth century, the mounting volume of exports of primary products passing through the major sea-ports (most of which were national capitals or near them) made these the recipients of foreign investment, thus accelerating the imbalance between them and the periphery. The metropolises had the monopoly of credit, communication facilities and each was the hub of the transport system and the seat of a *comprador* bourgeoisie of export-import merchants closely tied to foreign merchant houses. With their banks, insurance houses, transport communications, entertainment and cultural facilities, the metropolises attracted national capital, and the abler and more enterprising of the rural population, as well as diverting foreign capital away from less immediately profitable areas in the interior.

The drift from the land has been a phenomenon in all developed and underdeveloped countries in recent years. But even against this background the drift to the cities in Latin America is remarkable for its scale. After Europe, Latin America is now the world's most highly urbanized continent at the same time as it has one of the highest areas of empty land. A notable feature of this urbanization is that migration has been to the capital cities. Thus in Mexico, Mexico City now has approximately 10–12 million inhabitants, Montevideo has thirty-two per cent of the country's population and in Argentina, Buenos Aires has thirty-four per cent. Only in Colombia and Brazil do we find even urban growth. In Brazil, especially, and in spite of the spiralling growth of São Paulo and Rio de Janeiro, there are now more than 40 cities with over 100,000 inhabitants. The urban drift is graphically shown by the increase from thirty-one per cent of the total population classified as urban in 1940 to the fifty-six per cent of 1970. Thus Brazil, the fourth largest country in the world, is now predominantly urban.

A feature of this urbanization is that it outruns the pace of industrialization so that most Latin American cities are pre-industrial aggregations, with large inflated service sectors and high rates of underemployment and unemployed. Under the conditions of modern capital-intensive industrialization, industry absorbs only a minimal number of the new immigrants. Cities, where public services are unable to meet the needs of their poorer inhabitants, are visible symbols of the failure of the rural economy to provide a viable alternative.

The political legacy

Latin American frontiers have not provided fertile ground for democracy. The concentration of landed wealth and the absence of capital and of highly motivated pioneers effectively blocked the growth of independent smallholders and a rural middle class; even where the latter did begin to emerge, as on the frontier in northern Paraná, it encountered resistance from large landowners whose political influence could be exerted on national and state governments.

The newly independent republics were heirs to the centralism of the Spanish Empire, as reflected in the wide powers enjoyed by all Latin American presidents and in the artificiality of Latin American federal systems. But central control did not imply ability to control outlying frontier regions. In Mexico the hold of the central government was so tenuous that the northern provinces were easily prised away by the Americans in the war of 1846–8. The experience of Central America was little different for the assertion of particularist interests led to the breakup of the Central American Federation in 1838. In Argentina, the new government at Buenos Aires proved unable until the 1850s to prevent factional conflicts between provinces or between them and the central government.

These revolts against the central governments were not expressions of frontier democracy. Under centralist governments and where there is no ingrained system of municipal independence (and this depends on fiscal resources), local autonomy was not a sign of burgeoning democracy. Too often there was ample scope for the provincial governor, often a local magnate, to become a petty tyrant. The further a region was from the central power, the greater liberty was given to local landowners to dominate their work force and the underpaid, centrally appointed, government officials. During the colonial period in Brazil, for example, the powers of local policing were handed over to the *fazendeiros* who were appointed *coroneis* and undertook to police the areas under their control with private armies. For practical purposes they were virtually autonomous. The weakness of national governments, crippled by financial burdens, indebted to foreign powers and unable to raise income except by levying export and import taxes, limited their patronage resources to granting land or franchises in return for political support. But this only served to strengthen centrifugal tendencies. The conflict between regionalism and centralism has been a major theme in the politics of independent Latin America.

To some extent this has been reflected in the broad division between 'conservatives' and 'liberals', with the former representing centralist control by a landowning elite, supporting clericalism and in favour of a low tariff so as not to interfere with their freedom to export agricultural products in return for manufactured goods. The liberals, for their part, were mostly merchants, professionals, townsmen and industrialists wanting greater freedom for state governments, the breakdown of corporate organizations and privileges, and especially communal land ownership which impeded unlimited free access to it. Not all 'conservatives' though, were anti-tariff. In Mexico, for example, Lucas Alamán was the leading spokesman for protection, especially for the textile industry threatened by cheap English imports. Liberals, by definition, believed in *laissez-faire* and yet industrialists needed tariff barriers to protect them against foreign competition. Many liberals also aspired to become land-owners and so came to have a vested interest in rural traditionalism. Such were some of the anomalies in political alignments which were groupings of rival families or interest groups rather than parties with clear ideological bases. We need to be aware of the semantic trap involved in using European concepts in a different social and economic context where they lack analytical precision.[1]

During the colonial period the system of checks and balances operated by the imperial government prevented the development of a feudal-style challenge to royal authority; when the French invasion of Spain in 1808 caused the collapse of the monarchy and the withdrawal of Spanish power at the centre, a legitimacy vacuum was caused which strong men tried to fill. The break-down of the *casta* society created a fluid political system in which socially mobile and politically ambitious mestizos became vocal in their demands. In the ensuing struggle for power, violence was endemic and accepted as a legitimate means of effecting political change while the *macho* characteristics of *caudillismo* became a model to be emulated.

Caudillismo flourished in the anarchical conditions of the early independence period and included many ex-officers from the patriot armies who had been enriched by grants of land as reward for their services. The haciendas, with a tied labour force of peons, became the economic and political base for the *caudillos'* operations, directed either against their neighbours in the struggle for land or against the state itself.

The Conquest involved sexual domination of the indigenous inhabitants, bequeathing a legacy of family instability, acceptance of the double standard of sexual morality and the subjugation of women. The *caudillo* epitomized and, by his behaviour, perpetuated the attitudes of this male-dominated society. He acquired prestige in the eyes of his followers by his sexual prowess and regarded his own womenfolk as valuable property assets, marrying off his daughters to cement alliances with potential rivals in the style of the dynastic marriages of feudal Europe.

As an economic unit, the hacienda took on new life after independence, for its self-sufficiency enabled it to weather the hazards of an open market economy, allowing the ruling landowning oligarchy to dominate most of the newly independent governments. As the central state grew weaker after independence, so the hacienda gained in strength and in the process increased the difficulties of national integration. Unlike nationalism in Europe or the United States, where the idea of the nation existed in the minds of men before the territorial organization of the state, in Latin America the reverse was true. The new states were artificial creations—their political borders as often as not following the line of administrative divisions of the Spanish Empire. Each new state, therefore, had to generate its own nationalist ethos but this had to be done in the absence of a firm framework for institutionalized politics. Politics thus remained personalized with *caudillos* rather than the nation providing a focus for loyalty.

Those *caudillos*, like Porfirio Díaz in Mexico, Rufino Barrios in Guatemala and Juan Vicente Gómez in Venezuela, who were able to establish themselves as national rulers and guarantee political stability, were welcome to foreign powers anxious to obtain new sources of raw materials and fields for investment.

Until the last third of the nineteenth century most *caudillos* represented family or regional interests; *caudillismo* was essentially a personalized form of political control and as such distinct from militarism or from the army acting as a political institution, with an espirit de corps growing out of the professionalism consequent on modernization. Unresolved disputes over political frontiers on the Pacific coast or in the River Plate Basin, provided an excuse for large military establishments and European-style arms races. The 'free security' which enabled the United States to keep its military establishment to a minimum, releasing huge sums to be channelled into frontier expansion, was denied to many Latin American countries both because of their mutual suspicions and because of internal civilian-military rivalries. When wars over frontier disputes did break out they stimulated developments in regions which had previously languished. Western Paraná in Brazil, for example, benefited from road building during the war with Paraguay in the late 1860s, and the need to supply the Paraguayan army stimulated some of the hitherto isolated farming regions of the Chaco during the war with Bolivia in the 1930s. But wars in Latin America, unlike the US Civil War and subsequent American wars, have not had comparable multiplier effects on the economy. Indirectly, however, frontiers of settlement have gained advantages from the military (much as the American West did from the US army's involvement) in road-building, colonization schemes, and internal communications.

Latin America provides very few examples of rural populist movements, which have their origins and roots in the countryside and seek to reaffirm rural values against those of the city. A prerequisite for a viable populist movement of this sort is the existence of a body of farmers or peasants who are able to organize independently, but the expansion of haciendas and the concentration of landownership has whittled down those available for this type of movement. The difficulties of organizing any sort of peasant resistance can be related to the density of dependency relationships in the country in which social institutions such as *compadrazgo* played an important role, creating a sense of mutual interdependence and obligation.

The history of rural Latin America has shown the reluctance of peasants to break out of dependency relationships in the absence of any alternative form of protection. Another factor has been the comparative lack of interest shown by urban radical movements in seeking allies among the rural population in their struggle with landowning elites. Urban populist parties such as those supporting Vargas in Brazil or Perón in Argentina have shown little interest in rural problems or in agrarian reform. In origin, many of these movements have risen in response to massive migration from the countryside and a large part of their energy has been absorbed by the effort of trying to incorporate the new migrants into a social and economic milieu where the slow pace of capital-intensive industrialization cannot provide employment opportunities. In return for political support the populist leader offers both psychic security and material benefits. Thus populist movements in Latin America should not be confused with Russian or American agrarian populism. They should be compared with Boss Tweed's New York City machine-politics rather than with the communitarian agrarian populism of the *narodniks* or the credit-conscious agrarian populism of the Mid-West or the Canadian Prairies.

One consequence of the massive influx of rural migrants into the cities has been to create pools of cheap labour. These 'peasants living in the city' show more interest in finding a niche within existing society than in overthrowing it while orthodox Marxists tend to regard marginal city dwellers as an unreliable lumpenproletariat. With the expansion of the marginal unemployed and underemployed, the established working class has become a labour aristocracy concerned with defending its own privileges rather than playing the role of revolutionary vanguard. This unheroic posture underlines the irrelevance to many Latin American radicals of the orthodox Marxist revolutionary strategy which assigns the crucial role in the revolutionary process to the urban proletariat. For them, the Cuban model of an intellectual elite in alliance with peasants and marginal groups offers a better prospect for success than urban workers corrupted by compromises made in return for security and higher wages. In Cuba the Sierra Maestra, where the guerrillas established their *foco*, was the one part of Cuba which might be described as a frontier region, thinly populated by squatters, vagrants, descendants of runaway slaves and criminals on the run.

Where frontier regions are the refuge of desperados and the habitat of bandits or of peasants at the mercy of natural forces beyond their control and of powerful landowners, they may seem to contain revolutionary potential; but the primitive rebellions of such areas rarely have revolutionary political or social overtones. The Sierra Maestra was unpromising tinder but it was sparked off by dedicated revolutionaries from the outside who were able to direct generalized feelings of discontent into specific revolutionary channels. When Fidel Castro referred to the Andes becoming the 'Sierra Maestra of Latin America' he was both stressing the key role which he expected peasants to play in the coming struggle and holding up the Cuban Revolution as a model. But the Cubans over-estimated the revolutionary potential of frontier regions as the failure of guerrilla campaigns in the 1960s showed.[2] Why was this?

The Cuban myth of the rural guerrilla had been deliberately cultivated in order to stress the continuity of the struggles of the 1950s with those of the independence war against Spain in the nineteenth century; thus the role of the urban resistance against Batista was underplayed and did not take into account different conditioning factors elsewhere. Earlier, in the 1920s in Brazil, the failure of the Prestes Column to raise the peasants of the backlands had already shown the difficulties facing anyone trying to rouse their revolutionary consciousness. Although geographical isolation favours guerrilla fronts, it creates logistical problems, and what is gained from being inaccessible to counter-guerrilla forces is offset by the difficulties of widening the guerrillas' own sphere of operations and linking up with urban movements. A successful guerrilla campaign also needs a minimum population density to become self-generating by expanding its support. In any case, many who live in frontier regions through choice do so because of the wish to escape from the pressures of society or because they see the frontier as the road to advancement and so have no wish to be drawn into political conflicts, especially as these might expose them to retaliation by counter-guerrilla forces against which the guerrillas might not be able to provide adequate protection. It seems unlikely, at least in the near future, that frontier regions will become cradles of revolution comparable to the Sierra Maestra.

Frontiers of the future

A glance at any population distribution map of South America graphically illustrates the way in which settlement is still very largely concentrated within a hundred miles or so of the sea-board. The reasons for this have been primarily geographical. The Andes have been a deterrent to settlement except by mining communities although they still remain an area of high density for a predominantly Indian population as during the pre-Columbian period. An even greater deterrent has been the great tropical forest fringe from Bolivia to the Guyanas through which drains the Amazon and its manifold tributaries. This huge area constitutes the last frontier of any significance, apart from the Canadian north and Alaska, in the Americas. In so far as there has been any development in this region it has been stimulated by periodic booms—cacao, quinine and most spectacularly, rubber and now, in eastern Ecuador, oil and, in northern Maranhão, minerals.

The problem of these empty spaces is highlighted by the case of Colombia, where some ninety-eight per cent of the population live in the highlands and the western escarpments of the Andes and on the coast, while the eastern areas, comprising half the country, remain virtually uninhabited. A cattle frontier has pushed into the Casanare and the Colombian *llanos*, but otherwise it is still substantially the untamed jungle of Rivera's *La vorágine*; the road peters out 70 miles or so east of Bogotá and is continued by jungle tracks along which tropical products are brought out of the forest on muleback. It is a similar story in the jungle regions of the Guyanas, Venezuela, Brazil, Peru and Bolivia.

The most ambitious projects to open up this area are occurring in Peru and Brazil, where road building programmes are designed to act as feeders for settlement and colonization. In Peru, this was the vision of Fernando Belaúnde. During his presidency between 1963 and 1968, a beginning was made in building a road from north to south along the eastern slopes of the Andes from which roads would branch off to penetrate the tropical valleys running east and west. This strategy was in complete contrast to traditional thinking about development which considered that Peru's future lay in the coastal region where irrigation schemes could reclaim the desert comparatively cheaply and drain off the surplus population of the economically backward highlands. Belaúnde's plan was based on his admiration for the Inca's road system and on the need to tap the resources of a potentially rich region, but the costs have been prohibitive in view of the small return. A major difficulty has been to attract migrants to move into the jungle in large numbers. The scheme presupposes a pioneer spirit sufficiently strong among highland dwellers to overcome the considerable rival attractions of migrating to the coastal region where obvious economic opportunities seem to lie. In this respect, Bolivia has been more fortunate in not having a rival coastal attraction; any internal migration must move eastwards, either to the fertile tropical valleys of the Yungas or to the vast unsettled savannah country of the Oriente which comprises about sixty per cent of the country but has only eleven per cent of the population. There have been examples of spontaneous migration of highland Indians into the Yungas although this involves considerable psychological, biological and cultural adjustment. The Oriente is the region offering greatest scope for the Bolivian entrepreneur (or for foreign colonists such as the Japanese) who would be inhibited by the revolutionary land legislation on the densely populated *altiplano*. As in the case of Peru, there is a strong geopolitical motive for filling in these empty spaces in the face of Brazilian westward expansion as already the Oriente, like Paraguay, is coming within Brazil's economic orbit.

These examples of frontier expansion pale in comparison with the scale of what is occurring in Brazil; here, the massive road building programme fanning out from Brasília is beginning to link isolated settlements like Belém and Manaus with the Brazilian heartland as well as pushing into virgin territory. A long-term aim for this policy is to siphon off surplus population from the northeast and to shift the distribution of Brazil's inhabitants. The roads will also facilitate the economic penetration of Brazil's neighbours, thus providing one stimulus to Spanish American countries to draw closer together in some sort of economic union, as in the Andean Pact.

Although it is tempting to draw parallels between Brazil's Marcha para Oeste and the westward expansion of the United States in the nineteenth century these should not be overdrawn. Brazil's expansion is taking place under the auspices of a military authoritarian government, highly favourable to capitalist and foreign interests. Brazil cannot expect to receive millions of European peasants already conversant with the techniques of mixed farming. Most migrants from the northeast are not farmers at all and many lack the pioneering spirit as well as the expertise for jungle farming. Primitive methods of slash-and-burn cultivation will only destroy the rich humus and exhaust the soil as previously happened in the *sertão*. There is the danger, however, that in the present mood of exuberant expansionism coupled with the desire for quick profit, some of the ecological problems connected with the destruction of jungle cover will be overlooked. Faced with the need to feed a rapidly growing population and responding to the stimulus of growing world demand for meat, cereals and timber, it is difficult for planners in a technocratic environment to resist the temptations of economies of scale and the application of intensive farming methods which may not be suitable to the particular conditions of Amazonia. Under pressures from vested interests, both Brazilian and foreign, the considerations of market demand are given higher priority than the establishment of viable rural communities. Transnational companies may be reaping the greater reward leaving Brazil with an ecological problem of fearsome proportions.

The pattern which seems to be emerging on Brazil's frontiers of a two-class society based on the *latifundio*, or its modern equivalent, the capital intensive agro-industrial enterprise, and the *minifundio*, often with insecurity of tenure, indicates that the modernization of agriculture does not necessarily imply structural changes or contribute towards the reduction of social and political inequalities. The new rural poor may now in fact be worse off as they have not even the sense of security which could be generated by old-style patrimonial relationships. There is a sense, too, in which an expanding frontier on the periphery can perpetuate authoritarian rule at the centre, acting as a safety-valve for urban discontents and political pressures.

Another aspect of Brazilian frontier expansion is that it is the last Indian frontier as the hitherto isolated tribes of jungle Indians become casualties of expanding settlement. There is a tradition of trying to preserve them from the worst excesses of Western influence, running from the Jesuit missions in the seventeenth century to the remarkable work of General Rondon in the early twentieth century and to the Vilas Boas brothers of today. Attempts have been made by the Indian Protection Service to save Indians from extinction by setting aside reserves in order to protect them from contamination by civilization, but whether the small groups of Indians inhabiting them can survive in the drive to modernity is an open question.

6

Comparative Perspectives

The purpose of comparative analysis is twofold—to discover similarities between like situations and so deduce regularities and frame generalizations and, by tracing differences between dissimilar situations, to pose new questions and suggest possible new lines of enquiry. In both cases working hypotheses can be framed about frontier societies but at present the challenge has gone virtually unheeded and we are far from anything approaching a comprehensive sociology of the frontier. No one has proceeded far beyond the pioneering book of J. G. Leyburn, *Frontier Folkways*[1] in which he compared what he considered to be the four main types of frontier experience—small farm, settlement plantation, exploitation plantation and mining camp—taking his examples from Massachusetts, the Reconcavo of Bahia, Australia, South Africa and French Canada.

Frontier settlement has been a recurrent phenomenon throughout recorded history and there is no limit to the comparisons which could be attempted. Geographers, dealing mainly with the process of settlement and historians and political scientists, more concerned with the influence of frontiers on institutions, have explored some of these comparisons but usually Latin America has been excluded, either because of ignorance or because it was felt that as a unique case, especially in the matter of timing, the differences were too wide to permit valid comparisons to be made. Argentina, however, has attracted some attention as it was an area of predominantly white settlement in a temperate climate, primarily during the nineteenth century and, being unaffected by slavery or sedentary Indians, had much in common with the other main areas of white settlement. Brazil with its own frontier consciousness and sense of Manifest Destiny is now beginning to attract similar attention.

Only by a knowledge of other areas can the unique features of a particular frontier's development be appreciated and a hierarchy of significance be given to the variables involved. How decisive are geographical and climatic factors, and is environment more important than the cultural attributes brought by settlers to the frontier? How important is the role of institutions inherited from the parent society? How crucial is timing, and once a pattern has been established during the initial period of expansion is it possible to break it, given the imperatives of capitalist economic development? What is the relationship between frontier expansion and economic growth? These are some of the questions which comparative study should attempt to answer. Most of the issues are too complex to be discussed in this section which is simply concerned to sketch some of the aspects which might be worth treating comparatively in greater detail.

In any analysis of the reasons why people migrate there are a complex of 'push' factors which force people to move out of a particular social, political and economic environment and 'pull' factors which attract people to move into one society rather than another. On the nature of these motivations will depend the level of expectations. Not every migrant moves to a frontier. For many, probably the majority, opportunity will lie in the cities but for others, peasants avid to own land, restless adventurers seeking fortunes in mining camps, religious sectarians anxious to build a City on a Hill, the outer limits of civilization will prove more attractive.

Push factors include lack of political and religious liberty, absence of economic opportunity, restricted possibilities of social mobility, land hunger and unemployment in the countries from which immigrants move. Clearly, the factors operating in Spain were different from those elsewhere. Spain was not an exporter of religious and political malcontents although in the latter half of the nineteenth century political motives do assume some importance and the desire to escape conscription was a major motive. Inflexible social attitudes, which made *hidalgos* prefer to be unemployed than to enter commerce, drove many to emigrate, while both land hunger and lack of economic opportunity were motives for less hidebound social groups, attracted also by the prospect of a captive labour force after living in a society where manual labour was traditionally despised.

In a different category is forcible exportation—the *degredados* of Brazil, the convicts of Tasmania and Botany Bay, the prostitutes cleared off the streets of Paris and transported to Saint Dominique—as well as the enforced migration of slaves throughout the Americas. Between free choice and compulsion there is a range of semi-free migration. This includes indentured labour, such as that in the seventeenth century to the Caribbean and Virginia, and contracted labour where the early years must be worked out in subordination to the contractor, as in the case of workers on the coffee plantations of São Paulo, East Indians in British Guyana and Chinese in Cuba.

Pull factors explain the lure of new lands—the hope of total renewal in a different social and political environment, expressed in a restless yearning for change and nourished on myth. But the 'land of the free' and the 'land of opportunity' in the popular vision of the United States, with its dynamic economy and political stability, contrasts with the sluggish economy, political instability and recurrent violence of Latin America (although Latin American history has nothing to compare with the scale and devastation of the American Civil War). To emigrate to Latin America, therefore clearly involved greater risks. Nevertheless, the El Dorado myth and the belief that the majority of Latin Americans lacked entrepreneurial drive encouraged many to seek a quick fortune and to return to Europe with no commitment to the country which had admitted them. Once the migration process has started, family links become crucial and are probably the biggest single generator of further migration financed by the all-important remittances. One has to distinguish between the initial impulse to migrate and what sustains the migration process in its later stages.

Geographical factors obviously play a key role in determining the pattern of settlement and in easing or hindering communication. In the far north of Canada and Alaska, the Cambrian Shield and the tundra conditions have deterred all but the hardiest prospectors, educators and missionaries.

Climatic obstacles no longer need be a deterrent to frontier expansion as current developments in Alaska now show, but a boom based on oil can be as temporary as earlier gold and fur booms. Daunting physical conditions, difficulties of food supply and transport make Arctic frontiers capital- rather than labour-intensive. Transients may be attracted by inflated wages but few except those wishing to embrace the wilderness would agree to settle there. If the boom ends it will be left as a frontier for the recluse or a playground for simulated adventure in a world of ice and snow. The 'wilderness controversy' provoked by environmentalist and preservation lobbies, with its nationalist undertones in Canada, goes to the heart of the dilemma of what to do with empty spaces. Preservation is not simply a romantic dream but has ecological implications which even developers should not ignore. Nevertheless, with the prospect of high profits and voracious markets they are ignored as the Brazilian case also shows. In Brazil, in contrast to the nineteenth century, it is no longer a question of sealing off the frontier to retain the labour force on coastal plantations but to attract cheap labour to new rural settlements by building roads into Amazonia, the other great American wilderness, thus obviating the need to pour money into the arid *sertão*. Although this development strategy of relying on out-migration may be a rational solution to what has been an intractable problem, its effectiveness is limited because many of these migrants lack the traits and skills needed for jungle pioneering. In order to create viable communities, resources need to be channelled into technical advisory agencies but, at present, many of the large companies operating in Amazonia seem to be more interested in migrants as a source of cheap labour.

Neither Brazil nor Canada can resort to the forced labour expedient, employed in the initial opening of the forbidding northern Siberian frontier, nor to the draft system, comparable to the *mita* of Upper Peru, used to solve the labour problem in the tundra silver mining region of Lapland in northern Sweden in the seventeenth century.

In the 1920s, Canadian historians were encouraged by their awareness of the importance of climate and geography and of the potential wealth of unsettled regions to apply Turner's ideas to their own history. Like Turner's desire to break with the Eurocentric interpretations of United States history, this was a means of breaking with the dominant British-oriented interpretations then in vogue. But although it concentrated attention on the contributions of the Canadian frontiersman, the frontier thesis has never dominated Canadian historiography, partly because of a counter-school of 'metropolitan' historians who argue that the key role in Canadian development has been played by cities—Montreal and Toronto and later Winnipeg and Vancouver. Such a metropolitan interpretation could be fruitfully applied to Latin America where cities have also played a dominant role.

Similarly, the staple theory of economic growth, by which Canadian historians have explained their country's economic development in terms of a cycle of export staples (fur, timber, wheat), could be compared and contrasted with the monoproductive export economies of Latin America. The consequences in the two cases have been very different. In Canada, the close reliance on Britain as an exporter of capital, immigrants and expertise provided an expanding market which helped to make Canada a rich country; even so it is now to a great extent economically dependent on the United States. From this sense of dependence springs a determination to retain control of the exploitation of potential frontier riches. Latin America also shares this feeling of dependence and thus frontiers both there and in Canada are serving to generate a new assertive nationalism. Nothing has roused more ardent feeling in Canada than the activities of mining and oil companies operating in frontier regions, or in Brazil those of Protestant fundamentalist sects proselytizing isolated Indians. When new wealth is discovered in outlying regions there is a determination to prevent its undue exploitation by foreign concerns although often it is only the heavily capitalized transnational companies who can afford the investment.

The importance of river transport is underlined, in Canada, by the role of the St Lawrence in opening up the interior of the continent, given primacy as a determinant in Canadian economic history by the 'Laurentian School'. In Latin America rivers did little to ease the transport problem. Rare cases of rivers opening up frontiers are those of the São Francisco in northeast Brazil, the gold-diggings of Cuiabá in Mato Grosso reached by a network of rivers from São Paulo, and the Magdalena River in Colombia. The River Plate never carried the volume of traffic its size warranted. The Amazonian rubber frontier was totally dependent on river transport but although the Amazon led to the heart of South America it could not fulfil a role similar to that of the St Lawrence or the Mississippi. The Amazon shares with the St Lawrence a pattern of riparian settlement and what has been written in respect to Canada before the British occupation might be applied to the Amazon.

> In contrast to the English colonies where the frontier became ever more remote from the settled areas along the seaboard, Canada was part and parcel of an all pervasive frontier, for all the houses of the colony had the river at their doorstep and along it came the men of the wilderness into the homes.[2]

The French *habitant* could have moved into the wilderness but he chose not to do so (when French Canadians did migrate they tended to move to the textile towns of New England and not to the English- or Scottish-dominated frontiers further west); but for the Amazonian river dweller the jungle effectively hemmed him in. Australia also suffered from lack of riverways but this was offset by coastal traffic linking the scattered urban nuclei, much the same as along the South American Pacific coast. There is no similar relationship between the 'urban frontier' and strategic river sites comparable to St Louis, Pittsburgh, Louisville and countless others in the United States or Québec, Montreal and Toronto in Canada.

In comparison with North America, railways played a limited role in opening up frontiers. There are, of course, the all-important exceptions of the Argentinian pampas, the São Paulo coffee frontier, the far north and south of Chile, and with reservations, Mexico where railways were largely built to service the mining industry but, by increasing land values and opening up urban markets, became a contributory factor behind the rising number of Indian disturbances in the latter half of the nineteenth century. The line penetrating the Andes up to Huancayo in the Peruvian Sierra, the one linking Guayaquil and Quito and that linking the Bolivian tin mines with the Pacific coast all connected existing settlements. The problems facing railway engineers elsewhere were almost insuperable and defied even an indomitable railway entrepreneur like Percival Farquhar, whose plans for the Southern Brazilian Railway came to nothing. The problems were graphically illustrated by the Madeira-Mamoré Railway, 'going from nowhere to nowhere' but built to fulfil the terms of the 1903 treaty as compensation for Bolivia's loss of Acre in the conflict with Brazil three years earlier. The railway, reputed to have cost a life per sleeper, by-passed the cataracts on the River Madeira which used to cause twenty per cent losses among the crews of the clumsy ten-ton boats bringing rubber out of the Bolivian jungle. It gave Bolivia an outlet on the Amazon but it never fulfilled Farquhar's dream to open up one of the 'earth's potentially richest regions'. It is now an unused museum piece.

In a sense Latin America has missed the railway age. Although railways have been built recently, in the Bolivian Oriente for example, road and air traffic are relatively more important and less than one fifth of the continent is within 20 miles of a railway.[3] The railway has never quite enjoyed that position as a symbol of progress or alternatively as a destroyer of the pastoral idyll which we find in North America. It does, however, stand as a symbol of foreign capitalism, for instance in the network of the previously British-owned railways in the pampas and the American-built lines in Mexico.

Railways in Latin America never played the role of stimulating urbanization as they did in North America. The middle decades of the nineteenth century in the United States saw an unprecedented rise in the establishment of new towns. To find a comparable example we would have to go back to sixteenth-century Spanish America where the extraordinary spate of town-founding was due as much to the *pobladores'* desire to achieve fame and the belief that cities were synonymous with civilization as to functional need. Differences between the two were startling. Most Latin American 'cities' remained isolated outposts, many remaining static for a century or more, increasing by natural growth rather than by immigration from outside. Apart from mining cities, they tended to be commercial or bureaucratic centres. Spanish and English attitudes to city life are highlighted by the splendour of the Spanish Caribbean city like Havana, Santo Domingo, Santiago de Cuba, in contrast to the squalor of the urban outposts of the English Caribbean, and by the Georgian magnificence of planter residences in contrast to the poverty of Spanish rural architecture. In the Caribbean we can see coexisting two similar slave plantation systems but each with different conceptions about the merits or otherwise of rural life. These contrasts reflect traditions in the parent countries—as does the English addiction to and Spanish disinterest in landscape painting.

In the United States, the major part of trans-Mississippi urbanization was accompanied by industrialization. Industry, when it comes to the Spanish American town, has to be grafted on to a pre-industrial base. The combination of frenetic 'boosterism', real estate speculation (often by Easterners) and railway promoters is absent from Latin America. In

Argentina, railroads were given concessions in return for stimulating colonization but urban growth in the pampas remained minimal. In São Paulo state alone can we find some parallel, with *grileiros*, railway and settlement companies advancing in unison. Here we can talk of an 'urban frontier'. The Brazilian pattern of settlement is distinctive and Brasília remains the supreme example in Latin America of an 'urban frontier'—a deliberate artificial creation to serve as a magnet drawing settlers in to the uninhabited interior.

We should not be misled by similarities in grid-iron city groundplans which were common to both the United States and Spanish America. In the former, the motive was largely utilitarian—it meant ease of surveying; in the latter, it was a deliberate act of empire, symbolizing the bureaucratic desire for uniformity and order. The centrality of the plaza in Spanish American cities symbolizes the unity of Church and state which in a culture of religious pluralism would be impossible. Which sect could allow its rival to occupy the central site confronting the town hall?

The most striking feature of frontier expansion in the eighteenth and nineteenth centuries was the occupation of huge tracts of grasslands—the Canadian prairies, the Great Plains of the United States, the Argentinian pampas, the South African veldt, the Hungarian plain, the Russian steppes and the Australian outback.

Generally speaking, when grasslands were exploited as pastoral undertakings we find a 'big man's frontier', as in Australia, Argentina, New Zealand, and in the cattle areas of Texas, the Mid-West and Alberta. Cattle and horse frontiers produce independent herders who are often taken to symbolize the national virtues as, for instance, Martín Fierro in Argentina or Petöfi's glorification of the Gikos of the Hungarian plain; together with Cossacks and Tabuntchiks in Russia, the Mongolian herdsmen on Asia's inner frontiers, and the Boer herdsmen in the African veldt, they share many of the same values and culture traits. But although they may be taken as a criterion against which to measure degrees of freedom, they share the ambivalence (as the history of Cossacks amply shows) observed earlier of being pastoral democracies to the insider but despotisms to the outsider.

Where grasslands have become wheatland as in Canada and the United States, wheat can become a family farmer's crop. Argentina, however, is mostly an exception to this generalization. When large areas of the pampas were converted from cattle ranching to more profitable wheat growing, the size of the operating units was reduced, but *estancieros* retained control and rented out land. The shift from beef to wheat did not affect land tenure as previously it had in the case of the shift from sheep to dairy farming in New Zealand, a replacement of extensive by intensive farming.

Historians have explained the contrast between Australia's big man's frontier and the US family farm by the fact that the Australian government confirmed the holdings of the squatters, the sheep farmers, backed by banks linked to Yorkshire woollen interests, instead of implementing the homestead legislation of the Free Selection Acts. The fact that land had to be paid for enabled the pastoralists to win out over the agriculturists much as they had done, for different reasons, in Argentina in the 1820s. Land policy in Australia had been consciously dictated by the intention to recreate a hierarchical rural society, an image of the English gentry on whom the upstart squattocracy based themselves even to the extent of establishing English-style public schools, much as Argentinian *estancieros* did. Given inadequate rainfall and vast distances together with the demands of Yorkshire mills, the economy of scale in Australian pastoralism made sense. The persuasive arguments of Gibbon Wakefield in such writings as *Letters from Sydney* of 1829 were also an important influence; he claimed that only by keeping the price of land high would it be possible to subsidize immigration and put land beyond the reach of poor immigrants and so ensure a pool of cheap labour. Wakefield's ideas, specifically formulated to avoid the 'forced equality' of Americans who are 'rotten before they are ripe', were to exert some influence on Brazilian planters in the Land Law of 1850, anxious to seal off the frontier from European immigrants. In practice, however, this legislation failed to prevent extensive squatting although the difficulties of jungle farming kept most *posseiros* at a subsistence level.

The increase in the number of corporations in the Australian outback linked to British banks and Yorkshire woollen interests was paralleled in Argentina by the growth of speculative land companies whose successful pressuring of government nullified homestead legislation, and with some exceptions, as in Santa Fe's agricultural colonies, ensured that Argentina would remain a big man's frontier. In the Argentinian case, pastoralism expanded in a symbiotic relationship with British manufacturing exports (in Britain itself beef producers found their interests overridden by industrialists' desire to retain markets in Argentina). But unlike the Australian case where initial dependence on pastoral exports did not inhibit industrial growth, in Argentina the obverse was true. In Australia industrialization occurred as a complement to and not in competition with sheep-grazing. Part of the explanation for this divergence lies in the contrast between the success of the Australian Labour party with its residual Chartist and Irish radical tradition and the failure of the Argentinian Radical party (both of which grew up in opposition to the rural landed elite) to back protective tariffs and support a policy of industrialization. It required a Perón to implement industrial protection. The Radicals' failure between 1916 and 1930 throws light on the mentality of first- and second-generation immigrants who were content to leave the basic economic structure undisturbed so long as openings were available in commerce, government service and the professions.

A major consequence of the pastoral ascendancy in Australia and in Argentina, as with planter ascendancy in Brazil, was to give a further stimulus to urbanization and to deflect interest away from a concern with agrarian matters. In Brazil, for example, the writings of Alberto Torres in the early decades of the twentieth century placed a Jeffersonian emphasis on the need to encourage the growth of an independent yeomanry as the prerequisite for national regeneration; yet they went unheeded by those radicals like the *tenente* movement of young officers in the 1920s and 1930s who were otherwise deeply influenced by his nationalist ideas. In Argentina, radical movements, whether Radical, Socialist or Communist were comparatively uninterested in rural problems except for opportunistic reasons. Denied the support of urban groups small farmers throughout Latin America have been unable by themselves to assume active political roles. There has been no equivalent of the mass agrarian populism of the United States or Canada.

The newly formed Radical party in Argentina did champion the cause of discontented farmers in Santa Fe in 1893 but the farmers' protest shared very few of the characteristics of North American populism. It was not a rural-versus-urban phenomenon; it was not directed against financial interests which, in the United States, were held responsible for the farmers' plight; it was not underpinned by monetarist demands, for Argentine farmers stood to gain from the cattle sector's policy of expanding the money supply. The protest was directed rather against burdensome taxes and against high-handed action by provincial authorities; it was in favour of uncorrupt and responsible municipal government and against the monopoly of provincial power by a narrow 'political class'; it was essentially a farmers' movement and little interest was shown in either tenant-farmers or the agricultural proletariat. This example of political action among immigrant farmers, especially Swiss who were the most active, may have been exceptional; generally they tended to avoid political involvement, often preferring to move once an area became politically disturbed, like the Germans and Swiss in Misiones and Entre Ríos. The case of the German-Brazilians who organized Nazi cells in Rio Grande do Sul in the 1930s had racial and political not economic origins. The Canadian example shows how farmers' movements can swing either to the left as, for instance, Saskatchewan's CCF (Cooperative Commonwealth Federation) or to the right, as with Alberta's Social Credit party, the swing being determined by specific political traditions.

In racial terms many Latin American frontiers were frontiers of inclusion in contrast to the frontiers of exclusion in other areas of white settlement. The absence of stable family migration, coupled with the shortage of white women and the lack of an inhibiting Puritan sexual ethic encouraged widespread miscegenation which helped to break down racial exclusiveness. It is possible to talk of biological adaptation to the environment as mestizos and mulattoes acquired immunity to diseases, and a distinctive hybrid culture emerged in which Indian, European and African traits were fused. This, however, was mainly confined to areas of dense settlement or to those frontiers which were a haven to runaways and vagrants. Where there was a 'hard' frontier between settlers and nomadic Indians as in Argentina, the pattern of relations between the races was little different from other areas of white settlement. Argentinians showed themselves as skilled and ruthless in exterminating pampas Indians as the first settlers in Tasmania had been in wiping out the indigenous islanders.

One account of General Roca's War of the Desert 1879–83 puts it:

> the advance of civilizing forces crusaded into the desert in a decisive effort to defeat the tribes of savage Indians that terrorized, stole and killed Argentine settlers that struggled to build a peaceful and productive country on the Buenos Aires frontierland. Argentine soldiers established Christianity, order and the benefits of liberty to all that submitted to the way of life that their flag stands for.[4]

Whereas Mapuches or descendants of the Araucanians have recently led a revindication movement in neighbouring Chile, there are now no pampas Indians left to do so; such was one legacy of Sarmiento's brutalizing liberalism.

This was seen as part of the civilizing process. Attitudes towards Indians were not simply conditioned by fear and strangeness but often also by preconceptions formed even before crossing the Atlantic. Views on slavery in Latin America were shaped by experience of enslaving captives taken in the wars against the 'infidel' whose civilization was despised by the crusading mentality. Indians were enslaved in the English colonies but it was a rare practice, possibly because of the fear of reprisal but also because of ambivalent attitudes towards Indians in contrast to unequivocal attitudes towards negroes. To many frontiersmen, extermination was in any case a preferable alternative as Indian labour was not essential. Whether death occurred by disease, wars or through degeneration, caused as often as not by alcohol, was immaterial. The callousness of such attitudes was partly engendered by the 'pacification' of Ireland: wars of attrition against 'savage' Catholic peasants provided a schooling for future colonists, the lessons of which were put to good use by the Scots-Irish, many of whom were to be found on the outermost fringes of the frontier.

More tolerant attitudes by French settlers in North America may be partly due to the overriding importance of the trappers' frontier and the symbiotic relationship between French trader and Indian trapper which it engendered (paralleled in the case of the British in the Hudson's Bay Company and in the Ohio Valley, although British trapper-traders were outnumbered by agricultural settlers and this was not the case in New France). Moreover, France, unlike Spain and England, did not have a contiguous region of 'savages' at home against whom wars of pacification had been waged and in which attitudes had hardened. In Italy, the main area of French activity abroad in the sixteenth century (apart from the 'corsair-frontier' of the Mediterranean), it was the French who were *i barbari*. It would be heartening to think that their tolerance was also a result of the gentle humanism of Montaigne but that would be to overestimate the influence of secular intellectuals at that time.

However, the most devastating consequences of frontier expansion everywhere has been the impact of disease. If there is any common factor uniting the multifarious experiences of frontier expansion, it has been the impact of European-borne diseases on indigenous peoples. This, rather than the triumph of 'civilization' with all its putative advantages over 'barbarism', however this polarity is defined, has been the common experience of the conquered. The numbers of Europeans who died from tropical diseases or who were killed in frontier wars are a drop in the ocean compared to those who died from the simplest European diseases in what a historian, referring to the Americas, has graphically called the 'War of the Worlds'.[5] Paradoxically, those colonial policies designed to segregate indigenous peoples from Europeans, as in the United States reservation policy, have enabled many tribes to survive and to rebuild their culture. Whether attempts to move Brazilian Indians onto reservations will save them from extinction is seriously open to doubt. The humanitarian issue concerns foreigners more than Brazilians who are often irritated by critics from countries which have cared little for their own indigenous peoples in the past and whose propaganda is sometimes interpreted, together with arguments for population control, as part of a wider conspiracy on the part of developed nations to hinder Brazil's development. Unlike the Aleuts in Alaska, whose land rights have been recognized and whose future as nascent capitalists seems assured, the future for Brazilian Indians looks bleak—either extermination by heedless settlers, or a slow degeneration on the fringes of a non-caring society or as a spectacle for jaded tourists, gawping at the tribal ceremonies of a world lost.

Alcohol, as well as disease, was a weapon of conquest and a means of social control among migrant workers as the case of South Africa shows most graphically. Previously unknown to North American Indians, whose metabolism could not cope with its effects, its introduction helped both to destroy societal bonds and to create a stereotype of the drunken Indian which perpetuated the settlers' feeling of superiority. In Latin America, alcohol was a less decisive factor mainly because Indians had their own fermented liquor before Europeans arrived and because drinking had become ritualized. When these rituals begin to break down and are replaced by anomic drinking it is a sure sign that a society has come under severe strain. Alcohol was a staple in all frontier societies, from the whiskey mash accepted by curates on the Kentucky frontier in lieu of tithes, to the *cachaça*, or sugar brandy, which made life bearable in the jungle diggings of Cuiabá. It would be impossible to prove quantitatively that drunkenness was more rife in frontier societies than in overcrowded industrial towns but, in the absence of alternative pleasures, those of drinking figured very highly.

Racial attitudes were modified only where the skills of indigenous peoples were admired and coveted. For instance, on trapping frontiers the Mountain Men and more especially the *coureurs de bois* of French Canada depended on the cooperation of Indians for their success in tracking beavers. Mating with Indian women, wearing their native dress, speaking their language and adopting their superbly efficient birch-bark canoe, the *coureurs de bois* (or the *voyageurs* as they were known in the eighteenth century) became culture heroes for later generations much as the *bandeirantes* in Brazil. For French Canadians, the *coureur de bois* with his feckless, carefree ways was the antithesis of the penny-pinching, austere Scottish merchant of Montreal who came to dominate commerce after the fall of French Canada; for environmentalists concerned with preserving the wilderness, his respect for the natural habitat contrasted with the frontiersman as destroyer—the trader introducing natives to rum and whiskey, the axeman of the North American forests or the *machadeiro* of the Brazilian jungle, the slash-and-burn cultivators (copied from natives but carried out on a scale which created a wasteland as in the *sertão*), the Mid-West farmer making dustbowls through overcultivation—all those, in other words, for whom 'taming the wilderness' was too often a euphemism for destroying it.

The *métis*, the offspring of the union of French Canadians and Indian women, became a political problem in the 1860s and 1880s when their settlements in Manitoba and Saskatchewan held up the expansion of settlers moving west from Ontario. Defence of their hunting lands in 1869 and 1884 required the dispatch of troops and the execution of their leader Louis Riel, who has since become a French Canadian hero and a symbol of the resistance to bulldozing frontier expansion represented by the building of the transcontinental railway.

Religion often provided a justification for racial exclusiveness, as in New England and South Africa where Old Testament exhortations were taken literally. The presence of missionaries on the Spanish American frontier, symbolized in the solidity of church and mission buildings, played a more important role in 'civilizing' frontier areas than secular institutions. As the English North American frontier expanded, the absence of an educated clergy left the frontiersman dependent on a personal interpretation of the Bible or on no religion at all, and in so far as the church was interested in proselytization it was among godless settlers rather than savage Indians who were regarded as being beyond redemption.

In New England some Puritans took missionary activity seriously although paying little attention to Indian needs. A college was built at Harvard to educate Indians in the classical curriculum but the funds for this, raised in parish collections in England and also for a similar college in Virginia which never materialized, were diverted to offset company losses. Neither the Harvard experiment nor the Franciscan's college at Tlatelolco in Mexico to train an Indian priesthood, succeeded and the Harvard college was demolished in 1695 after graduating only one Indian student. In Mexico no Indian priest graduated. Early Puritan concern was swept aside by King Philip's war of 1675, which occurred just before the great Pueblo revolt of 1680 forced the Spaniards to evacuate New Mexico. Thus on both English and Spanish frontiers, almost simultaneously, Indian–white relations deteriorated and were to continue to do so throughout the eighteenth century—in the English colonies under pressures of ever increasing numbers of immigrants moving into Indians' woodland hunting grounds; and in northern New Spain from raiding Apache and Comanche horsemen goaded by Spanish attempts to enslave them. The British, concerned with the French threat, felt compelled to militarize their Indian policy, seeking allies among friendly tribes. The Spaniards also militarized their frontier policy, as settlements became exposed to horse-borne attacks: in the eighteenth century the *presidio* becomes more important than the mission.

Because missionaries in North America abandoned proselitizing among Indians and concentrated on converting settlers, there is little to correspond to that penumbral area of religious syncretism which is a feature of Latin American frontiers. Throughout Latin America, the hold of the Catholic Church on frontier areas became tenuous once the missions had been secularized and the Jesuits expelled, and with the shortage of priests and the low educational level of those there were, and with no alternative sect tradition, religion easily relapsed into primitivism. This might take an exaggerated form of folk Catholicism, an amalgam of Catholic and pre-Catholic beliefs, in which Mariolatry becomes confused with the worship of pre-Hispanic deities, spiritism echoing Iberian traditions, the frenzy of backlands messianism tinged with Africanisms or of withdrawal religions such as peyotism, in which the hallucinative properties of the peyote cactus induces trances. Apart from specifically religious communities like the Mennonites and Hutterites, religion has not inculcated economic virtues or legitimated economic success as it has with the Mormons or with ascetic North American frontier sectarianism. The frozen wealth of baroque church decoration and the ephemeral gaudiness of fiestas is evidence of the absence of the Protestant ethic.

The main parallel to Latin America's mission frontier is to be found in French Canada: the missions of the early seventeenth century in Huronia were run by the Jesuits and the Recollets, although Protestant and Catholic missions were also active among Indians and Eskimos from the 1860s. The failure to assimilate Indians into French society led to attempts to segregate French and Indians (the influence of the *coureurs de bois* was deplored by the missionaries), much as the Jesuits tried to do in Latin America. But the exigencies of the military frontier between rival French and British forces undermined the missionaries' efforts as each side sought to win over Indians by gifts of arms, alcohol and trade.

The importance of religion as a consolidating factor in successful settlement in the wilderness cannot be exaggerated. There is the supreme example of the Mormons and also the Welsh in Chubut and the 'Jewish gauchos' of the pampas. But there can come a point, as in the case of the Mennonite colony in Mexico, where inability to relate culturally to the surrounding population limits success.

Sects can be divisive; the byzantine intricacies of sectarian differences, with their complex sociological roots and equally complex theological justifications, were a feature of the North American frontier experience which does not seem to be paralleled on other frontiers. The anti-intellectualism and fervour of some sects may be explained as a reaction against the restrictions of East-Coast religious establishments, in Virginia for example, and this itself may have provided one motive for moving to the frontier, much as it had for the Puritans coming to America in the first place.

The frontier, in fact, became the breeding ground for enthusiastic evangelism, where the Great Awakening and the sects were to find their most passionate adherents in Canada as well as the United States, reflecting the aspirations of simple frontier folk against sophisticated Easterners. The itinerant preacher, the circuit rider, the hell-fire sermon, the frontier camp meeting—that 'unique American contribution to Christianity'—and a basic fundamentalism propounding simple pieties and simplistic solutions played an integral part in North American frontier life.

In frontiers in a Catholic culture, enthusiasm is harder to restrain. When it occurred, for instance, in the heretical implications of miracle-working and messianism in northeast Brazil or in the flagellatory excesses of the Penitentes in New Mexico the hierarchy intervened. There would seem to be a *prima facie* case for supposing that such religious tensions would provide a fertile breeding ground for Protestant sects. However, apart from missions among isolated Indians, many of whom had been untouched by Catholicism, the majority of converts to Protestantism in Latin America have been in poor urban areas. The comfort, sense of community and equality deriving from folk Catholicism and supporting institutions like *cofradías* outweigh the putative advantages of Protestant individualism. In the same way as Catholics have tended to concentrate on urban parishes in the United States (bishops encouraging Catholic colonies in the West did not meet with a great response) so Protestants in Latin America have had greater success in poor urban areas. Where the frontier provided opportunities, as in North America, a premium was placed on those values exalted by the Protestant ethic.

Some doubts have nevertheless been expressed about the innovatory features of frontier Protestantism. What can be said in positive terms is that rivalry in the educational field between Protestant sects was responsible for stimulating the growth of colleges throughout the West which were to become nuclei of future universities, with Yale patronizing Unitarian and Princeton Presbyterian foundations. Rivalry between Protestants and Catholics spurred on proselytization and, in the 1830s and 1840s, such fiery tracts as Beecher's *Plea for the West* expressed fears that the West was being won for Popery. In Canada in the nineteenth century and in Latin America in the twentieth, Protestants and Catholics engaged in missionary rivalry among Indians who often became casualties of a conflict they could not understand.

In French Canada where Protestants had very little influence, Catholic parish priests, anxious to prevent emigration from tightly controlled and overpopulated rural areas to New England textile towns, with the threat which this might imply to traditional social and religious ties, initiated their own colonization schemes. But these had only minimal effect: New England and New Hampshire rather than the cold wastes of northern Québec or infertile lands further east continued to be the frontier for migrant *québecois*, excluded by American, English and Scottish settlers from moving to Ontario and by the failure of Riel's rebellion from moving farther west.

In North America, wherever a Protestant Church was established it would be accompanied by a Protestant school. Literacy was essential to enable the Protestant to tap the solace and inspiration of the Bible. The schoolhouse was a symbol of community life and the school mistress a softening influence in what was often a harsh environment. From primary schools, to high schools and land-grant colleges, the North American frontier was amply served with educational institutions, complemented by the fringe activities of itinerant peddlers of culture selling self-improvement manuals. Not only schools but touring drama companies, libraries, together with temperance bands and other moral and mind-improving associations, flourished in the North American frontier environment.

Sarmiento, who visited the United States in 1847 was so impressed by the influence of education on democratic mores that on his return to Argentina he campaigned to improve educational standards, especially in rural areas, as the only way to stem the encroachments of 'barbarism'. Elsewhere in Latin America governments were slow to respond to educational needs. In Mexico, for example, it was not until the 1920s that any government responded to the challenge of illiteracy by inaugurating a rural school programme. Where there was any expression of cultural activity on Latin American frontiers it tended to emphasize the gap between the elite and the masses as reflected by the opera houses at Manaus, Iquique and Copiapó.

Literary forms reflected the way in which North American frontiersmen were people of the Book. In this literary culture much of the spontaneity of oral cultures was lost: the Bible became the source of imagery, of metaphor and of moral precept. In Latin America, illiteracy placed a high premium on memory: legends and myths were handed down verbally and often in song as in the frontier balladry of medieval Spain, the *chanson de gestes*, in Mexican *corridos* and the ballads of the Brazilian backlands. The rich variety and complexity of Latin American folk music and legend contrasts with the relative scarcity of its North American counterpart, although oral legends have their parallel among North American Indians, and to a lesser extent, Blacks.

School, church and family were the major socializing influences on the North American frontier where, in Turner's words, 'complex society is precipitated by the wilderness into a kind of primitive organization based on the family', inculcating the values of individual endeavour and self-help. If, in Latin America, this particular sense of democratic community with popular decision-making was absent, the extended family, kinship ties, *compadrazgo* (the Brazilian *compadresco*) and religious fiestas provided a compensating feeling of community as well as being a form of insurance, although its strength varied according to the density of settlement.

Compadrazgo implies mutual obligation and commitment. In Latin America it has been a device for cementing the relationship between patron and retainer as well as for integrating different ethnic groups (those which necessarily have to have contact with each other), as when

Spanish or mestizo settlers act as baptismal godparents for Indian children or adults. *Compadrazgo* also provides a form of sexual protection in scattered communities where the husband might have to leave his wife for long periods; thus a man can neutralize his wife's potential lover by forming a ritual relationship with him, as sexual intercourse is forbidden between *compadres* and *comadres*.

The area of family organization is one where comparisons are difficult. Detailed accounts of family life enable us to reconstruct sex roles on the North American frontier but faced with lack of evidence in Latin America the historian must beware of stereotypes and rely on the work of social anthropologists. One detailed study of family life in Ouro Preto in the eighteenth century seriously challenges the stereotype, too readily accepted under Freyre's influence, of the pervasiveness of the extended family, by showing that in this town at least it was an exception and that the nuclear or matrifocal family predominated. Mining communities may be an exception in this as in many things, and the Ouro Preto case might be simply a consequence of unstable cross-racial unions, but it is possible that women did play a more important role, as shopkeepers and even as mineowners, on the Brazilian mining frontier than in North America where they were often conspicuous by their absence.

It is on the gold and silver frontiers that some of the sharpest contrasts may be drawn between Latin America and elsewhere. In Latin America the mines were the motors of the colonial economy. They were also a major factor in extending the scope of royal power, as illustrated by the tight control exercised over the Brazilian diamond fields in the eighteenth century. Mines were a major stimulus to urban settlement and the architectural magnificence of Latin American mining cities, like Guanajuato, Zacatecas, San Luis Potosí, Ouro Preto and Potosí where the magnates vied with each other in their magnificent patronage of church building, could not provide a greater contrast to the makeshift, sleazy air of the mining towns of California, the Canadian Northwest, Victoria and New South Wales. Whereas Latin American mining magnates would take pride, like Renaissance princes, in embellishing the towns where their fortunes were made, the mining moguls of California or the Comstock Lode built their architectural extravaganzas, in true nouveau riche style, back on San Francisco's Nob Hill.

Differences between silver and gold mining cities may be explained by the greater need for organization required in high technology silver mining, dependent on a disciplined work force on one side and the individualistic nature of gold panning on the other. Even in Minas Gerais where the use of slaves and tight royal control brought a semblance of order into gold digging, there was always the freelance illegal activity of the *garimpeiros* and *faisqueiros* and in Central America of the *güirises*.

But whereas Latin America could produce its individualistic prospectors, like the protagonists of B. Traven's novel *Treasure of the Sierra Madre,* there was little to compare to the great cosmopolitan gold rushes of California, the Klondike and Victoria, drawing on a huge floating population of expectant miners many of whom were 'Old Californians'. The discovery of gold in Minas Gerais in the 1690s sparked off the first great gold rush of modern history but it was confined to drawing migrants from Portugal and Brazil's northeast coast and never reached the scale of the 80,000 persons who arrived in California in a single year in 1849. Although violent and brash, the mining camps of the United States had their schools and cultural activities and were imbued with a democratic, not to say at times anarchical, spirit, but there was another darker side. The mining camps brought to the surface the latent racism which was an integral part of the North American frontier experience. Mexicans, Peruvians and Chileans who had been attracted to the fields found themselves discriminated against and the object of crude nativist feeling.

The reason for this feeling initially was simple: Latin Americans had the mining skills lacked by the Anglos and so were envied for their early success. Once their techniques had been learnt they became pariahs, compelled to pay taxes under the Foreign Miners Tax Law of 1850, physically threatened and eventually driven out of the diggings. The alternatives were either to take to banditry—Joaquín Murieta was not simply a figment of Pablo Neruda's Yankeephobia and the *bandidos* of Southern California have become part of that state's folklore—or to drift to growing towns like Los Angeles, San Francisco or Sacramento, or to be employed as hired hands in the New Almadén mercury mines where a pattern was established of Anglo mechanics and skilled labour, overseeing Latin unskilled labour, which was to be repeated in countless mines throughout the southwest and even in Mexico itself.

In Australia the story was similar. The comparative lack of racial prejudice of the early years changed with the gold rush. The 40,000 Chinese, in particular, found themselves the object of abusive and violent treatment as their willingness to work for lower wages threatened to depress the general level. This was the case too in California but the Chinese had their uses, not only in the transcontinental railway gangs (which also recruited Mexicans), but also because, being more patient, they were prepared to work over claims which they bought from white miners who had deserted them. In Idaho in 1870s, for example, after strikes in Montana had drained away many white miners, some 4,274 out of a population of 15,000 were Chinese—well described as 'harbingers of decline'.

Some of the most violent nativist feeling was expressed by Irish Catholics who had themselves been subjected to discrimination in the

East. But, whereas in the United States and Australia nativist feeling was directed against those lowest in the social scale, in Latin America where few foreign miners were to be found, nativist feeling was directed against foreigners in managerial positions, or privileged and better-paid foreign technicians.

Latin American silver and gold mining frontiers did not generate the sort of grassroots radicalism which was such a feature of the Victorian gold diggings. There is no Latin American equivalent of the Eureka stockade. One of the reasons why the 'diggers' entered into Australian mythology was the legacy of bitterness felt among unemployed miners, after the boom burst, at the failure of land legislation in the 1860s to establish homesteads. This gave a fillip to that collectivist spirit which has been such a feature of Australian working class politics. There were frustrated gold miners in California too but many were able to squat on the uncultivated ranches of the *californios*. Fortunately for them, the California legislature was not inhibited by such considerations as Wakefield's doctrine of the sufficient price and many of their claims were upheld although often after complex legal wrangles. However, it was not so easy for Mexicans, expelled from the diggings, to acquire land in this way and those who did get land were often forced off. This seems to have been one motive for Joaquín Murieta turning to banditry. By no means all unsuccessful miners wanted land. Many were temperamentally maimed by the mining experience. There is a parallel between the 'buddy' or partner complex of mining prospectors and the male camaraderie of soldiers. Both find difficulty in readjusting to normal life and seek to recapture that heightened sense of comradeship which comes from shared excitement and danger. Migratory sheep shearers created a similar type of 'chum culture' and the Australian outback must bear some of the responsibility for producing the violent feminist reaction of recent years. 'Old Californians' felt a similar rootlessness and instability to those Civil War veterans who took to cattle work. Instability in Latin America fed the restless and malcontents into cattle herding but there was very little in mining experience to correspond with the mobile armies of miners of the American Far West.

The presence of women may have exercised a stabilizing and softening influence in male-dominated societies and their absence or shortage could become a pretext for disturbance as in the early days of Potosí, Ouro Preto or in the Far Western mining camps. Prostitutes inevitably figure prominently in these societies and brothels are social centres, perhaps specializing in those *Francesinhas* who, together with French nuns were the most active agents of French influence abroad in the nineteenth century.[6] It is too readily assumed though, under the influence of film and the dime novel, that frontier societies were necessarily violent and that the absence of restraints and of stable family life encouraged banditry and lawlessness. This is a misleading picture as studies of both cattle towns and mining camps in the United States have shown. Frontier violence, always excepting Indian wars and incidents like the Sand Creek Massacre, pale in comparison with violence in nineteenth-century American cities. The period between 1840 and 1860 may have been the era of greatest urban violence that America has ever experienced. Unfortunately, we lack comparable detailed studies of violence in Latin America, partly because its institutionalization (as the vocabulary of military coups reveals) means that it was too often taken for granted. Changes of power by violent methods did not incur the opprobrium similar coups would have done in North America.

Much of the work of social anthropologists has been concerned with explaining the infinitely complex mechanisms whereby 'primitive' societies seek to *avoid* conflict and to ritualize it when it is inevitable. What is difficult to determine is what constraints operate on those who are thrown into a frontier environment after being reared under the controls of a more ordered society, and what is the effect on their behaviour of prior conditioning factors. The outbreak of banditry in southern California in the 1850s, for example, has been explained in terms of an extension of the unsettled condition of northern Mexico after the wars of independence as well as of the inability of men, torn from tight village communities, to adapt to a more mobile existence. It is not sufficient to attribute outbreaks of violence to the much overworked concept of *machismo*. Male virtues might be praised in cowboy ballads, *payadas* and in *corridos* and the 'tough-guy' and *macho* may have been models to emulate, but their prevalence in reality should not be exaggerated. There is a sense in which the stereotype becomes the model on which subsequent behaviour is based and thus is self-perpetuating, but even in Latin America *machismo* is often regarded as an aberrant form of behaviour.

Nevertheless, there are degrees of lawlessness and violence and the opening of the Canadian West was a more orderly process than in the United States (whereas the contemporary Brazilian West may be surpassing it in disorderliness). A mining frontier which expanded first under the umbrella of the paternalist Hudson's Bay Company and then of imperial control in the Columbia River strike of 1858 was not to the liking of 'Old Californians' who left in disgust—as much at tighter controls than in the United States as at poor returns. The Canadian West was not opened up by laissez-faire but by systematic design on the part of the British government which feared American encroachment into unsettled areas and the draining off by American railroads of prairie wealth. Government intervention was also necessary as geographical obstacles deterring migrants prevented frontier expansion from attaining a self-generating momentum comparable to the United States. It is not surprising to find that *Tom Brown's Schooldays* with its model of the public-school ethos, was popular reading on the Canadian prairies. The founding of the Royal Canadian Mounted Police, the building of the Canadian Pacific Railway and the negotiation of treaties with Indians before there was a settler problem ensured a much tighter control of frontier development than in the United States. By comparison, colonial Latin America was closer to the Canadian example as strong control by church and state regulated an orderly process of frontier expansion, whereas in the nineteenth century when the writ of governments was weak, disorderly frontier expansion shared some of the characteristics of the United States.

The decline of Latin American silver mining after the destruction of the wars of emancipation at the beginning of the nineteenth century, bringing with it unemployment, contributed to the rural lawlessness of the early years of independence. Later in the nineteenth and early in the twentieth century, the development of a base metal mining frontier gave rise to political militancy among miners. The most radical of the continent's workers are to be found in the Chilean copper mines from the early years of this century and from the 1930s in the Bolivian tin mines (much as the IWW found its strongest support in the mining areas of the Far West). In contrast to the silver and gold mines of the colonial period in Latin America when capital was internally generated (less so after independence), the base metal frontier was stimulated by demand from the industrialized countries which provided the capital. As the majority of Latin American base metal mines have been foreign-owned, extractive mining has become a touchstone for nationalist feeling; thus the Cananea copper strike of 1906 in Mexico was caused by differential payments to American and Mexican workers. Although miners have been able to exert considerable pressure in situations where national economies are dependent on exports of one metal, the physical isolation of mines has enabled governments to control them. Nevertheless, the base metal mining frontiers of Latin America have exerted an important influence in national attitudes and governmental policies, as in the case of the Bolivian Revolution in 1952 and during Allende's regime in Chile.

Finally, to return to the starting point of this essay—the compulsive attraction of frontier mythology. In the United States the frontier has spawned the folk heroes of the industrial age, commercialized by the insatiable demands of a mass public for dime novels and Westerns— heroes like Daniel Boone, Kit Carson, Davy Crockett, General Custer and countless unsung anonymous frontiersmen who inhabit an imaginative universe of moral discourse where the issues of contemporary life can be debated within accepted conventions. Although other countries vicariously share this mythology, the subtler undertones elude easy comprehension.

But they have their own variants—Ned Kelly, Ben Hall and the bush-rangers of the Australian outback who epitomize values which urban dwellers may secretly envy or, in South Africa, the Great Trekkers who fuel the laager myth of Afrikanerdom.

Latin American equivalents do not come easily to mind. The symbolic *Martín Fierro* clearly has compulsive fascination for those trapped in the claustrophobic environment of Buenos Aires much as the dead Lampião is still a living reality for peasants in northeast Brazil, while for *paulistas* the *bandeirante* continues to be a folk hero. In Mexico, the bandit figure of Pancho Villa may embody yearnings of the rural poor but he is an embarrassment to a revolutionary establishment avid for respectability. In an age of romanticism the conquistadores had their admirers but they represent no positive values for a generation concerned with social injustice and economic inequality. Although it would be stretching a point to describe rural guerrillas as 'frontier heroes', for a decade or more after the Cuban Revolution they had an imaginative appeal, symbolized by Che Guevara, comparable to frontier myths.

Frontier myths derive their potency from the struggle of frontiersmen with the elements or with 'savages' who resist the onward march of 'progress', from creating order out of chaos and from their exaltation of individual effort and collective endeavour. Frontiersmen represent the primal vigour of the race and are the source for ideologies of rejuvenation. In Latin America, rural guerrillas operating in untamed wildernesses have fulfilled a similar function but with different expectations and assumptions. Whether these areas will become the foci of revolutionary change or will be tamed by the bulldozers of authoritarian technocracy is an open question—or is it one which has already been answered?

Notes

Preface

1. H. Bolton, 'The Epic of Greater America' in L. Hanke (ed.), *Do the Americas have a Common History?* (New York, 1964), p. 68.

Chapter 1

1. L. Fiedler, *Love and Death in the American Novel* (London, 1970), p. 464.
2. F. J. Turner, 'Contributions of the West to American Democracy' in R. A. Billington (ed.), *Selected Essays of Frederick Jackson Turner: Frontier and Section* (Englewood Cliffs, 1961), p. 95.
3. S. Elkins and E. McKitrick, 'Turner Thesis: Predictive Model' in E. N. Saveth (ed.), *American Historians and the Social Sciences* (New York, 1964), p. 380.
4. The relationship between frontier expansion and imperialism has been explored by W. A. Williams in his 'Frontier thesis and American foreign policy', *Pacific Historical Review* xxiv (1955) and developed in his *The Rise of the Modern American Empire* (New York, 1969).
5. V. A. Belaúnde, *The Frontier in Hispanic America*, Rice Institute pamphlets x (October, 1923).
6. Letters do exist which give an insight into colonial Spanish America as is shown by J. Lockhart and E. Otte, *Letters and People of the Spanish Indies: the Sixteenth Century* (Cambridge, 1976), but there is little comparable to those collections of letters which are so common in Anglo-American literary culture.
7. H. Bolton 'The mission as a frontier institution in the Spanish American colonies', *American Historical Review* xxiii (October 1917).
8. I. Bowman, *The Pioneer Fringe* (New York, 1931), p. 305.
9. F. J. Turner, 'The Significance of the Frontier in American History' in Billington, *Selected Essays*, p. 43.
10. R. M. Morse, *The Bandeirantes* (New York, 1965), p. 30.
11. W. P. Webb, *The Great Frontier* (Austin, 1964); I. Wallerstein, *The Modern World System: Capitalist Agriculture and the Origins of the European-World Economy in the Sixteenth Century* (New York, 1974) is the most ambitious attempt to survey the origins of an integrated world economic system from the sixteenth century on.
12. For peonage in the Deep South see P. Daniels, *The Shadow of Slavery: Peonage in the South, 1901–69* (New York, 1972).
13. T. Lynn Smith, *Brazilian Society* (Albuquerque, 1975), p. 188.
14. See G. Foster, *Culture and Conquest: America's Spanish Heritage* (Chicago, 1960).
15. Some historians have been struck by similarities between the enserfment on Latin America's frontiers and that in eastern Europe, the other great peripheral area of the expanding Western European world from the sixteenth century onwards.

16. A classic analysis of internal colonialism is P. González Casanova, *Democracy in Mexico* (New York, 1970. For an interesting application of the concept to Britain and its relevance to industrial societies see M. Hechter, *Internal Colonialism: the Celtic Fringe in British National Development, 1536–1966* (London, 1975).

Chapter 2

1. J. Lockhart, *The Men of Cajamarca* (Austin, 1972), p. 32–3. This is a key book for the analysis of Spanish social groups in early Spanish America although based on a very limited sample.
2. This estimate by S. F. Cook and W. Borah in *Essays in Population History: Mexico and the Caribbean* i (Berkeley, 1971), p. 487–8, is higher even than that of Las Casas who used to be accused of exaggeration.
3. Quoted in H. R. Wagner and H. R. Parish, *The Life and Writings of Bartolomé de Las Casas* (Albuquerque, 1967), p. 22.
4. E. Wolf, *Sons of the Shaking Earth* (Chicago, 1972), p. 204.
5. Brazil failed to benefit from the decline of British and French West Indian sugar early in the nineteenth century because of the absence of virgin land suitable for sugar. The persistence of slavery in Brazil hindered technological innovation but in Cuba virgin land combined with slavery, foreign capital and technology created the 'sugar revolution' which made Cuba the richest colony, for its size, possessed by any European power, comparable to Saint Dominique in the eighteenth century.
6. Quoted in Caio Prado Júnior, *The Colonial Background of Modern Brazil* (Berkeley, 1969), p. 325.
7. These were between followers of the rival Pizarro and Almagro families and centred on the distribution of *encomiendas* which were insufficient to satisfy the adventurers attracted by the legendary wealth of Peru.

Chapter 3

1. Quoted in P. Armillas, 'The arid frontier of Mexican civilization', *Transactions of the New York Academy of Science*, 2nd series xxxi no. 6 (June 1969).
2. Euclides da Cunha in *Rebellion in the Backlands* (Chicago, 1957), p. 43, refers to the early settlers as 'terrible makers of deserts', imitating the native habit of slash-and-burn cultivation. This method was highly efficient when used on a small scale but disastrous when applied indiscriminately. For a comparable example of environmental havoc we would have to go back to the invasion of North Africa by the Arabs, whose nomadic herds destroyed the granaries of the Roman Empire to create the desert of today or, of course, to the depredations of the Mesta in Extremadura.
3. Probably because this would have undermined the visible hierarchical structure on which conventional armies were based. During the wars of emancipation in the early nineteenth century and in the Cuban War of Independence the Spaniards, in spite of the guerrilla tradition of the Napoleonic War, were no different in this respect from other European troops.
4. See E. Montejo, *The Autobiography of a Runaway Slave* (London, 1969).
5. This is the theme of the Brazilian film *Ganga Zumba*.
6. M. MacLeod, *Spanish Central America: a Socioeconomic History, 1520–1720* (Berkeley, 1973).
7. L. Hanke, *The Imperial City of Potosí* (The Hague, 1956), p. 30.
8. Jane M. Loy, *The Llanos in Colombian History: Some Implications of a Static Frontier*, University of Massachusetts, International Area Studies Programme (1976), Occasional Papers series no. 2.
9. In the pre-1870 period the number of immigrants who became agricultural colonists was minimal: 4,200 out of 120,000 Italians; 1,900 out of 44,000 French; 500 out of 15,000 English; 1,500 out of 6,000 Germans; and only 200 out of 49,000 Spaniards. The Swiss provided the highest proportion with 5,900 out of 10,000.

J. Scobie, *Revolution on the Pampas: a Social History of Argentine Wheat* (Austin, 1964), p. 56.

10. A. Wallace, *Travels on the Amazon* (London, 1911), p. 230.
11. E. Hagen, *On the Theory of Social Change* (London, 1967), chapter 15.
12. C. Platt, *Latin America and British Trade 1806–1914* (London, 1972) p. 269. Peruvian bark, *cichona*, suffered a similar collapse after seeds had been taken to south India in 1859 and developed there to produce cheap quinine.
13. The violence of the Anglo reaction is understandable in view of clauses in the plan calling for all males over 16 to be shot and for assisting blacks to set up an independent state. A detailed study of this incident, based on new findings, is to be published in 1978 (see p. 177) by Professors C. Harris and R. Sadler who drew my attention to this incident.

Chapter 4

1. Sarmiento tells us that the *baqueano* could find his way in impenetrable darkness on the pampas by the taste of herbs. Rosas 'knows the pasturage of every estate in the south of Buenos Aires by its taste', D. F. Sarmiento, *Facundo or Life in the Argentine Republic in the Days of the Tyrant* (New York, 1961), p. 48.
2. Specific occasions may produce mining heroes as in the case of Pipila, the Indian miner who blew up the gates of the Alhóndiga in Guanajuato at the beginning of the War of Independence in Mexico in 1810; and clearly, too, the miner is a hero figure for the Trotskyist left in Bolivia.
3. Charles Darwin, *A Journal of Researches* (London, Ward Lock, n.d.), p. 59.
4. Familiar to urbanites through the films of the *cine novo*, especially those of Glauber Rocha such as *Black God, White Devil* and its sequel *Antonio das Mortes*. A brilliant sendup of this genre is the film *A Compadecida*. The film *O Cangaceiro*, the first of the bandit films, came out in 1953.
5. da Cunha, *Rebellion*, p. 110.
6. One need only point to the Cuban Carpentier, the Chilean Neruda, the Guatemalan Asturias and the Mexican Fuentes, four of the leading Latin American writers who have held the post over the past few years.
7. da Cunha, *Rebellion*, p. xxix.
8. A. Carpentier, *The Lost Steps* (Harmondsworth, 1968), p. 51.

Chapter 5

1. Latin American liberalism needs to be studied within a Hispanic tradition and not simply by reference to British or French practice. Spanish liberalism had its roots in the Spanish enlightenment but there was always tension between the economic doctrine of *laissez-faire* and the belief in a strong state as a political necessity to restrain local interests which were opposed to liberal modernization. Both Spanish Carlism and federal republicanism arose largely in response to the excessively centralist claims of the liberal state whereas in Latin America liberals were often the staunchest defenders of federal principles. But where the Catholic Church is an entrenched political power the 'passive state' of English example is a passport to suicide.
2. The problems of guerrillas operating in an isolated frontier region are graphically illustrated by Che Guevara's diary of the Bolivian campaign. *El diario del Che en Bolivia* (Buenos Aires, n.d.) xxi.

Chapter 6

1. J. G. Leyburn, *Frontier Folkways* (New Haven, 1935).
2. W. J. Eccles, *The Canadian Frontier, 1534–1760* (Albuquerque, 1976), p. 9.
3. Railway mileages at the end of the boom in railway building before 1914 were as follows: Mexico, 14,857; Argentina, 11,460; Brazil, 10,408; Chile, 2,800; Uruguay,

1,210; Peru, 1,146; Bolivia, 750; Venezuela, 529; Colombia, 411; Paraguay, 156; Ecuador, 125. Very few of these lines crossed political frontiers. In contrast, the United States had 232,046 miles and Canada about 30,000 miles of track.

4. *Retreta del Desierto*. From p. 1 of notes to accompany a record produced under the auspices of the Argentinian Army to relate the War of the Desert through bugle calls.
5. M. MacLeod, *Spanish Central America*, chapter 1.
6. C. Lévi-Strauss, *Tristes Tropiques* (Harmondsworth, 1976), p. 157. For a novelist's view see Vargas Llosa, *The Green House*, (London, 1969) and his *Pantaleón y los Visitadores*, (Madrid, 1973).

Bibliographical Essay

Bibliographies

There is a comprehensive 140-page bibliography on the United States frontier in R. A. Billington, *Westward Expansion* (New York, 4th edn, 1974). There is nothing comparable on the Latin American frontier. For specifically Borderlands history see the articles on 'Research on the Spanish Borderlands' in *Latin American Research Review* VII, no. 2 (summer 1972). The annual *Handbook to Latin American Studies*, University of Florida, is the standard bibliographical guide.

The Turner thesis and Latin America

In contrast to the dearth of material on the frontier in Latin America there is a huge literature on the Turner thesis and on the frontier in the United States. There are many editions of Turner's original essay. 'The significance of the frontier in American history'; for example, R. A. Billington (ed.), *Selected Essays of Frederick Jackson Turner: Frontier and Section* (Englewood Cliffs, 1961). Useful collections of critical assessments of the Turner thesis are G. R. Taylor (ed.), *The Turner Thesis* (Boston, 1956) and R. A. Billington (ed.), *The Frontier Thesis: Valid Interpretation of American History?* (New York, 1966). See also R. Hofstadter and S. M. Lipset (eds), *Turner and the Sociology of the Frontier* (New York, 1968).

The most comprehensive works on the frontier in the United States are those by Turner's major disciple, R. A. Billington; these include *Westward Expansion, op. cit.*; *The Far Western Frontier, 1830–1860* (New York, 1962); and *America's Frontier Heritage* (Albuquerque, 1974) which is one of the volumes in the *Histories of the American Frontier* series published by the University of New Mexico Press and edited by R. A. Billington. The volume by J. F. Bannon in this series, *The Spanish Borderlands Frontier, 1513–1821* (1970) deals with the northern Mexican frontier. Billington has also written a full-length biography of Turner, *Frederick Jackson Turner, Historian, Scholar, Teacher* (New York, 1973).

Two of the most perceptive critiques of Turner are R. Hofstadter, *The Progressive Historians* (New York, 1970) and D. M. Potter, *People of Plenty* (Chicago, 1966). For three useful but different discussions on the word 'frontier', see the chapter on *frontière* by L. Febvre in P. Burke (ed.), *A New Kind of History* (London, 1973); Fulmer Mood, 'Notes on the history of the word "frontier" ', *Agricultural History* XXII (April 1948) and J. T. Juricek, 'American usage of the word "Frontier" from colonial times to Frederick James Turner', *Proceedings of the American Philosophical Society* CX (February 1966).

There is a full literature on United States historiography. One of the most stimulating books is D. W. Noble, *Historians against History: the Frontier Thesis and the National Covenant in American Historical Writing* (Minneapolis, 1965). There is no comparable literature for Latin America but for the Brazilian racial myth see T. Skidmore, *Black into White: Race and Nationality in Brazilian Thought* (New York, 1974).

There is no book dealing specifically with the frontier in Latin America although A. Jara (ed.), *Tierras Nuevas: Expansión Territorial y Ocupación del Suelo en América* (siglos XVI–XIX) (México, 2nd edn, 1972) is a useful collection of essays. The essay by S. Zavala in W. D. Wyman and C. B. Kroeber (eds), *The Frontier in Perspective* (Madison, 1965) is seminal. A. R. Lewis and T. McGann (eds), *The New World Looks at its History* (Austin, 1963) is useful on the peninsular background and on comparisons. L. Hanke (ed.), *Does the New World have a Common History? a Critique of the Bolton Thesis* (New York, 1964) is a collection of readings. H. Bolton, *Greater America: Essays in honor of Herbert Eugene Bolton* (Berkeley, 1945) collects essays by his pupils together with an extensive bibliography of their writings. J. F. Bannon (ed.), *Bolton and the Spanish Borderlands* (Norman, 1964) collects some of Bolton's own essays. P. Chaunu, *L'Amérique et les Amériques* (Paris, 1964) is useful for comparative purposes. For the geographical background see P. E. James, *Latin America* (New York, 1959) and Harold Blakemore and C. T. Smith (eds), *Latin America: Geographical Perspectives* (London, 1971). One of the earliest treatments of a Latin American frontier was by the geographer Isaac Bowman, *Desert Trails of Atacama* (New York, 1924). For general background with much relevant material consult L. Hanke (ed.), *History of Latin American Civilization: Sources and Interpretations* (2 vols, London, 1969).

The Spanish background
The bibliographical articles by C. J. Bishko are fundamental: 'The Iberian background of Latin American history: recent progress and continuing problems', *Hispanic American Historical Review* XXXVI, no. 1 (February 1956) and 'The peninsular background of Latin American cattle ranching',

Hispanic American Historical Review xxxii, no. 4 (1952). There are two useful chapters in Lewis and McGann, *op. cit.*, one by Bishko, 'The Castilian as plainsman: the medieval ranching frontier in La Mancha and Extremadura' and by C. Sánchez Albornoz, 'The Frontier and Castilian liberties'. M. Góngora, *Studies in the Colonial History of Spanish America* (Cambridge, 1975) has stimulating insights. J. H. Elliott, *The Old World and the New: 1492–1650* (Cambridge, 1970) is packed with suggestive ideas. His general book *Imperial Spain, 1469–1716* (London, 1966) is crucial background reading as is J. Lynch, *Spain under the Habsburgs* (2 vols, Oxford, 1964 and 1969), especially volume ii, covering the little studied seventeenth century. For numbers and provenance of immigrants see P. Boyd Bowman, 'Patterns of Spanish emigration to the Indies until 1600', *Hispanic American Historical Review* xvi, no. 4 (November 1976). For a detailed social analysis of a small but crucial sample see J. Lockhart, *The Men of Cajamarca* (Austin, 1972). A. MacKay, *Spain in the Middle Ages: from Frontier to Empire, 1000–1500* (London, 1977) is excellent background.

The Caribbean frontier
The classic account for the early period is C. O. Sauer, *The Early Spanish Main*, (Cambridge, 1966). For the English Caribbean see C. and R. Bridenbaugh, *No Peace beyond the Line: the English in the Caribbean, 1624–1690* (New York, 1972). For the Dutch see C. Goslinga, *The Dutch in the Caribbean and on the Wild Coast, 1580–1680* (Gainesville, 1971) and articles and bibliographies in the *Boletín de Estudios Latinamericanos y del Caribe* published by the Centro de Estudios Latinamericanos, Amsterdam. A general introductory history is J. H. Parry and P. Sherlock, *A Short History of the West Indies* (London, 1956, reprinted 1971) and a popular readable account of early travellers in the Caribbean is T. Severin, *The Golden Antilles* (London, 1970). For the Caribbean generally the journal, *Caribbean Studies*, published by the *Instituto de Estudios del Caribe* of the Universidad de Puerto Rico, is fundamental. A useful overview which concentrates on Cuba is R. Guerra y Sánchez, *Sugar and Society in the Caribbean: an Economic and Social History of Cuban Agriculture* (New Haven, 1964). For the origins of sugar cultivation see M. Ratekin, 'The early sugar industry in Española', *Hispanic American Historical Review* xxxiv, no. 1 (January 1954).

El Dorado
A comprehensive study has yet to be written. V. S. Naipaul, *The Loss of El Dorado: a History* (London, 1969) is an unusual treatment by a novelist, based on historical records. Medieval legacies are covered in L. Weckman, 'The middle ages in the conquest of America', *Speculum* xxvi (1951). I.

Leonard, *Books of the Brave* (Berkeley 1949, reprinted 1964) is a pioneering book on the popular literature of the day which inflamed the conquistadors' imaginations. See also his 'Conquistadores and Amazons in Mexico', *Hispanic American Historical Review* xxiv, no. 4 (November 1944). S. Clissold, *The Seven Cities of Cíbola* (New York, 1962) deals with the Coronado expedition which is covered in greater detail in H. E. Bolton, *Coronado: Knight of Pueblos and Plains* (Albuquerque, 1949). Among treatments of specific myths see L. Olschki, 'Leon de Ponce's fountain of youth', *Hispanic American Historical Review* xxi, no. 3 (August 1941), E. Morales, *La Ciudad Encantada de la Patagonia* (Buenos Aires, 1944) and R. Coudyoudmjian 'La ciudad de los Césares: origen y evolución de una leyenda (1526–1880)' in *Historia* (Universidad Católica de Chile) vii (1968). For Brazil there is S. Buarque de Holanda, *Visão do Paraíso* (São Paulo, 1960). Werner Herzog's film *Aguirre-wrath of God* captures superbly the lure of Amazonian wealth.

Will to empire
Two short but useful introductions on the premisses of Spanish imperialism are J. H. Parry, *The Spanish Theory of Empire in the Sixteenth Century* (Cambridge, 1940) and S. Zavala, *The Political Philosophy of the Conquest of America* (Mexico, 1953).

Religious messianism
The key book is J. Phelan, *The Spiritual Kingdom of the Franciscans in the New World* (Berkeley, 2nd edn, 1970). The architectural expression is covered in G. Kubler, *Mexican Architecture in the Sixteenth Century* (2 vols, New Haven, 1945, reprinted 1972) which uses architectural history as an index of Indian acculturation. For the Portuguese variant of messianism see R. Ricard, 'Prophecy and messianism in the works of Antonio Vieira', *The Americas* xvii (April 1961). The messianism of Indian tribes is touched on in V. Lanternari, *The Religions of the Oppressed* (New York, 1965).

Colonization and early settlement
Basic texts are J. H. Parry, *The Spanish Seaborne Empire* (London, 1966), C. R. Boxer, *The Portuguese Seaborne Empire* (London, 1969), C. Haring, *The Spanish Empire in America* (New York, 1947) and C. Gibson *Spain in America* (New York, 1967).

Encomienda, hacienda and plantation
Fundamental is E. Florescano (ed.), *Haciendas, latifundios y plantaciones en América Latina* (Mexico, 1975) and K. Duncan and I. Rutledge (eds), *Land and Labour in Latin America: Essays on the Development of*

Agrarian Capitalism in the Nineteenth and Twentieth Centuries (Cambridge, 1977). Standard works on the *encomienda* are L. B. Simpson, *The Encomienda in New Spain* (Berkeley, 1950) and S. Zavala, *La Encomienda Indiana* (México, 1973). Modifications of older views are contained in R. G. Keith, 'Encomienda, hacienda and corregimiento in Spanish America: a structural analysis', *Hispanic American Historical Review* LI, no. 3 (August 1971) and J. Lockhart, 'Encomienda and hacienda: the evolution of the great estate in the Spanish West Indies', *Hispanic American Historical Review* XLIX, no. 1 (February 1965). The most recent literature is analysed in M. Mörner, 'The Spanish American hacienda: a survey on recent research and debate', *Hispanic American Historical Review* LIII, no. 2 (May 1973). The unusual case of Paraguay is treated in E. R. Service, 'The encomienda in Paraguay', *Hispanic American Historical Review* XXI, no. 1 (January 1951). The standard study of the northern Mexican hacienda is F. Chevalier, *Land and Society in Colonial Mexico: the Great Estate* (Berkeley, 1963). For Yucatán see A. Strickon, 'Hacienda and plantation in Yucatán', *América Indígena* xxv, no. 1 (January 1965). For late nineteenth-century Mexican haciendas see F. Katz, 'Labour conditions on haciendas in Porfirian Mexico: some tendencies and trends', *Hispanic American Historical Review* LIV, no. 1 (February 1974). For the case of Oaxaca see W. B. Taylor, *Landlord and Peasant in Colonial Oaxaca* (Stanford 1972). The central American plantation in the colonial period is covered very interestingly in M. MacLeod, *Spanish Central America: a Socioeconomic History, 1520–1720* (Berkeley, 1973). An important theoretical article is E. Wolf and S. Mintz, 'Haciendas and plantations in middle America and the Antilles', *Social and Economic Studies* VI (1957). S. Mintz, *Caribbean Transformations* (Chicago, 1974) is full of suggestive insights on plantation regimes. For a study of a late Brazilian plantation see W. Dean, *Rio Claro: a Brazilian Plantation System, 1820–1920* (Stanford, 1974).

Confrontation with the Amerindian
The basic work is R. Ricard, *The Spiritual Conquest of Mexico: an Essay in the Apostolate and Evangelizing Methods of the Mendicant Orders in New Spain, 1523–1572* (Berkeley, 1966). The 'Great Debate' is discussed in L. Hanke, *Aristotle and the American Indians: a Study in Race Prejudice in the Modern World* (London, 1959). C. Gibson, *The Aztecs under Spanish Rule: a History of the Indians of the Valley of Mexico, 1519–1810* (Stanford, 1964) is fundamental. A. W. Crosby, *The Columbian Exchange,* (Westport, 1972) is required reading for an understanding of the impact of the discovery of America on Indians and on the rest of the world. Mestizaje is discussed in C. E. Marshall, 'The birth of the mestizo in New Spain', *Hispanic American Historical Review* XIX, no. 2 (1939). For Brazil see the works of Freyre (below, p. 169); M. C. Kiernan, *The Indian Policy*

of Portugal in the Amazon Region, 1614–1693 (Washington, 1954); A. Marchant, *From Barter to Slavery: the Economic Relations of Portuguese and Indians in the Settlement of Brazil, 1500–1580* (Baltimore, 1942); C. Maclachlan, 'The Indian labour structure in the Portuguese Amazon, 1700–1800' in D. Alden *op. cit.*: J. Hemming, *Red Gold, the Conquest of the Brazilian Indians, 1500–1800* (London, 1976). N. Watchtel, *The Vision of the Vanquished: The Spanish Conquest of Peru Through Indian Eyes, 1530–70* (London, 1977) is fundamental.

The urban fixation

For the pre-Spanish city see J. Hardoy, *Pre-Columbian Cities* (London, 1973); P. Rivet, *Mayan Cities* (London, 1960) and G. F. Andrews, *Maya Cities: Place Making and Urbanization* (Norman, 1975). In the absence of any comprehensive treatment of the Latin American city the articles by R. M. Morse are crucial: 'Some characteristics of Latin American urban history', *American Historical Review* LXVII (January, 1962); 'Latin American cities: aspects of function and structure', *Comparative Studies in Society and History* IV (1962); and especially his 'A prolegomena to Latin American urban history', *Hispanic American Historical Review* LII, no. 3 August 1972). J. H. Parry, *The Cities of the Conquistadores* (London, 1961) is an introductory lecture. Z. Nuttall translates 'The royal ordinances concerning the laying out of towns' in *Hispanic American Historical Review* V (May 1922) and R. Ricard discusses the Plaza Mayor in 'La Plaza en Espagne et en Amérique Latine', *Annales* (1947). The growth of towns to protect the road to the silver frontier in New Spain is discussed in P. W. Powell, 'Presidios and towns on the silver frontier of New Spain, 1550–1580', *Hispanic American Historical Review* XXIV, no. 4 (November 1944). For later colonial urban growth see D. J. R. Robinson and T. Thomas 'New towns in eighteenth-century northwest Argentina', *Journal of Latin American Studies* VI, no. 1 (1974).

Brazil

There is good coverage on frontiers in R. Poppino, *Brazil: the Land and the People* (New York, 2nd edn, 1973), and also in Caio Prado Júnior, *The Colonial Background to Modern Brazil* (Berkeley, 1969). The various books by C. R. Boxer are fundamental for the colonial period: *The Dutch in Brazil, 1624–54* (Oxford, 1957, reprinted 1973); *Salvador de Sá and the Struggle for Brazil and Angola, 1602–86* (London, 1952) which stresses the South Atlantic links; and finally his account of the gold rushes, *The Golden Age of Brazil, 1695–1750* (Berkeley, 1962). The works of Gilberto Freyre are crucial, especially *The Masters and the Slaves* (New York, 1946) and *New World in the Tropics: the Culture of Modern Brazil* (New York, 1959). J. Normano, *Brazil: a Study of Economic Types* (Chapel Hill,

1935, reprinted 1968) is a suggestive older work. The best introduction to the bandeirantes is R. M. Morse (ed.), *Bandeirantes: the Role of the Brazilian Pathfinders* (New York, 1965). The mixed nature of the settlement process is brought out by A. Marchant in 'Feudal and capitalist elements in the Portuguese settlement of Brazil', *Hispanic American Historical Review* XXIII, no. 3 (August 1943). T. Lynn Smith, *Brazil: Peoples and Institutions* (Baton Rouge, 4th edn, 1972) is fundamental for background. S. B. Schwartz compares the leading cities of colonial Brazil and Mexico in 'Cities of empire: Mexico City and Bahia', *Journal of Inter-American Studies* II (1969). Geopolitical aspects are discussed by D. M. Davidson, 'How the Brazilian West was won: freelance and state on the Mato Grosso frontier, 1737–57' in D. Alden (ed.), *The Colonial Roots of Modern Brazil* (Berkeley, 1973). A very useful overview is Mary Lombardi, 'The frontier in Brazilian history: an historiographical essay' in *Pacific Historical Review* XLIV (1975). Later land policy is discussed in an important article by Warren Dean 'Latifundia and land policy in nineteenth-century Brazil', *Hispanic American Historical Review* LI, no. 3 (August 1970). There is an enormous and very good travel literature on Brazil. For a sample see H. Koster, *Travels in Brazil*, edited by C. Harvey Gardiner (Carbondale, 1966); R. F. Burton, *The Highlands of Brazil* (London 1869, reprinted New York, 1979). For modern accounts C. Lévi-Strauss, *Tristes Tropiques* (Harmondsworth, 1976) is a classic.

The mission frontier

H. E. Bolton, 'The mission as a frontier institution in the Spanish American colonies', *American Historical Review* XXIII (October 1917), is seminal. For northern Mexico, see J. F. Bannon *op. cit.* and on the Jesuits P. M. Dunne, *Early Jesuit Missions in Tarahumara* (Berkeley, 1948), *Black Robes in Lower California*, (Berkeley, 1968) and *Pioneer Jesuits in Northern Mexico* (Berkeley, 1944). Father Neumann's account of the Tarahumara revolt has been translated into French and edited by L. González in *Révolte des Indiens Tarahumars* (Paris, 1969). For the reductions, see M. Mörner, *The Political and Economic Activities of the Jesuits in the La Plata Region: the Habsburg Era* (Stockholm, 1953) and, for the expulsion, his edition of readings, *The Expulsion of the Jesuits from Latin America* (New York, 1965). P. Caraman, *The Lost Paradise: an account of the Jesuits in Paraguay, 1607–1768* (London, 1975) covers all the fascinating aspects of the Jesuit experiment. Spanish Amazonian missions are covered in J. Phelan, *The Kingdom of Quito in the Seventeenth Century* (Madison, 1967). For California, R. A. Billington, *Far Western Frontier, op. cit.* is a useful introduction. A. G. Kueth 'The pacification campaign on the Riohacha frontier, 1772–9', *Hispanic American Historical Review* L, no. 3 (August 1970) shows the shift in emphasis from missionary activity to armed force in the pacification process in late colonial Colombia. C. A. Hutchinson, *Frontier Settlement in Mexican California: the Hijar Padres Colony and its Origins, 1769–1835* (New Haven, 1969) deals with the transitional period. G. H. Phillips, *Chiefs and Challengers: Indian Resistance and Cooperation in Southern California* (Berkeley, 1975) deals with the aftermath.

The Amerindian frontier
There is an overlap with the above. For New Spain the works of P. W. Powell are crucial: 'The Chichimecs, scourge of the silver frontier in sixteenth-century Mexico', *Hispanic American Historical Review* xxv, no. 3 (August 1945), 'Spanish warfare against Chichimecs', *Hispanic American Historical Review* xxiv, no. 4 (November 1944) and his book, *Soldiers, Indians, and Silver: the Northward Advance into New Spain, 1550–1660* (Berkeley, 1952). The 'hard frontier' between sedentary and nomadic Indians is discussed in P. Armillas, 'The arid frontier of Mexican civilization', *Transactions of the New York Academy of Sciences*, series 2, xxxi, No. 6 (June 1969). The later period is covered in J. Forbes, *Apache, Navajo and Spaniard* (Norman, 1960) and M. L. Moorhead, *The Apache Frontier: Jacobo Ugarte and Spanish-Indian Relations in Northern New Spain, 1769–91* (Norman, 1968); for the defence problem in the same area, see Moorhead, *The Presidio: Bastion of the Spanish Borderlands* (Norman, 1975). Border conflicts with the United States are covered in C. Clendenen, *Blood on the Border: the United States Army and the Mexican Irregulars* (New York, 1969). For the final pacification of the Yaquis see E. Hu-Dehart 'Development and rural rebellion: pacification of the Yaquis in the late Porfiriato', *Hispanic American Historical Review* liv, no. 1 (February 1974). For Chile the key work is A. Jara, *Guerre et société au Chile* (Paris, 1961). An introduction is L. de Armand, 'Frontier warfare in colonial Chile', *Pacific Historical Review* xxiii (1954). More detailed is J. Rossignol, 'Chiliens et Indiens Araucanos au milieu du XIX siècle', *Caravelle* xx (1973). For Argentina, A. J. Tapson, 'Indian warfare on the Pampas in the colonial period', *Hispanic American Historical Review* xlii, no. 1 (February 1962) is useful. José Hernández's poem, *Martín Fierro*, conveys the atmosphere of the Indian frontier. For Brazil as above; for the current Indian problem there are many popular accounts as in R. Hanbury Tenison, *A Question of Survival* (London, 1973). For Paraguay see J. H. Williams, 'The deadly selva: Paraguay's northern Indian frontier' in *Americas* xxxiii, no. 1 (July 1976).

The Maroon frontier
There is a rapidly expanding literature on blacks and slavery. A useful overview for Spanish America is L. B. Rout Jnr, *The African Experience in Spanish America: 1502 to the Present Day* (Cambridge, 1976). H. Hoetink,

Slavery and Race Relations in the Americas (New York, 1973) is crucial. A useful book leading into Brazil is C. Degler, *Neither Black nor White: Slavery and Race Relations in Brazil and the United States* (New York, 1971). Specific books dealing with blacks on the frontier are rare but see N. Whitten, *Black Frontiersmen: a South American Case* (Cambridge, 1974) which deals with marginal black pioneers on the Pacific coast of northern Ecuador. Runaway communities are by definition frontier societies. For these see the key collection edited by R. Price, *Maroon Societies: Rebel Slave Communities in the Americas* (New York, 1973) and for Palmares, R. K. Kent 'Palmares: an African state in Brazil', *Journal of African History* vi, no. 2 (1965). Historians have started to work on the black experience on the US frontier; see, for example, P. Durham and E. L. Jones, *The Negro Cowboys* (New York, 1965) which shows that nearly one fifth of all cowboys were black—an interesting comment on the white cowboy myth. See also K. W. Porter, *The Negro on the American Frontier* (New York, 1971).

Silver frontiers

A useful if slightly technical discussion of Spanish mining methods is O. E. Young, 'The Spanish tradition in gold and silver mining', *Arizona and the West* vii (1965). Mexico has been well covered in P. Bakewell, *Silver Mining and Society in Colonial Mexico: Zacatecas, 1546–1700* (Cambridge, 1971); D. Brading, *Miners and Merchants in Bourbon Mexico, 1763–1910* (Cambridge, 1971); R. C. West, *The Mining Community in Northern New Spain: the Parral Mining District* (Berkeley, 1949); and R. W. Randall, *Real del Monte: a British Mining Venture in Mexico* (Austin, 1972) which examines one attempt to revive mining in the immediate post-independence period. The miners' equivalent of the Mesta is studied in W. Howe, *The Mining Guild of New Spain and its Tribunal General* (New York, reprinted 1968). Upper Peru has been less satisfactorily covered in English; L. Hanke, *The Imperial City of Potosí* (The Hague, 1956) is a useful introduction. His edition, with introduction, of Bartolomé Arzans de Orsua y Vela's *Historia de la Villa Imperial de Potosí* (in Spanish) (3 vols, Providence, 1965) is a vivid and detailed account up to 1737. G. B. Cobb, 'Supply and transportation for the Potosí mines, 1545–1649', *Hispanic American Historical Review* xxix, no. 1 (February 1949) illustrates the difficulties of mercury supplies. The crucial mercury mines are examined in A. P. Whitaker, *The Huancavelica Mercury Mines* (Cambridge, Mass., 1941).

Gold frontiers

The Brazilian gold rush is covered in Boxer *op. cit.* and in a series of articles by M. Cardozo: 'The collection of the fifths in Brazil, 1659–1709',

Hispanic American Historical Review no. 3 (August 1940); 'The guerra dos Emboabas, civil war in Minas Gerais, 1708–9', *Hispanic American Historical Review* XXII, no. 3 (August, 1942); and 'The Brazilian gold rush' *Americas* III, no. 2 (October 1946). For a revisionist view of the immediate economic effects see J. H. Galloway, 'Northeast Brazil, 1700–1750: the agricultural crisis re-examined', *Journal of Historical Geography* I, no. 1 (1975). Gold mining is studied as part of a wider process in J. T. Parsons, *Antioqueño Colonization in Western Colombia* (Berkeley, 1949). See also R. C. West, *Colonial Placer Mining in Colombia* (Baton Rouge, 1952). For a contrast see W. F. Sharp, *Slavery on the Spanish Frontier; the Colombian Chocó, 1680–1810* (Norman, 1976).

Base metal frontiers
A standard work for Mexico is M. Bernstein, *The Mexican Mining Industry, 1890–1950* (Yellow Springs, 1964). D. M. Pletcher, *Seven American Promoters in Mexico, 1867–1911* (Ithaca, 1958) illuminates the 'overspill' of the US frontier into Mexico.

Cattle frontiers
For Mexico see Chevalier *op. cit.*; W. Dusinberry, *The Mexican Mesta: the Administration of Ranching in Colonial Mexico* (Illinois, 1963); D. D. Brand, 'The early history of the range cattle industry in northern Mexico', *Agricultural History* XXXV (July 1961); R. J. Morrisey, 'The northward advance of cattle ranching in New Spain, 1550–1600', *Agricultural History* XXV (1951). For Argentina, H. Giberti, *Historia Económica de la Ganadería Argentina* (Buenos Aires, 2nd edn, 1961). A lively account of sheep farming in Tierra del Fuego is E. Lucas Bridges, *Uttermost Part of the Earth* (London, 1948). An interesting account by an anthropologist is P. Rivière's study of the 'fossilized frontier' in Roraima, cut off from the rest of Brazil, in *The Forgotten Frontier: Ranchers of Northern Brazil* (New York, 1972).

Agricultural frontiers
The standard works on Argentina in English are J. A. Scobie, *Revolution on the Pampas: a Social History of Argentine Wheat* (Austin, 1964); C. Taylor, *Rural life in Argentine* (Baton Rouge, 1948); and M. Jefferson, *Peopling the Argentine Pampas* (New York, 1926). For Brazil see M. W. Nicholls, 'The agricultural frontier in modern Brazilian history: the state of Paraná, 1920–65', in *Cultural Change in Brazil: Papers from the Midwest Association for Latin American Studies* (Muncie, 1969) and M. Margolis, *The Moving Frontier: Social and Political Change in Southern Brazilian Community* (Gainesville, 1973). For Cuban sugar see R. T. Ely, *Cuando Reinaba su Majestad el Azúcar* (Buenos Aires, 1963); R. Guerra y Sánchez *op. cit.*; F. Ortiz, *Cuban Counterpoint* (New York, 1947, reprinted

1970); H. Thomas, *Cuba: the Pursuit of Freedom* (London, 1971) covers sugar well. For a comparison between a sugar plantation in Morelos and Bahia see W. J. Barnett and S. Schwartz in Florescano, *op. cit.* See also W. Dean, *op. cit.*

Colonization schemes

There is a large bibliography; see T. Lynn Smith 'Studies in colonization and settlement', *Latin American Research Review* IV (1969) and the mimeographed 'Colonization and settlement' published by the Land Tenure Centre of the University of Wisconsin (1969 and 1971). For British colonization in Latin America, *Inter-American Economic Affairs* XVIII, no. 3 (1964) and XIX, no. 1 (1965), D. C. M. Platt, 'British Agricultural colonization in Latin America', parts I and II. His *Latin America and British Trade 1806–1914* (London, 1972) is fundamental for Latin American economic history in the nineteenth century.

The most detailed account of a British colony that failed—Nueva Liverpool in Guatemala—is given in W. J. Griffith, *Empires in the Wilderness: Foreign Colonization and Development in Guatemala, 1834–44* (Chapel Hill, 1965). The most detailed account of one that succeeded, that of the Welsh colony in Chubut, Argentina, is by G. Williams, *The Desert and the Dream* (Cardiff, 1975). See also J. E. Bauer, 'The Welsh in Patagonia: an example of nationalistic migration', *Hispanic American Historical Review* XXXIV, no. 4 (1954). A lively popular account of the Scottish failure in Darien in 1699 is I. Prebble's *The Darien Disaster* (London, 1968). The unusual story of the failure of the Nueva Australia colony in Paraguay is told by G. Souter, *A Peculiar People: the Australians in Paraguay* (Sydney, 1968) and by H. Livermore, 'New Australia', *Hispanic American Historical Review* XXX, no. 3 (August 1950). Jewish colonies in Argentina are discussed by M. D. Winsberg, *Colonia Baron Hirsch: a Jewish Agricultural Colony in Argentina* (Gainesville, 1964) and F. Schwarz and J. Te Valde, 'Jewish agricultural settlement in Argentina: The Ica experiment', *Hispanic American Historical Review* XIX, no. 2, May 1939). For a colourful account see A. Gerchunoff, *The Jewish Gauchos of the Pampas* (London, 1959). For a comparison with the U.S. see L. Shpall, 'Jewish agricultural colonies in the United States', *Agricultural History* XXIV. For Italians and Germans in Argentina see M. Jefferson *op. cit.* and E. Gallo, *Agricultural Colonization and Society in Argentina: the Province of Santa Fe* (unpublished D. Phil., Oxford, 1970) and R. C. Eidt, *Pioneer Settlement in Northeast Argentina* (Madison, 1971). His analysis of German immigration is complemented by two massive French studies on Brazil and Chile: J. Roche, *La Colonization allemande au Rio Grande do Sul* (Paris, 1959) and J-P. Blancpain, *Les Allemands au Chili 1816–1945* (Cologne, 1974). There is also a shorter study on Chile by G. F. W. Young,

Germans in Chile, Immigration and Colonization, 1849–1914 (New York, 1974). Wider in scope is C. Solberg, *Immigration and Nationalism: Argentina and Chile, 1890–1914* (Austin, 1970). There is an older but still useful general study for Chile by M. Jefferson, *Recent Colonization in Chile* (New York, 1921). For Mennonites in Mexico see H. L. Sawatsky, *They Sought a Country: Mennonite Colonization in Mexico* (Berkeley, 1971) and in Paraguay see J. Ogelsby, *Gringos from the Far North: essays in Canadian–Latin American relations, 1868–1968* (Toronto, 1976). For the British in Brazil see T. P. Bigg-Wither's personal account, *Pioneering in Southern Brazil* (2 vols, London, 1878, reprinted New York, 1968). A short introduction for southern Brazil is L. Waibel, 'European colonization in southern Brazil', *Geographical Review* XL (1950). For North American colonists, F. Goldman, *Os pioneros americanos no Brasil* (São Paulo, 1959). For the Japanese there is a useful chapter in T. Lynn Smith, *Brazilian Society* (Albuquerque, 1974) and the full length study by P. Staniford, *Pioneers in the Tropics: the Political Organization of an Immigrant Community in Brazil* (London, 1973) and N. R. Stewart, *Japanese Colonization in Eastern Paraguay* (Washington DC, 1967). See also H. D. Sims, 'Japanese agriculturists in Brazil and Paraguay: a review of the literature', *Peasant Studies Newsletter* (University of Pittsburgh) III, no. 2 (April, 1974).

The case of coffee
This has been well covered for Brazil in S. Stein, *Vassouras: a Brazilian Coffee County* (New York, 1970). For São Paulo there is P. Monbeig, *Pionniers et planteurs de São Paulo* (Paris, 1952) and for Paraná, M. Margolis, 'The coffee cycle on the Paraná frontier', *Luso Brazilian Review* IX, no. 1 (June 1972). Colombia is discussed in W. McGreevey, *An Economic History of Colombia, 1845–1930* (Cambridge, 1971) and the important case of Antioquia is thoroughly covered in R. Brew, *The Economic Development of Antioquia, 1950–1920* (unpublished D. Phil., Oxford, 1973). For Guatemala see D. J. McCreery, 'Coffee and class: the structure of liberal Guatemala', *Hispanic American Historical Review* LVI, no. 3 (August 1976) and for Cuba F. Pérez de la Riva, *El Café; historia de sau cultivo y explotación en Cuba* (La Habana, 1944).

The rubber frontier
A popular and readable introduction is R. Collier, *The River that God Forgot: the Story of the Amazon Rubber Boom* (London, 1968). J. V. Fifer discusses the greatest of the Bolivian rubber barons in 'The empire-builders: a history of the Bolivian rubber boom and the rise of the house of Suárez', *Journal of Latin American Studies* II, no. 2 (November 1970). For Julio Araña, the Peruvian rubber king, see H. L. Karno, 'Julio César

Araña, Frontier Cacique in Peru' in R. Kern (ed.), *The Caciques: Oligarchical Politics and the System of Caciquismo in the Luso-Hispanic World* (Albuquerque, 1973). J. Fifer examines the geopolitical problems of the Bolivian–Brazilian political frontier in *Bolivia: Land, Location and Politics since 1825* (Cambridge, 1972). Two useful articles are L. A. Tambs, 'Rubber, Rebels and Rio Branco: the Contest for the Acre', *Hispanic American Historical Review* XLVI, no. 3 (August 1966) and J. Melby, 'Rubber river: an account of the rise and collapse of the Amazon boom', *Hispanic American Historical Review* XXII, no. 3 (August 1943). For Manaus see B. Burns, 'Manaus 1910: portrait of a boom town', *Journal of Inter-American Studies* VII, no. 3 (July 1965).

The Anglo-Hispanic frontier

Carey McWilliams, *North from Mexico: the Spanish Speaking People of the United States* (New York, 1948, reprinted 1968) is still the best introduction. D. W. Meinig, *Southwest: Three Peoples in Geographical Change, 1600–1970* (Austin, 1971) is short but suggestive. N. Hundley (ed.), *The Chicano* (New York, 1975) is a useful collection of essays from the *Pacific Historical Review* with many bibliographical references. For California, L. Pitt, *The Decline of the Californios: a Social History of Spanish speaking Californians, 1846–1890* (Berkeley, 1966) is excellent. For Latin Americans in the Californian gold fields see J. Monaghan, *Chile, Peru and the California Gold Rush of 1849* (Berkeley, 1973). F. Swadesh, *Los Primeros Pobladores: Hispanic Americans of the Ute Frontier* (Notre Dame, 1974) is a model of what frontier historiography ought to be, written by a social anthropologist with a sense of historical change. Willa Cather's novel *Death Comes for the Archbishop* gives a sympathetic picture of New Mexico in the middle of the nineteenth century. For Texas, D. W. Meinig, *Imperial Texas* (Austin, 1969) is a stimulating introduction. P. S. Taylor, *An American-Mexican Frontier: Nueces County, Texas* (Chapel Hill, 1934) is very good on Texan attitudes. In the absence of any detailed studies of *bandidos*, P. Castillo and A. Camarillo (eds.), *Furia y Muerte: los Bandidos Chicanos* (Los Angeles, 1973) will have to do. See also A. Paredes, *With His Pistol in His Hand: A Border Ballad and its Hero* (Austin, 1958). D. J. Weber's article 'Stereotyping of Mexico's far northern frontier' in M. Servin (ed.), *An Awakened Minority: the Mexican Americans* (Beverley Hills, 1974) is useful, as is the whole collection. For the problems and progress of Chicano historiography see the various issues of *Aztlan, International Journal of Chicano Studies Research* (University of California at Los Angeles Chicano Studies Centre). A useful introduction to and analysis of American literary attitudes to Mexicans is C. Robinson, *With the Ears of Strangers: the Mexican in American Literature* (Tucson, 1963, reprinted 1973). For the Plan of San Diego see C. Harris and R. Sadler, 'The Plan of San Diego and the Mexican–United States War Crisis; a re-examination'—forthcoming in 1978 in the *Hispanic American Historical Review*.

Political frontiers
An overview of territorial disputes is S. Clissold and A. Hennessy, 'Territorial Disputes' in C. Veliz (ed.), *Latin America and the Caribbean: a Handbook* (London, 1968). The most detailed description in English of the disputes are the two volumes by G. Ireland—*Boundaries, Possessions and Conflicts in South America* (Cambridge, Mass., 1938) and *Boundaries, Possessions and Conflicts in Central and North America, and the Caribbean* (Cambridge, Mass., 1941). A lucid analysis of the developing balance of power in South America is R. N. Burr, *By Reason or Force: Chile and the Balancing of Power in South America, 1830–1905* (Berkeley, 1968).

Frontier society and culture
The two classics are D. F. Sarmiento, *Facundo or Life in the Argentine Republic in the Days of the Tyrant* (New York, 1961) and Euclides da Cunha, *Rebellion in the Backlands*, translated by S. Putnam (Chicago, 1957). The best discussions of cattle cultures are A. Strickon 'The Euro-American ranching complex' in A. Leeds and A. P. Vayda (eds), *Man, Culture and Animals* (Washington, DC, 1965) and Rivière, *op. cit.*

For a general overview of cattlemen see E. L. Tinker, 'The horsemen of the Americas', *Hispanic American Historical Review* xlii, no. 2 (May 1962) and *The Horsemen of the Americas and the Literature they Inspired* (New York, 1953). The best introduction to the gaucho is M. W. Nicholls, *The Gaucho: Cattle Hunter, Cavalryman, Ideal of Romance* (Durham, 1941) and her article 'The historic gaucho', *Hispanic American Historical Review* xxi, no. 3 (August 1941). R. Rodríguez has written on the gaucho in *Historia Social del Gaucho* (Buenos Aires, 1968) and 'El gaucho rio-platense: origen, desarrollo y marginalidad social', *Journal of Inter-American Studies* vi (1964); the gaucho mentality has been studied by A. J. Pérez Amuchástegui in *Mentalidades Argentinas* (Buenos Aires, 1965). Cattlemen elsewhere have not attracted comparable attention. The influence of the pampa on Argentinian society and character has been elaborated in a very suggestive manner in E. Martínez Estrada, *Radiografía de la Pampa*, translated as *X-ray of the Pampas* (Austin, 1971). The relationship between vagabondage and pastoralism with special emphasis on Chile has been studied by M. Góngora, 'Vagabondage et société pastorale en Amérique Latine', *Annales* (January 1969). R. M. Morse, *Bandeirantes, the Role of the Brazilian Pathfinder* (New York, 1965) is the best introduction. Vianna Moog, *Bandeirantes and Pioneers* (New York, 1964) is an impressionistic comparison between Brazil and the United

States and has some suggestive insights but takes a pessimistic view of the bandeirantes' influence. Cassiano Ricardo, *Marcha para Oeste: a Influencia da 'Bandeira' na Formação Social e Político do Brasil* (2 vols, Rio, 1959) is optimistic in contrast and is the nearest Brazilian equivalent to Turner.

Bandits and messiahs

E. Hobsbawm, *Bandits* (London, 1969) is an essential introduction. Da Cunha, *op. cit.* is essential reading. The meaning of *jagunço* is discussed in J. Calasans, 'Os Jagunços de Canudos', *Caravelle* xv (1970). The major historian of Brazilian messianic movements is Maria Pereira de Queiroz. See her 'Messiahs in Brazil', *Past and Present* xxxi (July 1965), 'L'influence du milieu social interne sur les mouvements messianiques brésiliens' and 'Classifications des messianismes brésiliens', both in *Archives de Sociologie des Religions* iii, no. 5 (January 1958). She has also written a standard account of bandits, *Os Cangaceiros: les bandits d'honneur brésiliens* (Paris, 1968). See also Amaury de Souza, 'The cangaço and the politics of violence in northeast Brazil' in R. H. Chilcote (ed.), *Protest and Resistance Movements in Angola and Brazil* (Berkeley, 1972) which is a stimulating attempt at comparative history. On Lampião there is A. Lima de Oliveira, *Lampião: Cangaço e Nordeste* (Rio, 1970) with graphic illustrations. For bandits generally there is the novel by Lins do Rego, *Cangaceiros* and the films *O Cangaceiro*, Glauber Rocha's *Black God, White Devil* and its sequel *Antonio das Mortes*. For an analysis of banditry, see P. Singlemann, 'Political structure and social banditry in northeast Brazil', *Journal of Latin American Studies* vii, no. 1 (May 1975). The ballad singers are analysed in R. Rowland, 'Cantadores del nordeste brasileño', *Aportes* iii (January 1967). For an analysis of *Antonio das Mortes* see T. M. Kavanagh, 'Imperialism and the revolutionary cinema: Glauber Rocha's *Antonio das Mortes' Journal of Modern Literature* iii, no. 2 (April 1973). For the Quebra-Quilo revolts see R. J. Barman, 'The Brazilian peasantry re-examined: the implications of the Quebra-Quilo revolts, 1974–5'. *Hispanic American Historical Review* lvii, no. 3, (August 1977). For an area other than the northeast, see M. Vinhas de Queiroz, *Messianisme e Conflito Social: a Guerra Sertanejo do Contestado, 1912–16* (Rio, 1966). The role of the church in the sertão it attracting attention as in D. P. Curry, 'Messiahs and protestants in Bahia's sertão', *Journal of Inter-American Studies* xii (1970); Eul Poo Sang, 'The changing role of priests in the politics of northeast Brazil, 1889–1964', *Americas* xxxi, no. 3 (January 1975); and especially R. Della Cava, *Miracle at Joaseiro* (New York, 1970) some of the challenging conclusions of which are contained in his 'Brazilian messianism and national institutions: a reappraisal of Canudos and Joaseiro', *Hispanic American Historical Review* xlviii, no. 3

(August 1968). A general introduction to messianic movements is V. Lantenari, *op. cit.* The Little Holy Cross of the Maya Indians is discussed in N. Reed, *The Caste War of Yucatán* (Stanford, 1967). Pancho Villa has been ill-served by historians. His own *Memoirs* (Austin, 1965) are none too reliable. We still await a detailed analysis of the economic and social basis of *Villismo*, comparable to Womack's study of Zapata. J. Reed, *Insurgent Mexico* (New York, 1969) gives some of the flavour of his motley following.

The frontier in literature

There is no critical study for Latin American literature comparable with H. Nash Smith, *Virgin Land: the American West as Symbol and Myth* (New York, 1950) or L. Marx, *The Machine in the Garden: Technology and the Pastoral Ideal in America* (New York, 1970) or the exhaustive and stimulating treatment of the frontier myth by R. Slotkin, *Regeneration through Violence: the Mythology of the American Frontier, 1600–1860* (Wesleyan University Press, 1973). The writings of Sarmiento, Gallegos, da Cunha, Carpentier, Güiraldes, Rivera, Quiroga, Hernández are discussed in general histories of Latin American literature. A useful introduction is J. Franco, *An Introduction to Spanish American Literature* (Cambridge, 1969) and her *The Modern Culture of Latin America: Society and the Artist* (London, 1973). She has also edited the short stories of Quiroga (London, 1968). Some novels have been translated into English: R. Gallegos, *Doña Bárbara* (New York, 1948); R. Güiraldes, *Don Segundo Sombra* (New York, 1935). For Brazil see J. Guimarães Rosa, *Devil to Pay in the Backlands* (London, 1971). For an insight into the life of a Portuguese immigrant on a coffee plantation see Ferreira de Castro, *The Emigrants* (London, 1962). There is a not very good paperback translation of *Martín Fierro* (New York, 1975) and a mass of critical literature about the author and his creation. A standard work is E. Martínez Estrada, *Muerte y Tranfiguración de Martín Fierro* (2 vols, Mexico, 1948, reprinted 1958) and one of many provocative studies, E. Giménez Vega and J. González, *Hernandismo y Martinfierrismo* (Buenos Aires, 1975). For Spanish frontier balladry see the excellent article by A. Mackay, 'The ballad and frontier in late medieval Spain', *Bulletin of Hispanic Studies* LIII, no. 1 (January 1965).

The rural crisis

The problem of the peasantry has been pungently analysed in E. Feder, *Rape of the Peasantry* (New York, 1971) and in R. Stavenhagen (ed.), *Agrarian Problems and Peasant Movements in Latin America* (New York, 1970). Agrarian problems are discussed in general studies of the Latin American economy such as C. Furtado, *Economic Development of Latin America* (Cambridge, 1970) and K. Griffin, *Underdevelopment in Spanish*

America (London, 1969). For peasants generally see A. Pearse, *Latin American Peasants* (London, 1975); H. Landsberger (ed.), *Latin American Peasant Movements* (Ithaca, 1969); and S. Forman, *The Brazilian Peasantry* (New York, 1975).

Frontier versus metropolis

The macrohistorical approach to the frontier-metropolis dichotomy finds its clearest expression in W. P. Webb, *The Great Frontier* (Austin, 1964), with a useful critique by G. Barraclough in Lewis and McGann, *op. cit.* Writing from a Marxist standpoint, Andre Gunder Frank develops the thesis of periphery versus metropolis in *Capitalism and Underdevelopment in Latin America: Historical Studies in Chile and Brazil* (London, 1971). For one of many critiques see D. Booth 'Andre Gunder Frank: an introduction and an appreciation' in I. Oxaal, T. Barnett, D. Booth (eds.), *Beyond the Sociology of Development* (London, 1975). For urbanization, see Morse, *op. cit.* and *The Urban Development of Latin America, 1750–1920* (Stanford, 1971) and, for bibliography, his 'Trends and issues in Latin American urban research, 1965–70', *Latin American Research Review* VI, no. 1 (spring and summer 1971). The problem of capital cities is covered in a special edition of *Caravelle* III (1964). There are few 'biographies' of Latin American cities in English apart from R. M. Morse, *From Community to Metropolis: a Biography of São Paulo* (Gainesville, 1958) and J. R. Scobie, *Buenos Aires: Plaza to Suburb, 1870–1910* (New York, 1974). For peasant migrations, see B. J. Sauers, 'Peasant migrations in Latin America: a survey of the literature in English' *Peasant Studies Newsletter* III, no. 2 (April 1974). For urbanization see J. Hardoy (ed.), *Urbanization in Latin America: Approaches and Issues* (New York, 1975).

The political legacy

A stimulating and perceptive analysis of *caudillismo* is E. Wolf and E. C. Hanson, 'Caudillo politics: a structural analysis', *Comparative Studies in Society and History* IX (1968). For a frontier *caudillo* in Mexico see R. Acuña, *Sonoran Strongman: Ignacio Pesqueira and his Times* (Tucson, 1974). An analysis of an Argentinian frontier *caudillo* is R. M. Haigh, 'The creation and control of a caudillo', *Hispanic American Historical Review* XLIV, no. 4 (November 1964). Sarmiento is essential reading. Rosas has generated an enormous literature, most of it revisionist and polemical. For an example see E. Astesano, *Rosas, Bases del Nacionalismo Popular* (Buenos Aires, 1960). The key work for Brazilian *coronelismo* is V. Nunes Leal, *Coronelismo, Enxada e voto: o Municipio e o regime representative no Brasil* (Rio, 1974, 2nd edn). There is an attempt at a typology of *coroneles* in Eul-Soo Pang, 'Coronelismo in Northeast Brazil' in R. Kern, *op. cit.*, which is a useful collection on clientilism generally. The politics of ranchers in the frontier state of Rio Grande do Sul is covered in J. Love, *Rio Grande do Sul and Brazilian Regionalism, 1882–1930* (Stanford, 1971). The problem of machismo and women's role in society has not attracted the attention its importance warrants, although there is a useful collection by Ann Pescatello (ed.), *Male and Female in Latin America* (Pittsburgh, 1973): for a bibliography see her 'Female in Latin America', *Latin American Research Review* VII, no. 2 (1972). The study of Latin American populism is attracting considerable attraction but for an introduction see A. Hennessy, 'Latin America' in G. Ionescu and E. Gellner (eds.), *Populism: its Meanings and National Characteristics* (London, 1969). The best way to appreciate the problems of guerrillas operating in frontier regions is to read Che Guevara's, *The Complete Diary of Che Guevara* (London, 1968) and his *Reminiscences of the Cuban Revolutionary War* (London, 1968). For a critique of Guevara's last campaign see R. Debray, *Che's Guerrilla War* (London, 1975). The standard work on rural guerrillas is R. Gott, *Guerrilla Movements in Latin America* (London, 1970). For peasants generally, see H. Landsberger (ed.), *op. cit.*, E. Hobsbawm, 'Peasants and rural migrants in politics' in C. Veliz (ed.), *The Politics of Conformity in Latin America* (London, 1967) and his 'A case of neo-feudalism: La Convención, Peru', *Journal of Latin American Studies* I (1969). The failure of the Brazilian 'Long March' is recounted in N. Macaulay, *The Prestes Column: Revolution in Brazil* (New York, 1974). An interesting analysis of a farmers' political movement is E. Gallo, *Farmers in Revolt: the Revolutions of 1893 in the Province of Santa Fe, Argentina* (London, 1976).

Frontiers of the future
See the T. Lynn Smith article under colonization. Two short overviews are P. E. James, 'Expanding frontiers of settlement in Latin America', *Hispanic American Historical Review* XXI, no. 2 (May 1941), where he discusses Costa Rica, Chile, Antioquia and South Brazil, and G. J. Butland, 'Frontiers of settlement in South America', *Revista Geográfica* (1966–7), with an emphasis on Brazil. There is also E. E. Hegen, *Highways into the Upper Amazon* (Gainesville, 1966). T. M. Nelson, *The Development of Tropical Lands: Policy Issues in Latin America* (Baltimore, 1973) surveys colonization projects from Mexico to Paraguay. B. J. Meggers, *Amazonia: Man and Culture in a Counterfeit Paradise* (Chicago, 1971) is a pessimistic evaluation of the Amazon's potential which is offset by the optimism of C. Wagley (ed.), *Man in the Amazon* (Gainesville, 1974). R. E. Crist and C. M. Nissly, *East from the Andes: Pioneer Settlements in the South American Heartland* (Gainesville, 1973) surveys projects in all the countries with Amazonian regions. D. B. Heath and H. O. Buechler (eds.), discuss the Bolivian Oriente and the effect of the revolution on

settlement in *Land Reform and Social Revolution in Bolivia* (New York, 1967). All the above works are mainly concerned with the practicalities and potentialities of frontier expansion. Two unpublished theses on the Brazilian frontier which are more concerned with the relationship between frontiers and political development are J. Foweraker, *Political Conflict on the Frontier: a Case Study of the Land Problem in the West of Paraná* (Oxford, 1974) and O. G. Velho, *Modes of Capitalist Development: Peasantry and the Moving Frontier* (Manchester, 1973). For a view which sees a viable rural middle class emerging in northern Paraná see E. Willems, 'The rise of a rural middle class in a frontier society' in R. Roett (ed.), *Brazil in the Sixties* (Nashville, 1972).

Comparative perspectives
In 1975 the University of Oklahoma started an occasional newsletter, *Comparative Frontier Studies*, the first issue of which listed recent books on the contemporary Latin American frontier. There have been few full-length contemporary studies and J. G. Leyburn, *Frontier Folkways* (New Haven, 1935) remains a pioneering work. Nor was there much follow up to W. Wyman and C. B. Kroeber, *op. cit.* or to H. Heaton, 'Other Wests than ours' in *Tasks of Economic History Perspective* (Madison, 1965). Two useful articles are M. Mikesell 'Comparative studies in frontier history', *Annals of the Association of American Geographers* (March 1960) and D. Gerhard, 'The frontier in comparative view', *Comparative Studies in Society and History* i (March 1959). A portent of reviving interest can also be seen in D. H. Miller and J. O. Steffen (eds.), *The Frontier: Comparative Studies* (Norman, 1977). An important theoretical contribution is M. Katzman, 'The Brazilian frontier in comparative perspective', *Comparative Studies in Society and History* xvii (July 1975). W. P. Webb, *The Great Plains* (New York, 1931, reprinted 1974) compares Anglo and Hispanic attitudes to the Great Plains problem. An important geographer's contribution is I. Bowman, *The Pioneer Fringe* (New York, 1931). J. Hellwege has made a direct comparison between the Thirteen Colonies and Spanish America in 'Frontier und *Conquista*' (mimeograph, University of Bielefeld, 1974). H. C. Allen, *Bush and Backwoods: a Comparison of the Frontier in Australia and the United States* (Michigan, 1959) follows up the earlier F. Alexander, *Moving Frontiers: an American Theme and its Application to Australian History* (Melbourne, 1947). The comparison was widened by P. A. Sharp, 'Three frontiers: some comparative studies of Canadian, American and Australian settlement', *Pacific Historical Review* xxiv (November 1955) and by R. Winks in *The Myth of the American Frontier: its Relevance to America, Canada and Australia* (Leicester, 1971) which is full of suggestive insights as is his 'On decolonization and informal empire', *American Historical Review* lxxxi, no. 3 (June 1976) with

a suggested comparison between Uruguay and New Zealand. Comparisons between Argentina and Australia are made in C. Goodrich 'Argentina as a new country', *Comparative Studies in Society and History* vII (1964). For a political comparison between the Australian Labour party and the Argentinian Radicals see T. H. Moran, 'The "development" of Argentina and the Labour party of Australia in the process of economic and political development', *Comparative Politics* III, no. 1 (October 1970). The 'Big Man's frontier' in Australia is discussed in B. Fitzpatrick, 'The big man's frontier and the Australian frontier', *Agricultural History* xxi (1947). For New Zealand see P. J. Coleman, 'The New Zealand Frontier and the Turner thesis', *Pacific Historical Review* xxvII (August 1958).

For the early Canadian frontier there is an excellent study by W. J. Eccles, *The Canadian Frontier, 1534–1760* (Albuquerque, 1976). For later French Canadian attitudes, see A. I. Silver, 'French Canada and the prairies frontier, 1870–1890', *Canadian Historical Review* L, no. 1 (March 1969). The spill-over of United States frontier expansion is covered in F. Landon, *Western Ontario and the American Frontier* (Toronto, 1941, reprinted 1967). Land distribution is dealt with in C. Martin, '*Dominion Lands' Policy* (Toronto, 1973). The north is covered in M. Zaslow, *The Opening of the Canadian North, 1870–1914* (Toronto, 1971) which has a comprehensive bibliography. For a comparison with Alaska, another northern frontier, see R. W. Paul, *Frontier Alaska, a Study in Historical Interpretation and Opportunity* (Proceedings of the Conference on Alaskan History, Anchorage, June 1967), and O. W. Miller, *The Frontier in Alaska and the Matanusha Colony* (New Haven, 1974). For discussions of the frontier concept see M. Zaslow, 'The frontier hypothesis in recent Canadian historiography', *Canadian Historical Review* xxix, no. 2 (1948); C. F. G. Stanley, 'Western Canada and the frontier thesis', *Canadian Historical Association Report* (1940); and J. M. S. Careless, 'Frontierism, metropolitanism and Canadian history', *Canadian Historical Review* xxxv (September 1954). For economic history and the staple approach, see W. J. Easterbrook and M. H. Watkins, *Approaches to Canadian Economic History* (Toronto, 1967, reprinted 1971).

An introduction to the frontier in South Africa is E. A. Walker's lecture, *The Frontier Tradition in South Africa* (Oxford, 1930) and a useful review essay, W. K. Hancock, 'Trek', *Economic History Review* x, no. 3 (1958). The early frontier is examined in D. Neumark, *The South African Frontier: Economic Influences 1652–1836* (Stanford, 1957).

The Russian frontier is discussed in D. Treadgold, 'Russian expansion in the light of Turner's study of the American frontier', *Agricultural History* xxvi (October 1952) and his book, *The Great Siberian Migration* (Princeton, 1957). For an earlier period, there is C. V. Lantzeff and R. A. Pierce, *Eastward to Empire: Exploration and Conquest on Russia's Open*

Frontier to 1750 (Montreal, 1975). For exploration in the US see W. Goetzmann's classic *Exploration and Empire* (New York, 1972). For frontiers in eastern Europe, see W. H. McNeill, *Europe's Steppe Frontier* (Chicago, 1964) and A. N. J. den Hollander, 'The great Hungarian plain: a European frontier area', *Comparative Studies in Society and History* III (1960). And for Asia's 'inner frontiers', O. Lattimore, *Studies in Frontier History: Collected Papers, 1928–58* (Oxford, 1962).

The only comparison of a Latin American mining frontier with one elsewhere is M. Mörner, 'Some comparative remarks on colonial silver mining in Lapland and Spanish America during the seventeenth century', *Bulletin de l'Institut Historique Belge de Rome*, Fascicule 44, (Brussels, 1974). Within Latin America, Peru and Mexico are compared in D. Brading and H. E. Cross, 'Colonial silver mining: Mexico and Peru', *Hispanic American Historical Review* LII, no. 4 (November 1972). C. H. Shinn, *Mining Camps: a Study in American Frontier Government* (New York, 1884, reprinted 1965) deals with Spanish influences. For United States mining frontiers the key book is R. W. Paul, *Mining Frontiers of the Far West, 1848–80* (Albuquerque, 1974). See also D. A. Smith, *Rocky Mountain Mining Camps: the Urban Frontier* (Bloomington, 1967). For the urban frontier generally in the United States see C. Bridenbaugh, *Cities in the Wilderness: the First Century of Urban Life in America, 1625–1742* (New York, 1955, reprinted 1964) and R. C. Wade, *The Urban Frontier: the Rise of Western Cities, 1790–1830* (Cambridge, Mass., 1959). For the urban-rural dichotomy see N. Harper, 'The rural and urban frontiers', *Historical Studies* (Australia and New Zealand) x, no. 40 (May 1963).

The influence of the frontier mystique of violence has been a major theme for United States historians and this is clearly a research need in Latin America, especially at the moment. For the United States see the excellent literary analysis by R. Slotkin, *op. cit.* A brief historical survey is E. Hollons, *Frontier Violence* (Oxford, 1974). Another largely unstudied theme is that of policing frontier areas—a comparison of Canadian Mounties, Texas Rangers, Mexican Rural Guards, Brazilian *capangas*, Argentinian *blandegues*, the Royal Queensland Constabulary and others, comparing recruitment patterns, popular images, etc. would be valuable addition to our knowledge. W. P. Webb, *The Texas Rangers: a Century of Frontier Defense* (Austin, 1935, reprinted 1965) studies one such force and P. Vanderwood has studied the Mexican Rural Guard in 'Genesis of the Rurales: Mexico's early struggle for public security', *Hispanic American Historical Review* L, no. 1 (February 1970). C. Clendenen, *Blood on the Border: the United States Army and the Mexican Irregulars* (London, 1969) is important for violence in the Borderlands. R. W. Paul compares social control on various North American frontiers in his chapter 'Patterns of culture in the American West' in *Frontier Alaska, op. cit.*

Nativism and anti-foreign feeling, comparing Anglo and Latin attitudes, has been studied in R. F. Heizer and A. J. Almquist, *The Other Californians: Prejudice and Discrimination under Spain, Mexico and the United States to 1920* (Berkeley, 1971). R. L. Seckinger has done a micro-analysis of one Latin American case in his 'The politics of nativism: ethnic prejudice and political power in Mato Grosso, 1831–4', *Americas* xxxi, no. 4 (April 1975). Different attitudes to Indians have been studied in E. H. Spicer's indispensable *Cycles of Conquest: the Impact of Spain, Mexico and the United States on the Indians of the Southwest, 1533–1960* (Tucson, 1962). See also E. A. H. John, *Storms Brewed in Other Men's Worlds: the Confrontation of Indians, Spaniards and French in the Southwest, 1540–1595* (College Station, 1975). It seems that the new assertiveness of United States Indians is beginning to stimulate comparative studies of Indians, in the way that Black Power encouraged comparative race studies.

The relationship between labour and racial attitudes is analysed by R. Beeman, 'Labour forces and race relations: a comparative view of the colonization of Brazil and Virginia', *Political Science Quarterly* lxxxvi (1971). For a contrast with Spanish Indian policy see A. T. Vaughan, *New England Frontier: Indians and Puritans, 1620–75* (Boston, 1965). From another perspective see the pungently written and cogently argued F. Jennings, *The Invasion of America: Indians and the Cant of Conquest* (Chapel Hill, 1975). For the English ideology of conquest see N. P. Canny, 'The ideology of English colonization: from Ireland to America', *William and Mary Quarterly*, 3rd series xxx (1973) and for the impact of disease see A. W. Crosby, 'Virgin soil epidemics as a factor in the aboriginal depopulation of America', *William and Mary Quarterly*, 3rd series xxxiii, No. 2 (April 1976) which complements his *Columbian Exchange, op. cit.*

Transportation problems such as comparative costs, etc. have been a major concern of United States historians. For an introduction see O. O. Winther, *The Transportation Frontier: Trans-Mississippi West, 1865–1890* (Albuquerque, 1974). For a superbly concise introduction to problems of US economic growth in the nineteenth century see P. Temin, *Causal Factors in American Economic Growth in the Nineteenth Century* (London, 1975). The problem of technology is analysed in H. J. Habbakuk, *American and British Technology in the Nineteenth Century* (Cambridge, 1962). For Latin America there is a pre-railway study by D. Ringrose, 'Carting in the Hispanic world: an examination of divergent development', *Hispanic American Historical Review* l, no. 1 (February 1970) which compares Spanish American experience with that of Spain. Railway entrepreneurs have attracted attention, mainly perhaps because most have been North Americans. See, for example, C. Gauld, *Percival Farquhar: the Last Titan* (Stanford, 1964). For Mexico see Pletcher, *op. cit.* and W. Coatsworth, 'Railroads, landholding and agrarian protest in the early Porfiriato',

Hispanic American Historical Review LIV, no. 1 (February 1974) and, for Argentina, W. R. Knight, *British owned Railways in Argentina and their Effect on Economic Nationalism, 1854–1948* (Austin, 1974), and P. B. Goodwin, 'Transportation, innovation and economic development in nineteenth-century Argentina', *Hispanic American Historical Review* LVII, no. 4, November 1977). For Canada see G. P. T. Glazebrook, *A History of Transportation in Canada* (2 vols, Toronto, 1970).

The considerable and growing literature on women on the North American frontier, ranging from popular works such as Dee Brown, *The Gentle Tamers* (London, 1973) to specialized articles like T. A. Larson 'Dolls, vassals and drudges—pioneer women in the West', *Western Historical Quarterly* III (1972) and J. Modell, 'Family and fertility on the Indiana frontier, 1820', *American Quarterly* XXII (1971) are not matched on the Latin American side although D. Ramos, 'Marriage and the family in colonial Vila Rica', *Hispanic American Historical Review* LV, no. 2 (May 1975) questions some of the suppositions of Freyre whose early recognition of the importance of the family has only recently been taken up by historians—largely under the influence of the women's movement. For current work on Latin America see M. Knaster, 'Women in Latin America: the state of research', *Latin American Research Review* XI, no. 1 (1976). There is no Latin American equivalent of the superb pictorial record of M. Lesy, *Wisconsin Death Trip* (New York, 1973).

A fruitful comparison of religion on the frontier would have to compare the sects of a predominantly Protestant environment with the cults of a Catholic culture. A useful view of African survivals is R. Bastide, *African Civilizations in the New World* (London, 1972). There is comparative material on millennialism in Lanternari, *op. cit.* B. Wilson, *Magic and the Millennium* (London, 1975) is fundamental for the wider view. S. Thrupp (ed.), *Millennial Dreams in Action* (The Hague, 1962) includes a chapter by R. Ribeiro on Brazil. There is no Latin American equivalent of L. B. Wright, *Culture on the Moving Frontier* (New York, 1961). L. Hartz's 'fragment theory' in *The Founding of New Societies: Studies in the History of the United States, Latin America, South Africa, Canada and Australia* (New York, 1964) is both relevant and suggestive.

There is an abundance of material on the imagery of the frontier hero in the United States fed by the bottomless market for the dime novel and the Western as, for example, K. L. Steckmesser, *The Western Hero in History and Legend* (Norman, 1965) and, with a different emphasis, *The Frontier Mind: a Cultural Analysis of the Kentucky Frontiersman* (Louisville, 1957, reprinted 1957). In Latin America this field has not yet been opened up apart from ballad genres such as the Mexican *corrido* or the Argentinian *payada*. A book which raises all sorts of possibilities is Russel Ward's superb *Australian Legend* (Sydney, 1958, reprinted 1965). The whole question of visual reaction to landscape awaits exploration in the case of Latin America but it is worth mentioning the paintings by José María Velasco, one of the great landscape painters of the nineteenth century and virtually unknown outside Mexico. Two, in particular, *El Citlatepetl* and *Puente de Metlac* are as perfect an image of the 'Machine in the Garden' as one is likely to find. For background to the 'wilderness controversy', which is exercising an increasing number of people, see R. Nash, *Wilderness and the American Mind* (New Haven, 1967).

Glossary

Adobe   sun-dried brick
Agave   a cactus plant
Aldeia (Braz.)   village; refers especially to the Jesuit controlled villages of
   Amazonia
Altiplano   highlands of Bolivia and Mexico
Anglo   popular term in the American southwest for someone of white
   Anglo-Saxon descent
Antioqueño   inhabitants of Antioquia in Colombia
Argentinidad   'Argentinity'; the sense of being Argentinian
Arrastre   mining mill
Arriero   muleteer; cf. *tropeiro*
Asado   Argentinian barbecue

Baqueano   pathfinder; especially on the *pampas*; cf. *rastreador.*
Barretero   face-miner
Barrio   suburb, district of a town
Beato, -a (Braz.)   religious zealot with priestly pretensions
Blandegue   frontier-guards on the *pampas* against Indians
Bolas   stones encased in leather fixed to a rope, used by *gauchos* to fell
   cattle
Bugreiro (Braz.)   slave-catcher

Cabanagem (Braz.)   guerrilla rising
Cabildo   town council
Cachaça (Braz.)   sugar brandy
Cacique   originally Indian chieftain but used later for any rural boss or
   rural agent for town politician
Cafetal   coffee plantation
Caipira (Braz.)   Rustic backwoodsman; sometimes used to mean thug;
   cf. *jagunço, sertanejo*

Câmara (Braz.)   town council

Camino Real   'Royal Road', running from Santa Fe in New Mexico to Vera Cruz via Mexico City

Campesino   generic term for rural dweller or peasant

Cangaceiro (Braz.)   bandit of the *sertão*, usually carrying the overtones of social banditry; after *cangaço*, referring to the bundle of arms which the *cangaceiro* carried round his neck

Cantador   ballad singer

Capangueiro (Braz.)   hired thug, a member of a *capanga* or bodyguard; employed by landowners to guard the borders of estates

Capitão do mato (Braz.)   bush-whacking captain, slave-catcher

Capitulación   agreement, contract

Casta   caste, applying to colonial Spanish society, stratified on racial lines

Caudillo, Caudilho (Braz.)   strong man whose power derives from exercise of strong arm methods; hence *caudillismo* and *caudillaje*

Cearense   inhabitant of Ceará, state in northeast Brazil, subject to periodic droughts

Charqueada   establishment where beef was sun-dried

Charro (Mex.)   a rural small proprietor with 'squirearchy' overtones

Chicano   someone of Mexican descent who feels a sense of ethnic identity and resists conforming to the cultural norms of white America

Chiclero   gatherer of *chicle*, the basis of chewing gum, especially in Quintana Roo, southeast Mexico

Chinampa   highly productive floating market gardens, valley of Mexico

Chinchona   quinine

Cimarrón   runaway slave; Jamaican maroon or bush-negro in Guyana

Cine Novo (Braz.)   the Brazilian 'New Cinema' movement dating from the early 1960s and largely based on themes from the northeast

Coca   dried leaves of the coca plant which, chewed together with lime, produces narcotic effect; used to deaden pain of hunger and fatigue by Andean Indians

Cofradía   religious confraternity

Colono (Braz.)   landless labourer

Comadre   godmother

Compadre   godfather

Comprador   buyer; hence *comprador bourgeoisie*, middlemen who managed trade between manufacturing and Latin American countries

Conquistadores   the original Spanish conquerors of the Indies

Conuquero   a landless labourer in Venezuela

Coronel(-eis) (Braz.)   rural boss, originally an official rank in the militia but from the early Empire became used for any rural notable

Corregidor   a Spanish magistrate; *corregidor de Indios*, a Spanish official overseeing Indian communities in the colonial period

Corrido   Mexican popular ballad
Cortes   representative assembly in Spain
Coureur de bois (Can.)   French-Canadian fur trapper; the term *voyageur* was more frequent in the eighteenth century
Cuadrilla   team

Degredado (Braz.)   convict
Desafío   challenge song
División del Norte   'Division of the North', the title of Villa's army in the Mexican Revolution
Donatorio (Braz.)   grantee of land in the early settlement of Brazil
Dorados   name given to Villa's crack troops, the 'gilded ones'

Ejido   literally, way out, referring to the communally owned lands at the exit of Indian villages
Encomienda   grant of Indians to a Spanish settler; an *encomendero* was a recipient of such a grant
Entrada   literally, entrance but used to describe expeditions into the jungle regions of the interior
Estancia   cattle farm owned by an *estanciero*; in southern Brazil he would be an *estanceiro*
Expresión oral   oral culture

Facón   *gaucho's* knife
Faiscador, Faisqueiro (Braz.)   gold or diamond prospector
Fazenda (Braz.)   large estate owned by a *fazendeiro*; cf. *hacienda*
Fidalgo   see *hidalgo*
Foco   rural guerrilla base
Frigorífico   cold-storage room in meat-packaging house
Fuero   privilege granted by the crown in return for service

Gambusino (Mex.)   professional mining prospector
Garimpeiro (Braz.)   gold or diamond prospector; in the eighteenth century implied being a smuggler although it has lost this connotation now
Gaucho   cowboy of the Argentinian or Uruguayan pampas; *gaúcho* is the southern Brazilian equivalent; a *gaucho malo* is an outlaw
Gente sin razón   literally, people without reason; hence those who in the view of the Church could be legally enslaved
Gobernar es poblar   'to govern is to populate', slogan coined by the Argentinian Alberdi, implying the need to encourage European immigration as a basis for stable government

Golondrina   swallow, name given to seasonal labourers, crossing over to
Argentina for the annual wheat harvest
Gran Apachería   the area in Texas, New Mexico and Arizona dominated
by the Apaches
Gran Minería   large mining companies
Grileiro (Braz.)   land speculator
Gringo, -a   slang description of English-speaking man or woman
Guacho   orphan
Guerra a fuego y sangre   war by fire and blood, war of extermination
against Indians
Guerra dos Emboabas   the civil war between settlers and foreigners in
Ouro Preto in early years of the eighteenth century; *emboaba* was
depreciatory term for foreigner
Guijaro (Cuban)   poor peasant
Güirises   individual gold prospectors in Central America; cf. *garimpeiro,
faisqueiro*

Habitant (Can.)   anyone below seigneurial rank holding land in French
Canada
Hacer América   'to make America', to make a fortune rather than to put
down roots and settle in America
Hacienda   large estate owned by an *hacendado*
Hechicero   witch doctor
Henequen   cactus fibre from which sisal is made, grown mainly in
Yucatan
Hidalgo   lesser nobility, from *hijo de algo*, 'son of someone'; cf.
Portuguese *fidalgo* who was not so exclusive in his social attitudes
Hispano   popular term in the American southwest for someone of Spanish
descent; cf. *chicano*. Current in northern New Mexico.
Huasipunguero   landless labourer in Ecuador
Huaso   Chilean cowboy

Indianismo   cult, especially literary, of the Indian
Indiano   someone who returns from Spanish America to settle in Spain
Indigenismo   the literary movement which exalted the culture of
indigenous peoples, especially in Mexico and the Andean countries

Jagunço (Braz.)   has a variety of meanings, sometimes generically as
'ruffian' or as a synonym for *sertanejo*
Junta dos Missões   'Junta of the Missions', set up to supervise missionary
activities among Amazonian Indians

Ladino Indian who adopts European ways

Latifundio generic term for any large landed estate, owned by a
latifundista

Letrado lawyer, someone trained in the law

Letra impresa the printed word

Límites territoriales political frontiers

Llanero cowboy of the Llanos, the plains of the Orinoco

Lo Real Maravilloso literally, marvellous reality, referring to the school
of writers including Carpentier, Asturias, Roa Bastos who believed
Latin American reality was qualitatively different from that of
Europe and North America

Machadeiro (Braz.) axeman who clears the Brazilian jungle

Macho virile male; hence *machismo*

Maloca slave-catching expedition; cf. *resgate*

Mameluco (Braz.) progeny of an Amerindian mother and white father

Marcha para Oeste (Braz.) 'Westward March', a slogan coined during
Vargas's presidency

Maroon runaway slave in English colonies; cf. *cimarrón*

Marronage (Haiti) state of being a runaway slave

Mayorazgo entailed estate

Mesquite desert shrub

Mesta sheep guild of medieval Spain and cattle guild in Mexico

Mesteña mustang or unbroken wild horse

Mestizo, Mestiço (Braz.) a mixed blood, Indian and European; *mestizaje*
is race mixing

Métis (Can.) French-Canadian mixed blood; *métissage* is race mixing

Mineiro (Braz.) inhabitant of Minas Gerais

Minifundio small plot, barely adequate for family subsistence, owned or
leased (could be share-cropped) by a *minifundista*

Mita tribute labour in Peru and Bolivia

Mitayo Indian who provides *mita* labour

Mocambo (Braz.) runaway slave hideout

Modo de Ser 'Mode of being', the essence of a particular country's
philosophy of life; cf. *Volksgeist*

Monção (Braz.) 'monsoon' or convoy of canoes

Montonero guerrilla fighter of Northwestern Argentina

Mulato a mixed blood, African and European

Municipio town council

Mutirão (Braz.) mutual help among farmers at harvest time

Novela de la Tierra 'Novel of the Land', referring to novelists who turned
to the rural regions for their themes, especially in the 1920s

Obraje   workshop for making up woollen or cotton goods
Ordenanza   decree

Palenque   runaway slave hideout; hence *palenquero*
Pampas   grasslands of the River Plate region; cf. *Llanos*
Páramo   desert, wilderness
Pardo   mixed blood in Venezuela, in Mexico black/European mix;
   pardocracia means rule by half castes
Patrón   boss, protector
Padroado, (Port.) **Patronato Real**   crown's privilege of presentation to
   benefices
Payada   Argentinian challenge song
Peón   landless labourer usually on an *hacienda*, hence *peonaje*; originated
   from *peonía*, a grant of land made to a *peón* in contrast to a *caballería*,
   a grant made to a horseman; *peonaje* came later to imply landlessness
Pepena   bonus earned by miners, usually in the form of Sunday working
   on their own account
Peruleiro (Braz.)   Portuguese merchant active in the Peru trade
Pícaro   literally, rogue, someone who lives off his wits; hence picaresque;
   the picaresque novel was popularized in sixteenth- and
   seventeenth-century Spain and enjoyed some vogue in early
   nineteenth-century Spanish America
Porteño   inhabitant of Buenos Aires
Posseiro (Braz.)   squatter, after *posse* meaning property or possessions
Presidio   frontier garrison
Pueblo   town or village (*pueblecito*), also 'the people'; cf. *le peuple*
Pulque   fermented drink made from cactus plant

Quilombo (Braz.)   runaway slave hideout; the most famous was the
   'Republic of Palmares' which existed as a virtually independent
   African nation in the Brazilian northeast for seventy or so years in the
   seventeenth century

Rancheador   literally, someone who dwells in a hut—slave catcher (Cuba)
Rancho   small rural property owned by a *ranchero*
Rastreador   track finder on the pampas
República de Indios   'The Indian Republic'; term used to describe
   segregated Indian villages supervised by the *corregidor de indios*
Resgate (Braz.)   slave raiding expedition
Rodeo   cattle round-up

Saladero   factory for salting beef
Senhor do engenho (Braz.)   sugar planter

Senhoria (Braz.)   lordship

Seringueiro (Braz.)   Amazonian rubber gatherer; a *seringalista* is the
   middleman who collects the rubber and takes it to the merchant

Sertão   the backlands of northeast Brazil; hence *sertanejo*, an inhabitant
   of the backlands

Sesmaria (Braz.)   grant of land

Tabareo (Braz.)   rustic backwoodsman; cf. *caipira, jagunco*

Tanatero   carrier, after *tanate* or the basket in which ore was fetched out
   of the mine

Tenente (Braz.)   lieutenant; hence *tenentismo*, the movement of radical
   young officers in the 1920s

Terra Roxa (Braz.)   the red earth of the São Paulo region, excellent for
   coffee growing

Tropeiro (Braz.)   muleteer; a *tropa* is a string of mules; cf. *arreiro*

Vaquejada, Vaquería (Braz.)   cow-hunt

Vaquero   cowboy; there are many words in Spanish for cowboy but this
   is general in Mexico; *vaqueiro* (Braz.) refers especially to cowboys in
   the northeast; cf. *gaúchos* in Rio Grande do Sul

Vicuña   Andean animal akin to llama, prized for softness of its wool

Villista   follower of Pancho Villa in the Mexican Revolution

Waldhufendorf   forest village, common in central Germany

Yanacona   Peruvian Indian who was a personal servant

Zapatista   followers of Emiliano Zapata in the Mexican Revolution

Index